Globalization and Finance

Globalization and Finance

Tony Porter

Polity

First published in 2005 by Polity Press

Polity Press
65 Bridge Street
Cambridge CB2 1UR, UK.

Polity Press
350 Main Street
Malden, MA 02148, USA

ISBN 0 7456 3118 5
ISBN 0 7456 3119 3 (paperback)

A catalogue record for this book is available from the British Library and has been applied for from the Library of Congress.

Typeset in 10.5 on 12 pt Sabon
by SNP Best-set Typesetter Ltd., Hong Kong
Printed and bound in Great Britain by MPG Books Ltd, Bodmin, Cornwall

For further information on Polity, visit our website: www.polity.co.uk

The publisher has used its best endeavours to ensure that the URLs for external websites referred to in this book are correct and active at the time of going to press. However, the publisher has no responsibility for the websites and can make no guarantee that a site will remain live or that the content is or will remain appropriate.

Contents

Preface

Globalization has become one of the most prominent and controversial features of contemporary life, and finance has always played a leading role, as in the images of exuberant international financial trading in New York or London or in the frightening disruptions of daily life that global financial crises can bring about in the most remote corners of the world. Often this has seemed like an epic conflict between the churning fluidity of cross-border financial flows, and the inertia of the state, anchored in its unchanging territory and the long-standing traditions of its people, and there has been intense debate about which of these forces will, or should, win out over the long run.

While taking this debate as a starting point, this book presents an alternative account that highlights the role of formal and informal social practices and institutions in the development and regulation of the globalization of finance. Social institutions and practices are sets of formal or informal rules that both shape and are reproduced by actors of all types as they engage in their ongoing interactions with global finance. Examining the complex network of institutions and practices in global finance is important for understanding the past evolution of global finance and the ways in which its future development may be shaped, and for drawing out relationships and comparisons with other non-financial aspects of globalization.

One of the remarkable changes in global finance over the past decade is the greater accessibility of detailed information about it. This is due to the growth of the internet, itself an aspect of globalization, to the centrality of knowledge production for global finance, and to the emphasis by regulators on transparency in response to the challenges that global finance has faced. Entering into an internet search engine even the most unfamiliar words or organizational names found in this book is likely to turn up pages and pages of information. This book may be read not as the final word on the subject, but rather as an entry point to a fast-developing phenomenon whose political, technical, and scholarly aspects will call for ongoing exploration.

In writing this book I have benefited enormously from the help of others, including Robert O'Brien and Ann Porter, who commented on portions of the manuscript, and Diana Cucuz, Heather McKeen-Edwards, Adam Pelissero, Ian Roberge, Nisha Shah, and Juliet Lan Zhang, whose assistance with research was crucial to the book's completion. The comments of two anonymous reviewers were also very helpful. This book was very much enriched by the interviews granted by busy regulators and other participants in global finance for this and other financial research I have conducted. The funding of the Social Sciences and Humanities Research Council of Canada was essential for the research upon which this book is based. I wish to express my great appreciation for all this help, and for that from others not mentioned here.

List of Acronyms

ABA	American Bankers Association
ABF	Asian Bond Fund
AIBD	Association of International Bond Dealers
ALOP	Asociación Latinoamericana de Organizaciones de Promoción
ASEAN	Association of South East Asian Nations
ATS	Alternative Trading Systems
ATTAC	Association for the Taxation of Financial Transactions for the Aid of Citizens
BCBS	Basel Committee on Banking Supervision
BIS	Bank for International Settlements
BIT	Bilateral Investment Treaty
CEMLA	Centro de Estudios Monetarios Latinoamericanos
CEO	Chief Executive Officer
CFA	Chartered Financial Analyst
CFP	Certified Financial Planner
CHIPS	Clearing House Inter-Bank Payments System
CIA	Central Intelligence Agency
CSO	Civil society organization with a social mission
CTC	United Nations Center on Transnational Corporations
CUFTA	Canada–US Free Trade Agreement
EMC	Emerging Markets Committee (IOSCO)
EMEAP	Executives' Meeting of East Asia–Pacific Central Banks
EU	European Union

EURODAD	European Network on Debt and Development
FDI	Foreign Direct Investment
Fed	Federal Reserve
FfD	Financing for Development
FLG	Financial Leaders Group
FSA	Financial Services Agreement
FSF	Financial Stability Forum
G7	Group of Seven
G8	Group of Eight
G9	Group of Nine
G10	Group of Ten
G15	Group of Fifteen
G20	Group of Twenty
G22	Group of Twenty-Two
G24	Group of Twenty-Four
G30	Group of Thirty
G33	Group of Thirty-Three
GAAP	Generally Accepted Accounting Principles
GDP	Gross Domestic Product
GFCF	Gross Fixed Capital Formation
HIPC	Highly Indebted Poor Countries
IAIS	International Association of Insurance Supervisors
IAS	International Accounting Standards
IASB	International Accounting Standards Board
IIF	Institute of International Finance
IMF	International Monetary Fund
IOSCO	International Organization of Securities Commissions
IPMA	International Primary Markets Association
IR	International Relations
ISDA	International Swaps and Derivatives Association
ISMA	International Securities Markets Association
LDCs	Less Developed Countries
LTCM	Long-Term Capital Management
MAI	Multilateral Agreement on Investment
MNC	Multinational Corporation
MOU	Memorandum of Understanding
NAFTA	North American Free Trade Agreement
NASD – R	National Association of Securities Dealers – Regulation
NASDAQ	National Association of Securities Dealers Automated Quotation system
NEPAD	New Partnership for Africa's Development
NGO	Non-Governmental Organization

NIEO	New International Economic Order
OECD	Organization for Economic Cooperation and Development
OPEC	Organization of Petroleum Exporting Countries
OTC	Over the Counter
PBC	People's Bank of China
PRSP	Poverty Reduction Strategy Papers
ROSC	Report on Observance of Financial Standards and Codes
SAP	Structural Adjustment Policy
SEC	Securities and Exchange Commission
TRIMs	Trade-Related Investment Measures
TRIPS	Trade-Related Intellectual Property Rights
UN	United Nations
UNCTAD	United Nations Conference on Trade and Development
UNDP	United Nations Development Program
WDI	World Development Index
WFE	World Federation of Exchanges
WTO	World Trade Organization
WWB	Women's World Banking

Part I

The Institutionalization of Global Finance

1

Introduction: Why Study Global Finance?

What is the Globalization of Finance?

Globalization can be defined as the intensification of interactions at a distance among people around the world such that humanity as a whole can be said to be aware of sharing a common experience to a significant degree. There are many previous periods in history in which people interacted across vast distances, including great empires, such as those of the Mongols, the Romans, and the European ones. The nineteenth century saw great inter-continental flows of people, trade, and capital, as for instance the flows linking the expanding American economies with the rest of the world. While some scholars refer to these earlier periods of integration as examples of globalization, this tends to obscure the distinctive meaning and utility of the term. Use of the word "globalization" began in the 1960s and exploded through the last quarter of the twentieth century, and this alone is an indication that there was a widespread perception that something new was afoot. Both the intensity of the inter-actions and the awareness of them are qualitatively different today than in previous historical periods of integration.[1]

It is useful to think of globalization as involving both extensive and intensive expansion. Extensive expansion refers to the incorpo-ration of ever wider geographic areas into the process, while inten-sive expansion refers to the growth in the density and complexity of interactions in any given geographic area. In the case of financial globalization one might refer to the opening of foreign bank branches in a country that previously had none as *extensive* growth, while the expansion of the range of financial products offered by those bank branches could be seen as *intensive* growth.

Both the intensity of the current period of globalization and people's awareness of globalization, and of sharing a common experience, make the current period unlike previous historical periods of internationalization. In earlier periods trade routes often extended around the world, but these usually involved luxury goods and accounted for only a small share of any particular country's economy. Exceptions include, for instance, the European colonization of North America, where furs (in Canada) and cotton (in the Thirteen Colonies) were vital for the economy as a whole. However, even in these cases, this level of interdependence was restricted to particular colonies' relationships to their colonizing power, and the types of cross-border flows were not nearly as varied as is the case today. Moreover, in none of these earlier periods was the popular awareness of being subject to *global* forces as strong as is the case today.

Finance can be defined with reference to its constituent parts: namely, money, credit, investments, and banking. More abstractly, it is the process by which savings are transferred from one entity to another for a period of time in exchange for a payment. Money, while important in finance, is typically defined by three other functions: it is a means of payment, a store of value, and a unit of account. Thus money is defined more by its use in facilitating payments and measuring value than by its connection to savings.

Finance can involve both public-sector and private-sector entities. Public-sector finance can involve the raising of funds by asking citizens to buy government securities – contracts that promise to make a stream of payments over time. It can also involve the lending of money by a public-sector international organization such as the International Monetary Fund to a national government. There is an enormous variety of types of private-sector finance, or financial "instruments," but these tend to fall into three main types: loans, securities, and insurance. Loans involve *intermediation* – a process by which an institution, usually a bank, takes the responsibility to gather savings and to make these available to borrowers in exchange for interest. The bank plays a key role in assuming the risk and responsibility for assessing and monitoring the creditworthiness of borrowers. Securities, by contrast, involve the direct purchase by an investor of a security issued by a firm or government that wishes to borrow. Insurance involves the selling of a contract to cover a risk, and is a form of finance because it involves the transfer of savings to an insurer in exchange for a future payment, a payment that is conditional on specified conditions, such as the destruction of an insured object.

Financial linkages have extended across large expanses of the globe in many previous historical periods (Germaine, 1997; Langley, 2002). The *bezant* gold coin introduced by Emperor Constantine in the fourth century AD was used as a remarkably stable international currency in the Mediterranean and Europe until the Middle Ages (Lothian, 2002). Beginning in the eleventh century AD the Italian city-states of Florence and Venice had well-developed international banking systems: the Bardi Bank of Florence had more than 30 offices in Italy, France, London, Bruges, Spain, North Africa, and the Greek, Latin, and Moslem Levant (Bautier, 1971), and in the fourteenth century the repudiation by the English crown of its debts to Italian banks, equivalent at one point to its annual war budget, triggered a financial crisis in Italy (Postan, 1973). A well-developed system for financing long-distance overland trade was created with the circulation of "bills of exchange" in the Champagne fairs. In the sixteenth century the German-based Fugger bank lent money, especially for financing wars, to kings around Europe. In the seventeenth century, when the Netherlands was the center of a vast system of global trade, much of this trade, including the sale of stock in the Dutch East Indies Company, was financed through the Amsterdam stock markets, which included futures contracts, margins, and short sales (Neal, 1990). In the nineteenth century London financial markets financed project after project around the world, including mining operations in Latin America, railroad construction across Russia and North America, the international cotton trade, and the operations of large international trading companies. In the early part of the twentieth century US banks were heavily involved in lending to Latin America.

This long history of international finance has been regularly punctuated by financial crises as well. The refusal of the British king to repay bank loans owed to Italian banks in the fourteenth century led to a crisis in the Italian markets. In the 1630s, when Amsterdam financial markets were at the center of the world economy, the tulip mania saw the prices of some rare tulip bulbs increase 60-fold, to the equivalent of five years' pay, and then cause havoc when they collapsed. In 1719 and 1720 stock market speculation in international investments, including the South Sea Bubble and the Mississippi Bubble, resulted in such severe crises across Europe that in the ensuing century joint stock corporations were banned in England and banking was discredited in France (Chancellor, 1999; Kindleberger, 1989; Neal, 1990; Porter, 1995).

The most recent period of international financial expansion – the period we call "the globalization of finance" – began in the 1960s. However, this occurred after a period in the middle of the twentieth century in which states had greatly increased restrictions on global financial flows. An early example was the Soviet Union's cutting all relations with international financial markets after the 1917 revolution that created it. After World War II the governments of most countries created strong controls over their financial systems in an attempt to make finance serve the priority of the time, which was rapid industrial growth and post-war reconstruction. These controls were also designed to try to prevent some of the serious financial problems of the earlier part of the twentieth century, that were seen as having contributed to the Great Depression of the 1930s and the war (Ruggie, 1982). Financial speculation and the stock market crash of 1929 had contributed to the Depression, and this in turn, along with the strict constraints imposed on governments by the gold standard, a powerful set of international monetary rules in force in the nineteenth and early twentieth centuries, had led to the excessive exposure of citizens to risks associated with the international economy. The post-World War II controls that governments used were designed both to insulate the domestic economy from the risks associated with cross-border financial flows and to reduce the negative effects of excessive financial speculation in domestic markets. A variety of measures, such as putting ceilings on interest rates or having governments own banks, were also designed to channel flows of cheap finance to the building of industry and infrastructure.

International monetary stability was further enhanced by the Bretton Woods monetary system, whereby countries pegged their exchange rates and the US dollar became the main international currency, backed by a commitment by the US government to exchange dollars for gold at $35 per ounce. At the meetings in Bretton Woods, New Hampshire, at which these arrangements were negotiated, the delegates also established the International Monetary Fund and the International Bank for Reconstruction and Development, now better known as the World Bank (Pauly, 1997). The former was designed to assist countries in maintaining their pegged exchange rates by providing short-term financing to governments facing downward pressure on their exchange rates (due to a shortfall in exports and the resulting decline in demand for the currency) and by approving periodic adjustments to the value at which the currencies were pegged. The latter was designed to facilitate the international mobilization of financial resources for national reconstruction and development, but these were envisioned as being channeled through and controlled by governments.

During the 1960s these controls over international finance that governments had created began to be eroded, and this launched the period of the globalization of finance that we continue to experience today. Firms and individual investors from different countries began depositing US dollars in accounts in London in order to escape various government regulations, and by the end of the decade these *Euromarkets* had become huge, appearing to many observers as if they were beyond the control of states. These international financial markets continued to grow rapidly in volume and complexity through the remainder of the twentieth century. From simple bank deposits, they grew to include international bonds, stocks, and a bewildering number of complex *derivatives* – contracts based on an underlying asset, such as a promise to make payments based on the future movement of an interest rate.

This period of rapid international financial expansion was accompanied by a series of severe financial crises, including collapses of international banks in the 1970s, the developing country debt crisis of the early 1980s, the Mexican peso crisis of 1994, and the East Asian crisis of 1997/8. At certain points in each of these crises it appeared to many officials as if the whole global financial system was at risk of collapsing. Financial globalization became one of the most prominent aspects of globalization more generally, with its images of frenzied international bond traders and enormous instantaneous movements of electronic money from one side of the world to the other.

Patterns of the international expansion of financial flows have corresponded closely to patterns involving other international flows, and thus the globalization of finance involves many of the same debates as over globalization more generally. Many people, noting the earlier historical periods of international financial expansion, have argued that today's international financial flows are nothing new. These skeptics have also pointed out that many measures of financial globalization begin with the mid-twentieth century, a temporary high point of state control of the economy, and if measures are extended further back in history, it becomes apparent that part of what appears to be rapid financial globalization in the post-World War II period is instead simply a return to the types of cross-border financial flows that characterized the period before this unusual mid-twentieth-century anomaly.

One way to address these types of debates is to try to measure cross-border financial flows and relationships. For instance, Lothian

(2002, p. 710) has measured international correlations of interest rates over the past three centuries, and his data demonstrate convergence – "more countries becoming more integrated as time has elapsed" – with a marked convergence from 1990 to 2000, even if earlier correlations, such as those between Dutch and British interest rates in the eighteenth century are surprisingly high.[2] While this book will provide some such measures, its primary focus is rather on analyzing the institutional linkages that constitute global finance. Data alone are inadequate for the analysis of the globalization of finance. For instance, foreign exchange trading is sometimes used as an indicator of the globalization of finance, but its volume declined following the creation of the Euro – a major instance of cross-border integration – since there was no longer any need to trade the European currencies that were replaced by the Euro. Similarly, a foreign investment by a multinational corporation can be taken either as a sign of increased financial integration or as an institutional arrangement to allow a firm to exploit ongoing gaps and barriers separating markets and jurisdictions. Such complications require us to pay careful attention to the significance of institutional arrangements. This book demonstrates that a complex set of institutions for facilitating and governing the globalization of finance have emerged over the past quarter-century, and this decisively distinguishes our current period of financial globalization from previous ones. Especially important is the inclusion in these institutional arrangements of decentralized sets of rules – social practices – that link the daily experiences of individuals of all types with the formal organizations and laws that we normally associate with political authority in the governance of financial markets.

In sum, the globalization of finance refers to the intensification of financial interactions at a distance among people around the world such that humanity as a whole can be said to be aware of sharing a common involvement with these cross-border financial flows to a significant degree.

Why Study Global Finance?

People have mixed feelings about finance. Finance may be needed to buy something we couldn't otherwise afford, to save for the future, to help the firm we work for avoid bankruptcy, or for our government to build a new road. We also know that finance does not just bring these good things, but can bring bad things as well: crushing debt, harrowing economic instability, massive fraud, the loss of one's life savings, and huge economic rewards for speculators that may seem very unjust. Our ambivalence about finance comes not just from this mixture of good and bad effects, but because, even though we know it is important, it often seems mind-numbingly boring or frighteningly complex – pages of fine print or mathematical formulas.

All of these feelings about finance have become magnified as finance has become more globalized. Every few years a major financial crisis breaks out somewhere in the world and washes across large expanses of the global economy, throwing people into sudden poverty as it goes. Now we have to worry not just about *local* con artists, but worldwide financial fraud carried out through the internet. Yet we know that the globalization of finance has brought new opportunities as well, including a wider range of financial products and new opportunities for mobilizing globally large amounts of investment for needed projects. Understanding global finance seems even more daunting than understanding finance closer to home: if the insurance policy we buy from a local broker seems complicated, then understanding the effects of derivatives sold in London on the volatility of our exchange rates and thus the insecurity of our jobs can seem impossible.

The complexity and risks associated with global finance are one reason why its management is left to experts. On the private-sector side, key financial decisions are often made by fabulously well-paid traders on the basis of complex transactions or mathematical models that even those who supposedly control the firm may not understand. On the public-sector side, regulators have difficulty keeping up with these transactions and models, and when they do, when they make plans to try to avoid a catastrophic collapse of the financial system, they seem to speak the same highly technical language as the private-sector traders – a language that the average citizen has trouble understanding. Fears that the global financial system is dangerously out of control come not just from the great sloshing global ocean of footloose money that can destroy whole economies in the space of days, but also from our nagging worry that no one really understands the destructive global forces that have been unleashed – or even worse, that those who understand these forces don't want us to know what they know.

As breakdowns in financial systems, such as the East Asian crisis of 1997–8 or the Enron collapse of 2001, begin to have increasingly severe consequences for the average citizen, this gap between those making financial decisions and those harmed by financial crisis, mismanagement, or fraud has become a more and more serious problem.

This gap between experts and non-experts is made worse because it can correspond to the gap between the wealthy and the poor, not just within countries but between countries as well. Traditionally, global finance has been managed by officials and firms from a small number of the most industrialized countries, such as the members of the Group of Seven or the Group of Ten, and it is only recently that officials from developing countries have been invited to participate in global policymaking. There is already widespread anxiety about the "democratic deficit" that accompanies globalization – the degree to which decisions are made in international institutions that appear remote and unaccountable to the average citizen. The large disparities in wealth and knowledge that are associated with this problem in global finance make the democratic deficit in this area especially troubling.

This book will argue that understanding global finance is not a task that should be left to the experts or to wealthy investors. Even if we just focus on financial transactions, global finance plays such a large role in the global economy and in the finances of the institutions on which we rely for our well-being, that it is valuable to learn about it. However, the book argues as well that understanding the evolution of global finance has many lessons that help us understand other important aspects of our contemporary world. These include lessons about how international institutions are formed in new areas of globalized activity, the contribution of knowledge to global governance, the role of risk technologies in controlling the future and in the unequal allocation across countries and social classes of the costs and benefits associated with contemporary risk, how confidence and trust are created when local traditions are incapable of doing so over the long distances that come with globalization.

This book does not just argue that knowledge about global finance should be more accessible, but aims as well to contribute to making it more accessible by avoiding overly technical language where possible, and by highlighting themes with relevance beyond the financial industry. At the same time it seeks to avoid excessive simplification. For those worried about the dangers of global finance, simple solutions that try to turn back the clock and shut down the global financial system are unlikely to work. This is not because there is something about the expansion of financial market forces that is natural and beyond human control, but rather that those who built the global financial system have constructed a huge, dangerous, and enormously complex machine that delivers, along with its often disastrous negative effects, enormous benefits for some powerful wealthy participants and smaller benefits for many smaller participants – and thus both the machine's momentum and the political con-figuration of forces associated with it make it more likely that change will come from altering the machine's functioning and direction rather than dismantling it.

This does not mean, however, that significant change in the gov-ernance of global finance is not on the horizon. Persistent global financial crises beginning in the 1990s put reform of the global finan-cial architecture high on the agenda of policymakers and non-governmental organizations. While other issues such as terrorism or global warming may displace global finance from the top of this agenda, these debates over reform have already produced a willing-ness to consider serious changes in global financial governance, and some of these changes have begun to be implemented. For instance, it is now widely accepted that rapid liberalization of cross-border capital flows without ensuring a state's capacity for strong domestic prudential financial regulation is a serious mistake, and that capital controls can be a useful policy instrument under certain conditions. Initiating organizational change in a system as complex and know-ledge-driven as global finance requires a strong understanding of how it works.

2

Debates and Controversies in the Conceptualization of Global Finance

Is the globalization of finance harmful or helpful to the well-being of those affected by it? Has the globalization of finance fatally undermined the power of states? What causes the globalization of finance? What options are available to ensure that we avoid global financial crises and the destruction they bring?

These questions, and others that we might wish to ask when studying global finance, cannot be answered by simply looking at financial statistics. Data and other empirical information are important, but without a theoretical framework we cannot know which empirical information is important, or what trends or structural characteristics this information is identifying. Evaluations of the effects of finance, and questions such as the fairness and legitimacy of the global arrangements for managing finance, require judgment and not just measurement: for instance, how do we weigh the greater risks and inequality that can come with the globalization of finance against the new opportunities for economic growth and increases in investment options? Such judgments require theoretical frameworks that can provide the reasons and criteria needed for evaluation.

This chapter focuses on theoretical issues that are important for understanding the globalization of finance. Theoretical reflection is rewarding because it allows us:

- to discern long-range patterns in an otherwise confusing mass of information;
- to connect our understanding of global finance to our understanding of globalization and our late-modern era more generally;

- to engage with ongoing debates about the future direction of the global financial system.

Theory is not just about understanding forces beyond our control, but more importantly about exercising our unique capacity as humans to chart our own future.

Many of the theoretical debates that have unfolded in the study of global finance are similar to those associated with globalization more generally. This is not surprising, since the globalization of finance is a key aspect of globalization, and indeed is often taken to be the quintessential case or driving force of globalization. However, as we will see below, there are scholars who have focused specifically on financial globalization, and there is much to be learned from their work. Following this introductory section, this chapter will start by discussing this work.

While it is useful to review existing debates, it is also helpful to go beyond these, and to try to take our collective understanding of the globalization of finance beyond its present level. Most of the existing debates have tended to characterize the key tension in global finance as one between centralized hierarchical self-interested states and fluid, atomistic, highly competitive markets. Debate has then centered on questions such as which of these two is or should be most powerful. This book takes a different perspective. It focuses upon the wide variety of institutions other than the two extremes of hierarchical states and fluid markets upon which most debate has focused.

These other institutions include, for instance, expert international committees that play a very important role in the governance of global finance. While these committees may be composed of public-sector officials, they have developed so much autonomy from the states that these officials ostensibly represent, that it is a problem to treat them as simply a negotiating forum for states. These institutions also include private-sector associations that are organized hierarchically and play an independent regulatory or lobbying role, and are therefore very different from the fluid anonymous market forces that are often thought to be the primary form that private-sector influence takes at the international level. These various public-sector and private-sector institutions are entangled with one another in complex ways. For instance, private-sector associations may provide influential reports to public-sector committees, or they may play a key role in implementing the guidelines of those committees. This institutional complexity at the international level requires us to use theoretical concepts that have not been adequately developed in the study of global finance.

The next sections start by looking at three traditions, before presenting a fourth approach that focuses on international institutions and social practices. The first, a liberal tradition mostly based in the academic discipline of economics, treats finance as an example of the expansion of markets. The second, a state-centric tradition mostly based in the academic discipline of international relations, treats finance as shaped by the initiatives of powerful states. The third, a critical approach drawing on insights from the Marxist tradition, sees the globalization of finance as closely connected to changes in capitalism as a whole, especially the organization of production and the unequal relationship between social classes. The chapter then draws on these concepts to develop a theoretical approach that is useful for understanding the complex set of new international institutions and practices that are developing along with the globalization of finance.

Market-Based Approaches

As discussed in chapter 1, by the late 1960s the Bretton Woods monetary system and the post-World War II control by governments of their domestic financial systems were beginning to be challenged by increases in cross-border financial flows. At the center of this expansion were the Eurocurrency markets, which by 1988 had grown to an estimated gross size of $4.6 trillion dollars (Goodfriend, 1998, p. 49). As the Euromarkets and other cross-border financial flows grew in importance, they began to attract more attention from those wishing to understand their growth theoretically. One prominent theme that emerged was the idea that financial globalization was an expression of a long-range tendency of markets to expand, assisted by technological advances, and thereby to undermine the power of governments. This theme was consistent with, and drew inspiration from, the overlapping traditions of liberal economic theory and liberal political theory.

In the liberal theoretical tradition, the expansion of markets tends to be seen as inevitable. Markets by definition involve the bringing together of sufficiently large numbers of buyers and sellers so that prices can be determined by the competitive interplay of supply and demand. In this competitive environment, inefficient high-cost producers will go out of business, leaving only the most competitive. This competitive imperative will make markets the most efficient form of economic organization – a form that will then be able to out-compete other forms, such as centralized state planning or traditional communal economies.

The inexorable expansion of markets can be also be linked rhetorically to the idea that "market forces" or "the invisible" hand operate like natural laws, independent of the volition of humans, or to the idea that markets are an irrepressible expression of individual human freedom – including the freedom to possess property, the freedom to exercise choice in buying and selling, and the freedom to be innovative (and to be economically rewarded for innovation) in entrepreneurial or technical activities.

From a liberal perspective this expansion of markets relative to governments and other forms of social organization is not just inevitable, but beneficial as well. Economic efficiency means that outputs are maximized relative to inputs, and thus a more efficient economy will make more goods available for consumers to enjoy. Traditionally, as well, liberal theory has seen business and market transactions as part of civil society, the realm in which citizens exercise their freedom, and the government has been seen as always at risk of becoming too large or repressive, and so to threaten freedom. Bureaucrats, because they are not held accountable by competitive pressures, seek to exploit their control over markets and to maximize their own self-interest – to "extract rents." Thus the displacement of state-controlled activity by market-driven activity is seen as positive for both its economic and its political effects.

These liberal ideas have been very prominent in much analysis of the globalization of finance. The Euromarkets were portrayed as a wonderful example of how well markets could work when they were free of the regulatory interference of territorial states. They were seen as a place where investors and firms could pursue their freedom to use their financial resources as they wished. The expansion of the Euromarkets was explained with reference to the ideas of market inevitability set out above. State regulation over domestic financial systems began to be portrayed as backwards, traditional, and inefficient, and the undermining of these regulations by financial actors was applauded. The technological innovations that were facilitating the globalization of finance – such as the expansion of cross-border electronic networks or new computer programs that facilitated trading of financial instruments – were seen as an expression of the restless individual innovation that markets encouraged.

The competitive imperative with regard to cross-border financial flows was also explained in this liberal tradition by treating these flows as driven by the search for higher returns that could be generated by maximizing their efficient use. Financial resources would flow from areas of the world where they were relatively abundant to areas in which they were scarce, and this scarcity would raise the price (such as interest rates) that people would be willing to pay for the use of these resources, a price that was sustainable because of the greater potential productivity of financial resources in areas of scarcity where they were desperately needed.

The competitive imperative could also be understood as driven by the need for over-regulated jurisdictions to move to a more market-oriented financial system if they were to survive in their competition with the greater efficiency of more lightly regulated jurisdictions. Finance is crucial to economies not just as an industry in its own right, but because it supplies the financial resources that are essential to the success of other industries. In liberal theory it is not just the low cost of these resources that is important, but also the efficiency with which they are allocated across a variety of potential uses. Market forces, with their search for higher economic returns, are seen as better in making these allocation decisions than are government bureaucrats, with their tendency to follow inefficiently their own self-interests, or the interests of political actors to whom they owe their position.

These liberal analyses of the globalization of finance fit well with an important tradition in liberal international relations theory that saw international institutions, including non-governmental actors, as creating an interdependent world in which competitive territorial states would decline in importance. The international activities of investors and multinational banks could be seen as yet another example of the rise of a set actors competing with the nation-state, and of increases in complex interdependence.

As global financial markets continued to grow through the 1980s and 1990s, the challenge they posed to the power of states appeared to grow and to be more direct and conscious. One aspect of this was the stronger and more organized response of financial markets to government policies they did not like. Whereas in the 1960s the effect of the growth of the Eurobond market was a subtle and gradual increase in competitive pressures for the national economies over which states presided, by the 1980s there were well-organized private-sector mechanisms for financial actors to make known their displeasure with government policies they did not like and to put pressure on states to change those policies. For instance, private-sector bond-rating agencies would judge the performance of governments against a set of market-oriented criteria, issue ratings of those governments' bonds, influence the sale or purchase of those bonds, and thereby put tremendous pressure on governments to pursue policies that international bond markets favored. This included lower taxes and lower government spending. Other sophisticated financial information systems, such as Reuters and other financial news services, had a similar effect. This private-sector capacity to influence states was further enhanced by the increased tendency of some public-sector bodies to work with private-sector actors to put pressure on states and other actors that were not following liberal prescriptions with regard to encouraging the expansion of markets, as with the International Monetary Fund pressuring developing country governments to go through painful market-oriented economic restructuring.

All of the changes described above were consistent with liberal economic and political theories. To liberals it seemed that the world was being transformed for the better as the positive power of global financial markets was unleashed, bringing promise of faster economic growth, greater efficiency, and beneficial constraints and accountability for big bad old-fashioned states (McKenzie and Lee, 1991).

Many theorists from traditions other than liberal ones drew similar conclusions about the degree to which global financial markets were constraining states, even if they did not agree with the liberal view that these constraints were beneficial. For instance Gill and Law (1989), working in a Marxist tradition, developed the concept of the "structural power of capital," and Andrews (1989), working in the political realist tradition, developed the concept of the "structure of capital mobility" to refer to the ability of mobile capital to put pressure on states. Cerny (2000) coined the term "competition state" to highlight the notion that states were increasingly compelled to orient their policies towards fostering national competitiveness in a global market.

Market-oriented theories of the globalization of finance are attractive. They come as a coherent, powerful package that can be used from the grandest mega-historical scale down to the micro-level experience of individual transactions. The fact that powerful wealthy actors using highly sophisticated economic models vigorously promoted liberal analysis of the globalization of finance further added to the approach's stature. In the next sections, however, we shall see that more state-centric and critical approaches have a different story to tell, and one that is also attractive theoretically.

State-Centric Approaches to the Globalization of Finance

The academic field of International Relations (IR), which has been engaged in organized study of international affairs for the past century, has always been interested in the interaction between states and their international environment, and thus it is not surprising that the rapid globalization of finance discussed above sparked much scholarly attention in the IR community. For most of its history IR has seen war as the most important international challenge facing states, with international law being seen as a relevant but relatively ineffective feature of the international system that aspired to offset the system's susceptibility to war. In war-related matters it has always been clear that states are the most important actors, and the prerogative for policymaking in this area has been more zealously guarded by the upper levels of the state against the encroachments of nongovernmental actors than is the case for other types of international interactions. Thus the dominant tradition within which IR scholars have worked is very different than the liberal tradition discussed above, even if, as noted above, some liberal international relations theories differed from this dominant tradition.

Four key insights from state-centric approaches to the globalization of finance can be identified. First, the globalization of finance did not come about simply because there is an inherent tendency of markets to expand. Rather, at key moments powerful states took decisions and self-interestedly deployed their power in order to bring about this globalization. As Helleiner (1994) has demonstrated, the emergence of the Euromarkets in London came about because the British government, after World War II, wanted to restore London to its position as the world's financial center, a position that it had enjoyed for more than a century before the War. The British and US governments saw further advantages in having the Euromarkets, because it gave their multinational corporations access to US dollars needed for their international activities. Both governments had restrictions on cross-border financial flows in the post-World War II period that were designed to foster the growth of their domestic economies, but the Euromarkets provided a way for their most internationally active firms to circumvent these restrictions without requiring their governments to dismantle them.

A second insight consistent with a state-centric approach to finance is that the degree to which financial globalization has taken place is often grossly overstated, because territory continues to be much more important than liberal approaches acknowledge. This point can be made in part by citing statistics. Cross-national differences persist in interest rates. Savings and investment rates continue to be more correlated within countries than one would expect with fully integrated markets (Herring and Litan, 1995; Held et al., 1999, pp. 216–19). Theoretical arguments can also be made for why territory continues to play a key role. Financial transactions are distinctive in the degree to which they rely on trust and coordination. Because they are intangible and complex, there is a high potential for fraud. Because they may involve huge sums, often they involve close coordination among many partners. Taken together, this means that financial markets require face-to-face interaction, and cannot simply operate through far-flung electronic networks, as is implied by much liberal analysis.

Scholars such as Sassen (1995) and Thrift (1994) have pointed out that one solution to this challenge has been to construct centralized financial districts. These districts bring participants in financial markets together and reinforce their capacity to recognize one another through the well-established buildings, clubs, and routine practices that are embedded in the physical structure of the district. They point out that finance has become more centralized in particular financial districts – London and New York – as some aspects of it have become more globalized. Thus territory continues to matter even for the most globalized aspects of finance. For less globalized aspects of finance, such as car insurance, territory matters even more, since local face-to-face interaction may be even more important for these.

A third and related point consistent with a state-centric approach is that the organization of the state continues to be much more important than liberal approaches recognize. The state is an enormously powerful institution that can mobilize huge quantities of resources, including money, people, knowledge, regulations and laws, and coercion. As Kapstein (1994) has shown, international bank regulation has relied to a significant degree on the ability of powerful states to regulate banks headquartered on their territory. Mooveover, states build on national cultures and traditions that strengthen their own capacity to foster their citizens' loyalty and that create challenges for financial firms that seek to operate globally. Citizens continue to be more comfortable conducting business within the borders of the state whose regulations and law they know well.

A fourth insight from state-centric approaches builds on this point about the importance of regulation and law. Contrary to the tendency of liberal analysis to focus on the capacity of market transactions to take place independent of, or even in opposition to, the state,

state-centric approaches point out that markets need rules and laws in order to operate. The most important such rules and laws are property rights, since goods and services cannot be exchanged unless there is a clear and enforceable system in place to identify who owns what. In financial markets involving huge sums of intangible assets this is especially important. In these markets basic property rights need to be supplemented by vast bodies of other regulations that set out the rights and obligations of those involved in financial transactions. For instance, while electronic networks are managed by banks and other private-sector actors, they are also governed by laws – if they were not, people would not entrust trillions of dollars to these networks. The Clearing House Inter-Bank Payments System (CHIPS) in New York, which handles 95 percent of dollar transactions between banks worldwide, more than $1.2 trillion daily, is governed by a set of rules put together by the banks that manage the system, but these rules in turn are backed up by the law of New York State.

At the international level the stabilizing and regulatory initiatives of states have been much more important than the liberal view set out in the previous section acknowledges. Throughout their history both domestic and international financial markets have been vulnerable to panics, crises, and collapses. A number of features of financial markets contribute to this instability, including the inter-dependence of financial actors (banks frequently lend huge sums to one another – in 2003 the international interbank market was valued at $4.6 trillion, 31 percent of all international lending),[1] the potential for mismatches between the sources of funds used by financial firms and the uses they make of these funds (for instance, banks that finance long-term illiquid loans through short-term liquid deposits), and the difficulty of accurately assessing risks when transactions are complex and intangible. At the international level it has been more difficult for states to carry out their stabilizing and regulatory functions than it is at the domestic level. Nevertheless, states have played a very important stabilizing and regulatory role at the international level, as will be evident in chapter 3.

Scholars have also pointed to the way in which the continued aggressive pursuit of self-interest by states can shape global finance. For instance, Macey (2003) argues that international financial regulation is best treated as the outcome of regulators successfully engaging in cartel-like collusion with one another in order to turn back challenges to their power and influence from regulatory competition. Oatley and Nabors (1998) argue that the Basel Capital Adequacy Accord, the most important agreement on international bank regulation, was the result of the US government self-interestedly creating international rules to redistribute income from Japanese banks to US banks. The next chapter argues that this picture of the international regulatory arrangements is inadequate. Nevertheless, state-centric analyses such as these highlight the importance of power and powerful states that is overlooked by the type of liberal approach set out in the previous section.

The Marxist Tradition and Critical Approaches to the Globalization of Finance

Throughout the twentieth century a long tradition developed of criticizing the social inequality associated with international financial flows and connecting these flows to transformations in the capitalist system. Many of these criticisms drew inspiration from the work of Karl Marx, who saw money and capital as a form of alienation that results when the products of labor are no longer created for their intrinsic value for those who create them, but rather for the value that they are assigned in extended circuits of exchange, a value which is appropriated by the owners of the means of production: "the object that labour produces, its product, confronts it as an alien being, as a power independent of the producer" (Marx, 1844, p. 78). This concept of money as "fetish" has been applied to contemporary global finance (Altvater and Mahnkopf, 1997, p. 452). Marx's linking of money and capital to exploitation and class inequality was further linked to the domination of poor countries by wealthy ones in Lenin's (1917) influential pamphlet *Imperialism: The Highest Stage of Capitalism*. Lenin saw a transformation "from the domination of capital in general" to "the domination of finance capital" (Lenin, 1917, p. 41), with the latter involving the control of banks over an increasingly monopolistic industrial sector, the export of finance capital, and the competition among the great powers for control of the world and its markets.

One major way in which the globalization of finance has been linked theoretically to social inequality has been to highlight the way in which financial transactions can generate enormous wealth for some and terrible hardship for others. The extreme contrast in the 1980s between the exuberant wealth enjoyed by New York and London financiers and the desperate hardship of impoverished citizens from whom developing countries were extracting resources in order to pay back loans to multinational banks and the IMF was an especially strong stimulus to this type of analysis.

Sometimes this inequality is portrayed as a cause (Kotz, 2003) or an effect of speculation: "the trend in the organisation of the flows of finance has been increasingly one which privileges the interests of rentiers and speculators over the functional requirements of productive investment" (Gowan, 1999, p. 9). The wealth generated by financiers is seen as like the proceeds from gambling in not coming from productive work – and, as with gambling, the risks associated with speculation are seen as damaging others. Financial speculation creates a global casino capitalism (Strange, 1996) in which the lives of ordinary citizens are whipsawed by crises and volatility. Speculation shifts attention and resources from the type of long-range industrial and social investment that societies need into short-term wasteful activity that benefits a wealthy minority.

Finance and social inequality has also been highlighted by those who focus on the way in which finance plays an organizing role in the capitalist economy more generally, a point that was an important aspect of Lenin's argument. In this view, those controlling financial firms, the leading fraction of the capitalist class, have a degree of cohesion that is constituted not just by their shared interest in maintaining their dominance of an exploitative system, but also by their common membership in certain clubs or networks, or their linkages through boards of directors. Their social cohesion and influence draw in key figures in governments as well. At the international level certain groupings, such as the Bilderberg meetings or the Trilateral Commission, can be seen as examples of sites in which this class power is solidified and exercised (Fennema and van der Pijl, 1987; Gill, 1990).

Leading financial firms may work closely with their governments, especially in the USA, in aggressively pushing international rules and ideas that help these firms profitably expand their activities around the world, such as rules and ideas supporting unrestrained cross-border capital mobility and requiring debtor countries to adjust to the demands of global financial markets (see, for instance, work by Soederberg such as Soederberg, 2004).

Gowan has argued that the US government worked aggressively to promote its own interests and those of Wall Street by bringing about the globalization of finance through what he calls "the Dollar Wall Street Regime." He suggests that the US government engineered price increases in dollar-denominated Middle Eastern oil in order to generate a flow of US dollars into US banks active in the Euromarkets and to create a dependence on US dollars of oil-importing developing countries. With the collapse of the Bretton Woods system, "the new centrality of the dollar turned people towards Wall Street for finance" (Gowan, 1999, p. 18). Subsequent initiatives of the US government and the crises that resulted reinforced these relations of power and dependence: "The story since the 1970s has been one of growing pressures from the Wall Street centre to weaken the barriers to its penetration into domestic financial systems. . . . In a crisis within a national financial system, the American state itself could open the whole capitalist system of the state concerned to being re-engineered in the interests of American capitalism" (Gowan, 1999, pp. 20, 23).

The dominant social role played by finance can be seen, therefore, not only in the actions of wealthy individuals, but also in the structural character of this domination. This structure involves not just states, but also the organization of the capitalist economy. For instance, finance has shifted from simply funding industrial firms to shaping their conduct, as evident in the use of mergers and other financial strategies by those industrial firms obsessed with their quarterly performance in stock markets. The participation of wealthy households in mutual funds and other forms of institutional investment is a part of this structural change, in which "the capital market moves from intermediation to regulation of firm and household behaviour" (Froud, Johal, and Williams, 2002, p. 126). As Altvater and Mahnkopf (1997, p. 459) note, the "capitalist economy creates a specific hierarchical order of markets: the money market directs the goods market whose development directs the labor market – i.e. the system (and the level) of employment."

One of the distinctive themes of the Marxist tradition has been the linkage of historical changes in the organization of the capitalist socio-economic system as a whole to changes in global finance. For instance, Arrighi (1994) sees the emergence of high international finance in the Italian city-states in the first half of the last millennium as following on their ability to master international production and trade, and to take advantage of the competition among territorial states, a pattern that he identifies in Dutch, British, and US hegemonies as well (Arrighi, 1994, p. 106). Harvey (1989) argues that the contemporary globalization of finance is an aspect of a system of flexible accumulation that has replaced the more Fordist and Keynesian systems that had become excessively rigid. Fordism refers to the match between mass production and high wages that balanced supply and demand, in concert with the stimulation of demand through the government spending that was a defining feature of Keynesianism. Harvey connects the fast-paced flexible restructuring of industry, the cultural carnival of post-modern style, and the fluidity of cross-border financial flows as related aspects of a post-Fordist phase of capitalism.

The Institutional Character of Global Finance: An Alternative Approach

The prevailing sets of approaches discussed in the previous sections are very useful in highlighting the role of competitive markets and of states in the globalization of finance. In their purest forms they are not compatible, since the market-oriented approaches see the state becoming irrelevant and the globalization of finance as consistent with expansions of freedom – claims that are challenged by the state-centric and critical approaches. However, it is not difficult to blend elements from each set of approaches. For instance, one could argue that states initiated the process of financial globalization, but that, once started, the process involved so much growth of financial markets that the market-oriented insights became relevant. Alternatively, one could argue that some powerful states are strengthened and take significant initiatives with regard to global finance, while weaker states are further weakened in the way in which some market-oriented and critical approaches suggest. Yet another alternative is that states are in control at critical junctures, such as at times of global financial crisis, or under particular conditions, such as when they are not indebted to foreign lenders, but that at other times – or in particular markets – market forces rule.

Yet even with such flexible efforts to integrate insights from both sets of approaches, there are important aspects of global finance that are not adequately captured by these theories. The picture these theories paint is one in which the relevant forces have an enduring structural character, whether these are the fluid competitive markets of liberal theory, the competitive state system of traditional international relations theory, or the logic of capitalism and the enduring dominance of the capitalist class of critical approaches. The problem with these ways of conceptualizing global finance is that they can obscure the way in which finance is associated with new forms of global organization that do not fit with conventional conceptions of states, markets, or the control of the system by finance capitalists. Critical approaches, because of their efforts to analyze finance as an aspect of the larger social system, provide an alternative to the fluid market/bureaucratic state dualism that is common in the other approaches; but even critical approaches tend to see finance as an expression of a more fundamental unified force – capitalism or the capitalist class – that either undermines states or works with them, a model in which the organization of global finance itself has little autonomous significance.

This section sets out an alternative approach that focuses on the institutional character of global finance. In the social sciences *institution* refers to a set of recognized rules that can be informal or formal. Marriage is an example of an institution that has formal and informal rules: some are codified in highly detailed laws, and some are widely shared expectations and understandings about how wives, husbands, and children should relate to one another, that are a set of rules, but not ones that are necessarily written down.

An institutional approach treats sets of rules as making an independent contribution to explaining activities such as global financial transactions. Without rules it would be impossible to organize complex interactions, especially over long distances. Although the rules associated with institutions can change over time, as is the case with expectations associated with marriage, even informal rules can have a great deal of independent momentum if they are widely used. In the case of marriage, for instance, no single individual can change the recognized rules, even if he or she can decide not to follow them. Often effective action requires voluntary compliance with recognized formal and informal rules, as is the case with someone who wisely chooses not to wear a swimsuit to an interview for an office job. With certain institutions, effective communication may require voluntary compliance with distinctive rules of language, mathematics, or science.

Perhaps because they are impressed by the apparently effortless way in which money moves around the world, people often assume that global finance lacks institutions. In fact, the intangible character of contemporary financial transactions has made rules and institutions even more important. Most markets require rules that define the grade or quality of the products that are being exchanged, and that make clear the procedures by which ownership of the product is transferred from seller to buyer. Most financial products are constituted by the rules they involve, such as agreed payment schedules, rather than by their material properties. No one is going to transfer millions of dollars electronically without being confident that the transaction is governed by a wide variety of rules, including the technical rules ensuring the integrity of the hardware and software and the legal rules that reduce the likelihood of successful fraud.

What types of institutions and rules are likely to be important in global finance? The *state* and the *firm* are two types of institution that are important, as the state-centric and critical approaches discussed above make clear. However, it is also important to recognize the role played by other types of institutions. Three types that have not been adequately considered in the above approaches are especially important: *international regimes*, *business associations*, and *social practices*. It is useful to look in more detail at each of these in turn.

International regime   This refers to an international institution that provides formal and informal rules in a particular issue area, such as global finance. The concept differs from traditional ideas about how international order comes about. There are two main traditional approaches. One, a *liberal internationalist* tradition, has hoped that formal international organizations, such as the United Nations, and international law would supplant the war-prone state system. The other, *state-centric* approach has assumed that international organizations and law are irrelevant, and has seen order as coming about either as a result of rules promoted by a powerful state or from the equilibrium that results from a balance of power among powerful states. Neither tradition is adequate for understanding the complex sources of international order that are emerging today. The concept of an international regime draws on elements of both traditions in suggesting that the conduct of states can be shaped by formal and informal understandings among them (Hasenclever, Mayer, and Rittberger, 1997).

International regimes may involve international organizations, but regime analysis usually goes beyond the formal aspects of international organizations, such as their articles of agreement, to examine the formal and informal rules in the issue area as a whole within which the organization functions. Thus one would look at the role of the World Trade Organization within the international trade *regime*, the role of the International Monetary Fund within the international monetary *regime*, or the United Nations Human Rights Commission within the international human rights *regime*.

One of the advantages of the regime concept is that it is used to refer to both formal and informal rules in a particular issue area. In the literature on regimes there are useful distinctions between types of rules, such as principles, norms, and decision-making procedures, and there are many theories to account for regime formation and performance. For the purposes of this book it is not necessary to go into these theoretical discussions. Instead, the regime concept is used to draw attention to the complex and interrelated set of formal and informal international institutions that contribute to the governance of global finance. Although the regime concept has most often been used to refer to the rules created by states to govern their interactions, it has also been expanded to include the rules created by private-sector actors (Porter, 1993; Cutler, Haufler, and Porter, 1999), and this expanded usage will be employed in this book.

Chapter 3 uses the term *international regime* to analyze the set of international arrangements that have been constructed to regulate global finance. These involve a complex set of interconnected rules and groupings that are often overlooked because they do not conform to traditional conceptions of international institutions. This emerging regime for regulating global finance has developed sufficiently to have an impact on global finance that is independent of the actions of the states involved, even if the political power of those states continues to be very important.

Business associations   A second type of international institution that has been underestimated is business associations. *Association* here refers primarily to formal organizations, such as stock exchanges or trade associations, but can also refer to more informal business groupings or networks. Global markets do not only consist of atomistic firms and individuals competing with one another; nor is private-sector governance in markets exercised only by powerful firms operating on the basis of their individual organizational capacity alone. There are hundreds of private-sector associations that are involved in global finance, and they often contribute to the making and management of rules that are significant for governance of global finance. These associations are the focus of chapter 7.

Social practices   A third type of institution that is useful in understanding global finance is social practices. *Practice* means a set of activities that are governed and constituted by a shared set of rules. Law and medicine are well-recognized practices, but the word can also be applied to less formalized activities, such as the international practice of sovereignty or the playing of chess (Keohane, 1988). In each case, actors are recognized as engaged in the activity in question only if they follow the rules governing it: the identities of lawyers, doctors, sovereign states, and chess-players are constituted by the rules that define their respective practices.

The concept of a *practice* is useful because it highlights a decentralized source of rules that is becoming increasingly important in international affairs and contemporary life more generally.

Traditionally in international affairs the only rules that were considered important were international laws negotiated by states. Law may play an important role in the operation of practices – for instance, the rules involved in the practice of medicine are backed up by laws prohibiting actors not following those rules from practicing in the jurisdiction of the government that has enacted the law. However, the practice can have a high degree of autonomy from governments: in the case of medicine, the most significant rules are created by doctors and are usually administered by a professional organization of doctors. Even government regulations concerning medicine are usually heavily shaped by actors with medical expertise.

Some aspects of global finance are easily recognized as similar to well-defined practices such as law or medicine. For instance, the practice of financial planning involves a set of rules managed by the Certified Financial Planner Board of Standards. The CFP Board manages the CFP professional designation through its links to financial planning associations, which, as of 2002, existed in 17 countries. The globally oriented CFA Institute (formerly the Association for Investment Management and Research) similarly manages the Chartered Financial Analyst designation. The International Accounting Standards Board and the International Federation of Accountants manage the rules governing accountancy. These are quite similar to the professional bodies that manage the practices of medicine or law.

Other aspects of global finance also are usefully treated as practices, even if they aren't as well defined as financial planning, financial analysis, or accountancy. For instance, the issuing of international bonds involves a set of well-recognized ways of doing things, many of which have been written down by the International Primary Markets Association (IPMA) in the form of recommendations. Although these are not formal regulations, they are a set of rules that govern the market. Despite the important role played by IPMA in codifying informal rules, most of the effectiveness of these rules comes not from the organization itself, but from the shared understanding by a relatively small community of firms that if one wants to participate in this market, one has to follow certain recognized practices that have evolved over the history of the market.

Although the concept of practices will be useful throughout this book, it will be especially important in chapter 10, which analyzes the role of gender, and chapter 11, which analyzes risk practices. Both gender and risk involve an important set of rules and expectations that shape global finance in particular ways, and both are reproduced primarily in a decentralized manner by their use in daily activities of global financial actors rather than by deliberate rule making. Thus gender and risk are forms of institutionalized rules, rules that fit best with the concept of practices rather than the types of institutions to which the regime and association labels refer.

How do the above types of institutions fit together? While there is overlap between internatonal regimes, associations, and practices, they differ significantly, with regimes referring to the institutions governing global finance as a whole in which states are involved, associations referring primarily to organizations of firms, most of which focus on a particular aspect of global finance, such as bond trading, and practices referring to decentralized sets of rules that are routinely reproduced in the daily operations of global finance. Taken together, these institutional concepts allow us to identify and analyze important patterns in global finance that would not otherwise be visible, as subsequent chapters will show.

What is the relationship between these institutionalist concepts and the other approaches to global finance discussed above? This book argues that while each of the other approaches provides important insights, it is not possible to really understand the globalization of finance without considering the way in which institutions support or inhibit particular activities. Efficiency, state power, and social class, the key concepts of market-oriented, state-centric, and critical approaches respectively, are all highly relevant to global finance, but they do not operate automatically or consistently without having to make use of, or work around, the sets of rules identified by an institutionalist approach. The institutional concepts set out above are important in identifying aspects of power and inequality that can be missed by focusing on states and social classes alone, as is the case, for instance, in the unequal distribution of dangers that result from risk practices or the negative effects of gendered financial practices.

The Conceptualization of Global Finance: Conclusion

This chapter started out by discussing market-oriented, state-centric, and critical approaches to the globalization of finance. Each of these approaches provides useful insights into aspects of the globalization of finance. However, these approaches tend to overlook the way in which the conduct and regulation of financial transactions are governed by rules created by public-sector and private-sector participants in financial markets as they engage in their ongoing interactions. The concept of social institutions is useful in highlighting the role played by such rules. Considering global finance as a set of institutionalized rules provides opportunities to creatively challenge market-oriented or state-centric assertions that nothing can be done to control global finance because the forces driving it are so powerful. Institutional concepts draw our attention away from the idea that actors' behavior is determined by these forces and instead urges us to look at how financial globalization is sustained by a wide variety of systems of rules, many of which are routinely reproduced in daily activity, that could, with more reflexivity, be modified. At the same time, a sensitivity to institutional factors encourages modesty and care in discerning the range of options that are feasible, given the dependence of future practices on past ones. Treating global finance as a set of social institutions and practices also allows us to begin to think of global finance as exhibiting many of the characteristics that are distinctive features of our late-modern world more generally.

3

The Emerging Regime for Regulating Global Finance

Often global finance is portrayed as a vast uncontrollable ocean of money that washes back and forth across borders unaffected by government regulations. While there certainly have been cases of serious economic destruction caused by inadequately regulated cross-border financial flows, the idea that global finance is unregulated is seriously misleading. This chapter provides an overview of the arrangements that have been constructed to regulate global finance. These are far stronger and more sophisticated than was the case in the 1970s when serious efforts to construct such arrangements first began. The focus of this chapter is on *prudential* regulation of private global financial flows. *Prudential* regulation is regulation concerned with financial stability, as opposed to rules designed to encourage cross-border financial flows, a topic addressed in chapter 6.

One of the reasons why the significance of the international arrangements for prudential regulation is often overlooked is that these arrangements involve a complex, interrelated set of informal committees, formal international organizations, and decentralized networks engaged in highly technical collaboration. This does not fit at all with the image that most people have when they think of strong, effective political authority. The concept of an international regime that was developed in chapter 2 is useful in analyzing the complex set of international institutions that have been developed to regulate global finance.

The Origins of the Current Regulatory Regime

As discussed in chapter 2, the globalization of finance that we are experiencing today can be traced back to the weakening of restrictions on cross-border financial flows that had been put in place in the mid-twentieth century. The political factors that encouraged the emergence of the Euromarkets, together with technological and organizational creativity of market actors, had, by the late 1960s, created a large enough quantity of lightly regulated financial assets outside the jurisdiction of the US and other governments responsible for the currency in which these assets were denominated, that some public-sector officials began to consider the implications of these cross-border financial activities for the stability of the system as a whole.

The Group of Ten (G10) and the Bank for International Settlements (BIS) played the most important role in initiating the current regime for international financial regulation. The G10 was created in 1962 to manage the General Arrangements to Borrow of the International Monetary Fund (IMF), a supplementary source of IMF financing provided by the G10 members. The G10 included central bankers and finance ministers from the 11 countries that were playing the most prominent role in international finance at the time. The BIS, originally set up in 1930 to handle German reparations for World War I, is a central bankers' bank, and is unusual for an international institution in that it has a revenue source from its own banking operations that it controls. Central bankers have helped one another and have contributed to international financial stability by swapping money through the BIS, but the most important contribution of the BIS to global financial regulation is its hosting of specialized and highly technical committees. In the 1960s a number of officials at the BIS were asked by the G10 to monitor the size of the Euromarkets – a group that would be more formally constituted as the Eurocurrency Standing Committee in 1971. Through the 1970s, 1980s, and early 1990s other similar initiatives were launched by the G10 and housed at the BIS. These BIS-based intergovernmental bodies involve sets of officials who have particular responsibilities and expertise, and some autonomy from the larger portfolio of responsibilities of the national central banks or regulators from which they come.

Three new institutions were launched in 1975 that would come to play an increasingly central role in international financial regulation (Porter, 2003). The first, created by the G10, was the Basel Committee on Banking Regulations and Supervisory Practices, which would subsequently be renamed as the Basel Committee on Banking

Supervision (BCBS), the most important international body concerned with the regulation of international banks. The BCBS's secretariat was hosted by the BIS, and its members consisted of central bankers and bank regulators from the G10 member countries, plus Luxembourg. The second institution launched was the Group of Seven (G7), an informal annual gathering of the leaders of the seven most industrialized countries designed to address the economic problems that accompanied the breakdown of the Bretton Woods system. Subsequently, in the mid-1990s, the G7 became much more institutionalized and took over the leading role played by the G10 Central Bank Governors in launching new initiatives with regard to international financial regulation. The third institution was the awkwardly named Inter-American Organization of Securities Commissions and Similar Organizations, initially designed to foster the emergence of stock markets in Latin America, but destined to be renamed the International Organization of Securities Commissions (IOSCO) and given a global mandate in 1984, after which it became the leading international body responsible for the regulation of securities markets.

Of the three institutions created in 1975, the BCBS proved to be the most important for financial regulation. Although the G10 and the G7 were higher-level from the point of view of political authority, they both had a broader responsibility for the global monetary and economic systems respectively, and concerned themselves only with the longer-range trajectory of prudential regulation, not the practical details – and the G7's interest in prudential regulation really became significant only in the midst of the international financial crises of the 1990s. The BCBS, while at first glance simply a boring technical committee, has worked out a series of concrete agreements on bank regulation that have been the biggest achievements of the emerging regime for international financial regulation.

The Evolution of the Regime since 1975

The purpose of this section, as of this chapter more generally, is to provide an overview of the evolution of the emerging regime for financial regulation. More detailed accounts of the work of the BCBS and IOSCO will be provided in chapters 4 and 5, which focus on international banking and securities regulation respectively. This chapter is more interested in the interrelationship of these and other institutions involved in international financial regulation. We shall see that this evolution involves a gradual coalescence of a regulatory regime from practically oriented developments in a set of bodies that initially operated relatively autonomously – not the deliberate construction by states of an elaborate international organization or body of international law. We see a high level of informality both in the relations among the bodies involved in the regime and in the character of many of the most important bodies themselves, including the G7 and the BCBS, neither of which have founding treaties, formal decision procedures, or independent secretariats.

It is useful to think of the evolution of the regime for international financial regulation as involving three main developments. The first is the development of bank regulation, which is the most advanced of all types of international financial regulation in its effectiveness. A second main development is the emergence and growth of other types of financial regulation, including especially securities and insurance, and the horizontal integration that linked them with the work on bank regulation. A third main development is the process of vertical integration that strengthened the links of the technical bodies to more political or formal sources of authority, including the G7 and formal intergovernmental organizations such as the IMF, World Bank, and the Organization for Economic Cooperation and Development (OECD). Each of these main developments is examined in turn.

There are a number of reasons why international bank regulation is more advanced than other types of international financial regulation. The Euromarkets began as bank deposits of US dollars in London, and only later expanded to include securities such as bonds and stocks, which required more complex infrastructures than banks. Thus banking has been at the leading edge of financial globalization.[1] Banks also have traditionally been more closely regulated by governments than other financial firms because their role in payments is central to the daily functioning of an economy, because smaller depositors can be vulnerable to bank fraud and mismanagement for which they cannot be expected to be responsible, and because the mismatch in time-frame between short-term deposits and long-term lending makes banks, who cannot quickly liquidate their assets, prone to bank runs, in which the bank collapses simply due to a lack of confidence, rather than a real problem with its solvency.

As noted, international collaboration among bank regulators has centred on the work at the BCBS. One function of the BCBS has been to foster exchange of information among its members, a task that is facilitated by the lack of formal structure and the focus on practical problems. The BCBS has also produced an ever-increasing number of technical reports that serve not just to identify problems, but to point towards recommended solutions. However, its most important accomplishments have been in creating agreed regulatory standards that are subsequently widely implemented in the jurisdictions of its members, and beyond.

The first regulatory standard addressed by the BCBS soon after it was established concerned the division of labor between regulators in different jurisdictions. A major concern with the globalization of finance is that banks would play one jurisdiction off against another, or move from one jurisdiction to another, in order to escape regulation. This could lead to a "race to the bottom" as states, seeking to retain banking activities in their jurisdictions, engage in a competitive process of deregulation, leaving the world with a dangerously low level of regulation. The BCBS sought to address this problem through a 1975 Concordat, which was revised in 1983 and 1992. The solution it settled on was to make the home regulator (the regulator in the jurisdiction in which the bank's head office is located) responsible for the regulation of the worldwide activities of international banks, a responsibility facilitated by an agreed requirement that those banks report on a consolidated basis (drawing together data from all their offices around the world). Since most of the internationally active banks have been headquartered in the 12 member countries of the BCBS, this has been quite effective.

The second type of regulatory standard addressed by the BCBS concerned the level of capital held by banks. Capital, which can be thought of as the difference between assets and liabilities, is an important safety cushion that helps protect banks from failing. The BCBS launched the first set of internationally agreed capital adequacy standards with its 1988 Basel Accord, and in the late 1990s efforts began to revise this accord. This process is examined in detail in chapter 4. The Basel Accord remains the most ambitious and successful example of international financial regulation.

From the point of view of its role in the emerging regulatory regime, another important feature of the BCBS has been its ability to construct a worldwide network of regional committees of bank regulators in order to extend its reach beyond its 12 member states. These are examined in more detail in chapter 8. This network remains very informal, with no written public rules governing either the very varied organizational character of the regional groups or the relationship of these groups to the BCBS.

Turning to the second main development in the regime for international financial regulation, the emergence and growth of other types of financial regulation than bank regulation and the horizontal integration that linked these with bank regulation, the most important body is IOSCO. As noted above, IOSCO took on its present name and global mandate in 1984. In contrast to the informality of the BCBS and its relations with the regional groups of bank regulators, IOSCO follows very closely the standard formal structure of an international organization. It has its own secretariat and secretary-general, a 19-member Executive Committee, and an assembly of all members that meets annually, called the Presidents' Committee. It publishes an organization chart, and it includes within it four well-defined regional committees. Unlike the BCBS, it is open to regulators from all countries and includes non-governmental actors as associate members. There is some parallel with the BCBS in the leading role played in IOSCO by its 15-member Technical Committee, composed of regulators from the most important markets, which focuses on the production of highly technical reports and standards, and which is engaged in asymmetrical interactions with developing and transition country regulators through the latter's involvement in IOSCO's Emerging Markets Committee. However, even these two committees of IOSCO are more formally defined than the BCBS and the regional groups associated with it.

The international regulatory body for insurance that corresponds to the BCBS for banking and IOSCO for securities is the International Association of Insurance Supervisors (IAIS). Like the BCBS, it has a secretariat at the BIS. It was formed relatively recently, in 1994, although it built on work on insurance regulation that had been going on for some years previously at the OECD. The IAIS is open to public-sector insurance regulators from any country, and in 2003 it had members from about 100 jurisdictions. More than 70 private-sector associations and other private-sector actors participate in the IAIS as observers, a category that excludes them from some discussions. The IAIS has a formal committee structure similar to IOSCO's.

As noted, one of the distinctive features of the emerging regime for international financial regulation is increased horizontal integration. In part this has been driven by organizational developments within markets that have broken down barriers between banking, securities, and insurance, as firms from those jurisdictions that have traditionally separated these sectors have sought to expand the range of financial products they offer. The first cross-sectoral regulatory collaboration involved IOSCO and the BCBS, at the initiative of the BCBS, which wanted to encourage the negotiation of capital standards at IOSCO to prevent activity migrating to securities markets in response to the BCBS capital standards. There were also worries that the blurring of boundaries in the activities of market actors could lead to new problems, either as a result of the difficulty of monitoring the more complex financial transactions and flows or because of the danger that problems in one sector would more easily and dangerously spread to other sectors. These concerns led to the creation of the informal Tripartite Group in 1993, which was reconstituted as the Joint Forum in 1996, by the BCBS, IOSCO, and IAIS, with a secretariat at the BIS. Aside from encouraging information sharing, the Joint Forum has primarily focused on regulatory issues related to conglomerates.

As noted above, the third major development in the emerging regime for international financial regulation has been a process of vertical integration in which high-level political authority and the daily technical work of bodies such as the BCBS have been brought more closely together. Until the 1990s international prudential regulation proceeded with relatively little high-level political involvement. There was some political accountability through periodic legislative review of the international initiatives of regulators, but this was minimal for two reasons: the highly technical character of the regulatory work which made it difficult for non-experts to monitor, and the deliberate efforts of regulators to keep politics out of their work through practices such as confidentiality or reliance on informal agreements rather than formal ones requiring legislative approval. Political conflict among financial regulators, while not insignificant, was much more muted than in other international issue areas, such as trade negotiations.

The lack of political involvement in international prudential regulation prior to the 1990s was also a result of the separation of two of the more conflictual aspects of global finance from the work on prudential regulation: the resolution of the Third World debt crisis that broke out in the early 1980s and conflicts over direct foreign investment. The first was handled through the IMF, as discussed in chapter 4, and the second through bilateral and regional agreements or at the OECD and UN, as discussed in chapter 6.

In the 1990s a key change in the character of the emerging regime for international financial regulation was the increased integration of the technically oriented international work with higher-level and more formalized forms of political authority. This involved two main aspects. The first was the increased involvement of the G7 in the governance of global finance, including its creation of two new bodies in 1999: the Financial Stability Forum (FSF) and the Group of Twenty (G20). The second was the increased linkages between the technical bodies doing work on prudential regulation and four large formal intergovernmental organizations: the IMF, World Bank, OECD, and the World Trade Organization (WTO). We now look at each of these aspects in turn.

As noted above, the G7 summit meetings began in 1975 and were initially intended to be an informal opportunity for leaders of the participating countries to exchange ideas for addressing the international economic problems of that decade. Although the G7 devoted considerable attention to international monetary issues, such as the value of the dollar relative to other currencies, and commented on the debt crisis of the early 1980s, it did not involve itself with the emerging regime for international financial regulation until the 1990s.

One factor that contributed to the G7 turning its attention to the emerging regime was the evolution of the institutional capacity of the G7 itself.[2] In the early years the G7 was almost entirely focused on the yearly summit of leaders, and when the expertise or interests of these leaders moved away from monetary and financial matters, the G7 did as well. However, over time there were enough officials in each country involved year-round in preparation for the summit and in communicating with one another, that the G7 began to be a much more robust institution, less dependent on the expertise and interest of the leaders, and more capable of handling more technically complex issues such as global financial regulation. A particularly important step in this process of institutionalization was the initiation of independent meetings of the G7 finance ministers in 1986.

The most important reason for the increased involvement of the G7 in the emerging regime for international financial regulation in the 1990s was the severity of a series of international financial crises in that decade. An early glimpse of the decade's problems was provided by the instability in the European monetary system in 1992, when rapid cross-border financial flows knocked the European Community members off their plan to align their currencies more closely. However, the Mexican crisis of 1994 was even more serious, as it not only caused trouble for the Mexican government but began to spread to other countries, threatening to damage the US financial system very seriously, and beginning to cripple the Mexican banking system and, consequently, the Mexican economy as a whole. This was a new type of crisis for the global financial system, because it involved the rapid flight from Mexican financial assets of widely dispersed private investors transferring money through securities markets, as compared to the more concentrated bank lending of the debt crisis of the early 1980s. A similar crisis broke out in East Asia in 1997, which subsequently spread to Russia, and in less severe form to Central Europe, Latin America, and the USA. The character of these crises is discussed in more detail in chapter 8.

Beginning with the first G7 summit after the Mexican crisis, the Halifax summit of 1995, the G7 began to devote a great deal of high-level attention to the emerging regime for international financial regulation. Initially a variety of responses were considered, including some serious consideration on the part of the Canadian and French governments of the idea of a tax on international financial transactions, often called the "Tobin tax" after the Nobel-winning economist who first proposed this idea as a way to "throw sand in the wheels of international finance" (Eichengreen, Tobin, and Wyplosz, 1995). However, the G7's focus moved quite quickly to the idea of strengthening prudential regulation and improving the information and standards in global securities markets, rather than options that would have involved government interference with cross-border financial flows. The G7's policy was consistent with the type of globalized financial activity that wealthy and powerful firms and governments, especially the US, had been aggressively promoting. However, the policy was also a recognition that if cross-border financial flows were to continue, the current phase of financial globalization, with its greater involvement of dispersed investors and securities markets, had brought with it serious new problems that required more complex responses than governments had previously considered.

A number of important institutional changes accompanied this increased attention to the international financial system of the G7. The first was a more regular and systematic reporting and decision process, in which the G7 finance ministers would set out quite detailed priorities, and the G7 summit would check up yearly on the progress on existing priorities, and endorse new ones that had been proposed by their ministers. An even more important institutional development, however, was the creation by the G7 of two new institutions in 1999: the Financial Stability Forum and the G20.

The Financial Stability Forum was created after Hans Tietmeyer, then head of the German central bank, issued a report recommending such a body after consulting with the G7 governments and key participants in the emerging regime for international financial regulation. The FSF brought together three representatives from each of the G7 governments, along with representatives from all the key international bodies involved in international financial matters. These now include the BCBS, IOSCO, IAIS, IMF, OECD, World Bank, European Central Bank, the International Accounting Standards Board, the Eurocurrency Standing Committee, renamed the Committee on the Global Financial System in 1999, as well as the Committee on Payments and Settlement Systems, a BIS-based committee that had been created in the 1970s to address potential prudential problems associated with electronic banking networks.

The stated purpose of the FSF was to provide a more coordinated international capacity to anticipate global crises. It was an expression of both the horizontal and the vertical integration of the emerging regime that have been identified in this chapter. On the horizontal dimension, it further enhanced information sharing among technically oriented bodies in the manner already begun with previous initiatives such as the Joint Forum. Its organizational character, including its reliance on a secretariat at the BIS and its informality, also closely resembled that of the other BIS-based technical bodies. On the vertical dimension, by bringing in political representatives from the G7, it connected these technical bodies more closely to higher-level political authorities. In the months following its launch, it began to be criticized for its lack of representation outside the G7 countries, and it has responded by adding Australia, Hong Kong, the Netherlands, and Singapore as members and by including developing countries on an *ad hoc* basis in its working groups and consultations. Despite this, the wealthy G7 countries still closely control it.

In its first years the FSF devoted itself to two main tasks. The first was to produce lengthy reports on key aspects of global finance that had seemed to be implicated in the crises of the 1990s. These included *highly leveraged institutions*, better known as hedge funds, organizations of very wealthy investors that speculated on financial fluctuations, including currency movements, and that contributed to international instability as a result. They also included *offshore centers*, lightly regulated jurisdictions like the Cayman Islands or Vanuatu, which were seen to have contributed to instability by weakening global regulatory standards. Other reports were written on cross-border capital flows and on exchange rates. These reports were quite technical, but made some important political contributions in following through on the promise to include developing countries in their formulation, and in proposing changes that previously would have been unacceptable to the USA and its G7 partners, including more rigorous monitoring and pressuring of offshore centers, more regulatory efforts to reduce bank lending to hedge funds, and serious consideration under certain circumstances of the merits of controls over cross-border capital flows.

The second of the FSF's major tasks was to try to pull together work on financial standards and codes that was being carried out in a variety of uncoordinated locations. This included, for instance, the BCBS, IAIS, and IOSCO standards, OECD work on international codes on corporate governance, the International Accounting Standards Board's accounting standards, among others. The FSF produced a Compendium of international financial standards and codes which it made available on its website, and began producing a series of reports addressing implementation issues. Much of the emphasis in this process was on producing standards that could be more easily incorporated into the calculations of market actors. For instance, an extensive FSF survey of market actors found that analysts and large investors would be more likely to use measures of compliance with standards that could be expressed as a numerical figure, so that these could be integrated into their mathematical risk modeling.

The G20 consisted of finance ministers and central bankers from the G7 plus 12 "systemically important" countries in global finance, along with representatives from the IMF, World Bank, and EU.[3] Participation by developing countries was therefore much greater than in the FSF. The G20 grew out of a more *ad hoc* grouping called the G22, which had been called together by the USA in the wake of the East Asian crisis, and which produced three major reports in 1998 on the reform of the international financial architecture. Each report was produced by a working group co-chaired by one developed market country and one emerging market country, although in practice the process was dominated by the former. The G22 was seen as a better way to address global financial problems than the IMF, because of its greater flexibility and informality and its inclusion of only the most relevant countries, and in this sense it resembled the G7. However the *ad hoc* character of its creation by the USA undermined its legitimacy, and by the end of its report-writing process, after it had been expanded to the G33 in response to demands from other countries to be included, it was ended, to be replaced a few months later by the G20.

The G20, during its first two years, was heavily influenced by its first chair, Canadian Finance Minister Paul Martin, and the G20 Secretariat provided by his Finance Department in Ottawa. The G20 was envisioned as a place where top policymakers from developed and developing countries could meet in an informal setting and set out broad initiatives, which their collective voting strength and national implementation capacity would allow them to carry out through the IMF, World Bank, and – through their national policies – in the world's major financial markets that they represented. The G20 meetings were restricted to three representatives from each country, to encourage a frank and informal exchange of ideas, modeled, like the G22, on the G7. In its first year the G20 focused mostly on the types of technical issues that the FSF was also discussing, but in its second year it expanded its agenda to include globalization more generally. While the G20 seemed to fulfill an important function in bridging the gap between the G7 and the large number of countries that had become important for the international financial system, it had some weaknesses with regard to legitimacy, both because of the many countries it excluded and because its membership of finance ministers and central bankers was not necessarily the best suited to address non-financial aspects of globalization. Beginning in 2002 the chair of the G20 began rotating yearly, to India, Mexico, Germany, and then China in 2005. The deputies to the ministers and central bank governors also began meeting regularly. In the 2003 Mexico ministerial meeting a range of issues, including financial stability, tax evasion, and financing for development, were discussed.

As noted above, in addition to the FSF and the G20, the other way in which the vertical integration of the technical bodies concerned with prudential regulation and the world of high-level political authority was strengthened was through the closer links established with four formal intergovernmental organizations: the IMF, World Bank, OECD, and WTO. The IMF was the most important of these. In addition to sitting on the FSF, the IMF strengthened its involvement in financial matters by bringing financial standards and codes into its conditionality processes. *Conditionality* refers to the way in which the IMF requires countries to meet certain requirements before receiving loans, and before the 1990s these mainly concerned macroeconomic matters such as budget deficits and exchange rates, while by the end of the 1990s they began to include compliance with international financial standards such as those created by the BCBS. The IMF also began carrying out Reports on Observance of Financial Standards and Codes (ROSCs), intensive audits of countries carried out by foreign regulators that countries were encouraged to make public. Although these ROSCs were ostensibly voluntary, the hope was that peer and market pressures would lead an increasing number of countries to participate. By 2003, 85 countries had ROSCs done, with many countries submitting to multiple ones. Most were posted on the IMF website. This willingness of sovereign states to submit to intensive and transparent peer review is remarkable, since even as recently as the G22 reports of 1998 it was not clear that such an intrusive process would be accepted.

The other three organizations played a more limited role. The World Bank began to devote much more attention to questions of domestic and international financial stability in its publications, research, and lending. The OECD contributed though its involvement in standards of corporate governance, a high-profile issue after "cronyism" and other types of corporate governance problems were blamed by many for the East Asian crisis. The OECD also hosted the Financial Action Task Force, the body responsible for standards to prevent money laundering and terrorist financing. The WTO's involvement was limited to negotiations on the degree to which prudential concerns could be a reason to restrain the liberalization of cross-border trade in financial services. In the 1997 WTO agreement on financial services there was a "prudential carve-out," which sought to clarify this issue. Following that agreement, negotiations slowly proceeded in the WTO's Committee on Financial Services, and in the Working Party on Domestic Regulation on the broader question of the relationship of domestic regulation to trade, a process that was carefully watched by the financial industry.

Conclusion

Looking back over the history of efforts to regulate global finance, it is clear that the primary form that these have taken is the creation of relatively informal and highly technical international bodies by states. States are important in the creation, implementation, and ongoing maintenance of these arrangements. Members of these bodies are usually representatives of states, and once a regulatory standard is agreed, it is mostly up to national governments and regulatory agencies to implement it. This is consistent with the state-centric analyses discussed in chapter 2. Additionally, it is clear that formal bureaucratic international organizations, including IOSCO, the BIS, IMF, OECD, and World Bank, play an important role, as liberal internationalist approaches suggest. However, it would be a mistake to see these arrangements as simply the product of the type of rationalistic competitive bargaining among states that we usually associate with international negotiations, or as relying on the capacities of formal bureaucratic international organizations. What are more significant are the networks of regulators and other market actors that cut across the formal structures of states and international organizations and that display considerable autonomy from them, as suggested by the institutionalist approach developed in chapter 2.

Much of the autonomy of these networks stems from the technical practices in which they are heavily engaged. For instance, in developing the capital adequacy standards at the Basel Committee on Banking Supervision, regulators and market actors engage in complex quantitative modeling of risks in which the national interests of the states from which they come play no explicit role. The ongoing development of this work is shaped much more by the practical technical problems it seeks to address than by the preferences of the leaders of governments back home. These leaders would find it difficult to follow the detailed progress of the regulators and to explain to voters why they should be enthusiastic about a leader devoting time to do so. When they do pay attention to the work of these international regulatory bodies, government leaders also generally believe that there is more to be gained by allowing them to operate relatively autonomously rather than by seeking to manipulate them. The autonomy of the international bodies and networks is further reinforced as the technically oriented participants get to know one another. When the technical body is located at an international organization and receives administrative support from it, then its autonomy from national governments can also be increased.

The members of these technical bodies consult carefully with leading financial firms, but many of the standards that they create impose significant costs on those firms. Wealthy owners of capital are certainly listened to very carefully, as predicted by the critical approaches discussed in chapter 2; but the ways in which the international institutions concerned with global financial regulation have been constructed do not allow these owners of capital to dictate the outcome of the regulators' work. There are serious problems with this process in the degree to which it sidelines democratic processes for addressing political issues, and this is discussed further in chapter 12. The emerging regulatory regime discussed in this chapter is focused on improving the performance of global finance, and restrictions on the growth of global finance, such as the Tobin tax, some of which might be beneficial to the general public, tend not to be given serious consideration, consistent with critical approaches that argue that the system remains dominated by wealthy states and firms that benefit from capital mobility. All the same, it is important to recognize that the institutions discussed in this chapter provide a much greater capacity to regulate global finance than most people realize. These institutions are likely to play a crucial role in any successful effort to control the harmful effects of global finance.

The emerging regime for global financial regulation is of interest not just for understanding how global finance is likely to continue to be regulated in the future, but also for what it tells us about global governance more generally. The role of practically oriented networks has been noted in other issue areas as well – for instance, in a UN-sponsored project on global policy networks (Reinicke and Deng, 2000). As in other areas of contemporary life, shared systems of abstract knowledge are an increasingly important source of social organization, and at the international level they can substitute for more formal legal structures that have been difficult and costly to construct, and that are often too rigid to cope with global change. Taking these types of social practices seriously, rather than just focusing on the conflicts involving centralized states and anonymous fluid markets, is important if we are to understand the future of governance in this and other globalizing issue areas.

Part II

Sectoral Developments

4

International Banking

Understanding international banking is important for understanding the globalization of finance, because this type of international financial activity has been the leading edge of the current wave of globalization, and because, as noted in the previous chapter, the arrangements for international bank regulation are at the heart of the larger emerging regime for international financial regulation. This chapter looks in more detail at the changes that international banking has experienced with globalization and at the efforts to regulate international banking, especially with regard to the Basel Capital Adequacy Accord. These developments tell us a great deal, not just about banking, but about globalization and regulation more generally. We shall see that the character of banks as institutions, which differs from the institutional character of other aspects of global finance such as securities markets or direct foreign investment, has a big impact on the globalization and regulation of international banking.

The Distinctiveness of International Banking

While banks have been involved in a wide variety of financial activities, the heart of the banking function involves the conversion of relatively short-term *liabilities*, such as the type of deposit the average person puts into their local bank, into longer-term *assets*, especially loans. Banks are able to do this because, in contrast to individual depositors, they possess substantial organizational capacity: they can find clients needing loans, they can assess the creditworthiness of those clients, they can monitor their performance in using and repaying the loan, and they can put pressure on delinquent borrowers, including taking legal action. The trustworthy reputation they may have built over many years allows them to collect deposits from relatively unknowledgeable depositors in a way that may not be possible for the firms to which banks extend loans. This institutional function of transforming short-term liabilities into longer-term assets is called *intermediation*.

Banking can be contrasted especially with securities markets, in which activities are financed not by loans, but instead by a firm or government issuing securities, such as stocks and bonds, which are then bought directly by dispersed investors. With regard to institutions, securities markets require a more sophisticated market infrastructure than banking, including mechanisms for providing information to investors and arrangements to sustain a sufficient volume of ongoing securities trading so that investors can sell their securities should they lose confidence in the borrower or need their money for something else (since they generally have neither the capacity to influence the borrowers nor the resources for long-term investments that banks have). In periods of increased international financial integration, including our present period of globalization, bank-intermediated financing usually precedes international securities markets, because the bank's organizational capacity can more easily be constructed and extended across borders than the infrastructure needed for securities markets. We shall see below that, as finance has become more globalized, there has been a shift from banking to securities markets, a process called *disintermediation*, with the latter surpassing the former in international finance in 1982.

Because of the way in which banks borrow short-term money from dispersed and relatively unknowledgable depositors, and lend this money for longer-term projects, there is an inherent danger that banks might collapse even if their assets outweigh their liabilities. If depositors start quickly withdrawing their deposits, the bank will probably not be able to liquidate its assets, most of which are long-term loans, quickly enough to provide the money demanded by depositors. The fact that most of the knowledge upon which the bank makes its assessment is internal to the bank and not accessible to depositors means that confidence in banks can be fragile, and panic can set in among depositors, with each depositor rushing to get money out before the bank collapses. The confidence problem is exacerbated by the tendency to fraud that is encouraged by lack of information available to depositors about the bank's internal operations. Since banks are able to obtain higher interest rates from lending to high-risk borrowers, there is also an inherent danger that some banks will take advantage of the reputation of the banking community of which they are a part to attract depositors, without exercising the prudence that is needed to maintain that reputation. As a consequence of these types of problems, the history of banking is littered with problems of fraud, panics, and bank collapses. In domestic settings this problem has been addressed by banks banding together to provide deposit insurance, and by governments regulating banks and providing emergency financing to banks that are in trouble – the "lender of last resort" function. The lack of a government at the international level has made it difficult to organize measures such as these.

Banks and the Euromarkets

The present period of financial globalization, as discussed in previous chapters, began with the Eurodollar markets – US dollar bank deposits in London and other jurisdictions outside the USA. This type of financial globalization was facilitated not just by the organizational capacity of the banks but also by a set of relations that existed among international bankers. These relations helped facilitate the flow of information about banks and borrowers, thereby helping in monitoring borrowers, building the reputation of banks, and the other functions that are part of banking, including building the type of confidence that might otherwise require government initiative. One way in which these relations were sustained was through the informal ties among bankers in the City of London that had evolved over the hundreds of years in which the City had been the centre of international finance. These ties were reinforced by family and social class identities, by distinctive styles of dress, by the well-defined physical boundedness of the City, and by the clubs to which bankers belonged (Thrift, 1994; Sassen, 1995). The relations were also sustained by the practice of syndication, in which banks regularly banded together to finance particularly large projects that would typically seek out financing in the Euromarkets. A bank that failed to meet the expected standards of conduct could be shunned, thereby crippling its ability to operate in the Euromarkets.

By the early 1970s, this informal set of relations among international banks began to erode and to be inadequate for maintaining the stability of international finance, contributing to imprudent behavior and an upswing in efforts by governments to begin playing a more active stabilizing role, as they had for many years for domestic banking. In London this was experienced as the intrusion of aggressive new players from the USA who did not share the ties or expectations of the traditional London banking community (Moran, 1984). This tendency would continue in ensuing years and decades as international banking spread from its original base in London to involve locations and banks around the world.

During the 1970s three other developments had an enormous impact on the globalization of banking. The first was the volatility in exchange rates that followed the breakdown of the Bretton Woods monetary system, and which encouraged many banks to engage in risky speculation, as described in chapter 2. In the ensuing years international banks were drawn into all sorts of new activities, either to try to make money by speculating themselves on this sort of volatility, or by selling products to firms that wanted to speculate or to risk-averse firms that wanted to pay to shift the risks from volatility onto speculators.

A second development was the oil price shocks of 1973 and 1979, the first connected to actions of the Organization of Petroleum Exporting Countries (OPEC) and the second to the aftermath of the 1979 revolution in Iran. In each case the rapid increases in oil prices led to massive inflows of money – "petrodollars" – into oil-exporting countries. These countries could not make good immediate use of this money, and saw the Euromarkets as an attractive place to put it, since they would not be vulnerable to political interference from the US government. At the same time developing countries that were oil importers were desperate to borrow, to cover the unexpected costs they were facing from the oil price increase. International banks therefore became key participants in the "recycling of petrodollars" that was carried out in this way in the Euromarkets.

A third development involved interest rates. With the collapse of the Bretton Woods monetary system, volatility in interest rates also increased, as governments felt freer to alter interest rates without regard to their potential impact on exchange rates, and this added to the volatility that arose from floating exchange rates. For this reason and others, governments allowed the money supply to grow, which led to high inflation and low or even negative real interest rates (the interest rate after the effect of inflation is deducted). This, together with the petrodollars, led to a boom in international lending, and stories are told of young bankers flying around the world eagerly urging developing governments to borrow, on the assumption that governments could never go bankrupt. Governments liked to borrow from banks, because the money seemed to come with fewer strings attached than loans from governments or from the International Monetary Fund or World Bank.

The LDC Debt Crisis of the 1980s

Interest rates climbed sharply upward following a surprise move to curb inflation on the part of the US Federal Reserve in 1979. The Fed's emphasis on countering inflation was subsequently followed by central banks in other countries as well. Developing countries that had borrowed heavily from banks during the 1970s suddenly found it difficult to repay their loans with these unexpectedly high rates. The effects of the higher interest charges were exacerbated by the global recession that accompanied the Fed's initiative, which sharply curtailed the exports of developing countries, leaving them without the foreign currency needed to cover the cost of their debt.

In August 1982 Mexico unilaterally declared a moratorium on its debt, and it subsequently became apparent that other heavily indebted countries such as Brazil and Argentina were also in crisis. It soon became apparent as well that the viability of many very large banks that had lent heavily to developing country governments was at risk. Since the collapse of these banks could bring down other banks, it began to look as if the global financial system as a whole was at risk.

At first it was not at all clear how the costs associated with this debt crisis would be distributed. The banks and their supporters argued that the loans must be repaid at any cost, because for developing countries to renege on their financial obligations would undermine a fundamental principle, that financial commitments should be honored, that was essential for the global financial system to operate. They argued that default would be harmful to the defaulting country, since it would be unable to obtain credit in the future. Many argued that the developing countries had been imprudent in borrowing so heavily and were having difficulty repaying because they had wasted the money on large inefficient projects, such as the building of unnecessary national airlines, rather than ensuring that it was used to generate the revenue needed to pay back the loans. Along with these general statements of high principle was the basic fact that the banks self-interestedly wanted to be repaid and not to have to shoulder the costs of the crisis.

Others supportive of the developing countries argued that the interest rate increases initiated by the Fed's action could not have been anticipated by the developing countries and were not their fault. Banks should have been more cautious in lending. In domestic economies banks that have lent money to companies that become bankrupt often bear some of the costs of that bankruptcy, as do other creditors.

In the end, the allocation of costs in the debt crisis was determined not by standards of fairness or efficiency, but instead by the organizational and political capacity of the creditor countries and banks, on the one hand, relative to the indebted developing countries, on the other. The US government, the IMF, and the banks worked hard in the midst of the crisis to ensure that indebted countries did not refuse to maintain their commitment to pay back the loans and interest that they owed to the banks. In particular, they successfully insisted that indebted countries negotiate individually, thereby reducing the likelihood that they would band together in a debtors' cartel to extract concessions from the banks.

The IMF used its expertise to identify a set of policies that would allow indebted countries to obtain the financial resources needed to repay their debt, policies which included reducing subsidies and social spending, selling off state-owned enterprises, encouraging export-oriented industries, and devaluing currencies to make imports more expensive for citizens and exports cheaper for foreign buyers. The IMF used its own lending to demand that governments make these structural adjustments, and to signal to the commercial banking community which governments they should continue to lend to, thereby increasing the pressure on indebted LDCs (less developed countries). The US government and the IMF put some pressure on banks to roll over their loans in order to avert a panicky flight as each bank tried to get its assets out while there were still some left. Overall, however, it looked to many observers that the US government, the IMF, and the banks had exercised their power to arbitrarily protect the interests of the banks at the expense of the citizens of indebted LDCs, who were being forced to cut back their already inadequate standards of living to solve a problem they had not created.

As the debt crisis continued, the IMF policies of loan conditionality and structural adjustment became more elaborate and well-recognized, and attracted more and more opposition, including a series of riots in places where they were implemented. Critics have compiled a list of 104 anti-IMF riots from 1976 to 2001 (<lists. essential.org/pipermail/stop-imf/2001q3/000488.html>). The 1980s were a lost decade for Latin America and Africa as living standards declined dramatically. In Latin America the number of people living in poverty rose by at least 40 million, or 22 percent, during the 1980s (IADB, 1997, p. 1). Net capital flows reversed, so that financial flows out of much of the developing world exceeded inflows.

By the late 1980s it began to be clear to everyone that the debt burden was so crushing that it would be impossible for developing countries to repay it all. Following the unsuccessful Baker plan of 1985, in 1989 US Treasury Secretary Nicholas Brady called for indebted LDCs to convert bank loans with high interest rates to long-term bonds with lower interest rates, backed up by a guarantee from the US and Japanese governments and the World Bank. More than US $160 billion face value of Brady bonds have been issued, typically involving a 30–50 percent discount on the face value of the loans (<www.emta.org>). A secondary market in developing country bank loans also developed in the mid-1980s with heavily exposed banks selling the bad loans they possessed, at a significant discount, to other banks that potentially could have made a lot of money should the indebted LDC end up paying back the loans in full. Exchanges of debt for equity in state-owned enterprises and other indebted-country assets also developed. From the end of 1985 to the end of 1988, before the Brady plan, banks retired $26 billion dollars worth of debt through debt–equity swaps, exit bonds, debt-buybacks, and discount restructurings (Cline, 1995, p. 210). In 1994 $1.7 trillion of emerging market debt was traded, of which 61 percent were Brady bonds (<www.emta.org>). This produced a bonanza on Wall Street (Molano, 1996).

These market-based efforts to address the debt crisis signaled a massive shift in global finance away from bank lending to securities markets, a shift that would lead to new types of global financial crises in the 1990s. Developing countries began to promote their stock markets, both for selling their government bonds and for selling stocks and bonds of domestic firms, including newly privatized ones. These changes in LDCs took place in a larger context involving complementary factors, including a general worldwide ideological shift in favor of market forces, the rapid growth of institutional investors (such as pensions and mutual funds) in developed countries that were eager to invest in foreign stocks and bonds, the growth of the type of financial infrastructure needed to sustain global securities markets, the inefficiency of banks, and the premium that banks needed to pay to attract financial resources given their perceived riskiness during the debt crisis. By the early 1990s phenomenal volumes of financial resources were flowing into developing countries through securities markets, with stock and bond financing increasing from $32.6 *million* in 1984 to almost $89 *billion* in 1993 (Haley, 1999, p. 75). According to the World Bank's World Development Index (WDI) data, the value of stocks traded as a percent of GDP in these countries had increased from 7.5 percent in 1991 to 37 percent in 2000.

We return to the global financial crises of the 1990s, which involved securities markets to a much greater degree than the debt crisis of the 1980s, in chapter 5. Amidst the massive inflows of the 1990s a new label for the developing and post-Communist transition host-countries was devised, "emerging markets," and the debt crisis seemed to be easing in severity. Nevertheless, there were a number of indications that the 1980s debt crisis was not resolved. Booming securities markets were concentrated in only a subset of indebted countries, and many of the poorest LDCs, especially in Africa, continued to be trapped under the debt burden, never able to earn enough after paying the interest on the debt to stimulate growth or foster their citizens' education and economic capacities in the way needed to promote sustainable long-term development. Protest at IMF structural adjustment and the LDC debt burden continued to be a prominent feature of the global political scene, as evident in the Jubilee 2000 initiative to forgive debt that was promoted by church groups and celebrities such as Bono.

While remaining remarkably impervious to the growing influence of global social movements that were criticizing them, the IMF and G7 began taking further steps to address the problems associated with the debt crisis and structural adjustment. The Highly Indebted Poor Countries (HIPC) initiative was agreed in 1996, and was enhanced at the Cologne G8 summit in 1999 in response to criticisms of the original initiative's inadequacy. As of 2002 the debt stock of the 26 countries qualifying for the program, mostly in sub-Saharan Africa, had declined by about two-thirds, and the debt service was estimated to have declined from over 27 percent of government revenues to below 15 percent.[1] However, problems remain in fully funding the initiative, in the administratively burdensome conditions involved in getting the money, and in the ongoing economic difficulties experienced by the HIPC countries. A related IMF initiative is the Poverty Reduction Strategy Papers, which has the borrowing LDCs setting out plans not just for the type of structural adjustment that had drawn so much fire from critics, but also for reducing poverty. The PRSP process also called for greater involvement of developing country NGOs in this planning process. These two initiatives are significant in their recognition, even two decades after the debt crisis of the 1980s, that the effects of this crisis were still damaging. According to the World Bank's WDI data, debt service as a percent of gross national income of developing countries, which was less than 3 percent through the 1970s, remained above 6 percent in 1999 and 2000.

The Regulation of International Banks

The Basel Committee on Banking Supervision has been the main international body responsible for standards for international bank regulation. As noted in chapter 3, it was formed in 1975, following the Herstatt and Franklin National Bank crises, and its major accomplishments have been to agree, through its Concordats, on a division of labor among regulators, and through its 1988 Basel Accord on capital adequacy on international standards for regulating bank capital, which thereby reduce excessive unmitigated risky behavior on the part of banks. As also noted previously, the Basel Committee has established linkages with a worldwide network of regional bank supervisory groups, and this organizational accomplishment, together with the Committee's regulatory accomplishments, has made it one of the most important and successful parts of the emerging regime for international financial regulation.

This section focuses on what the experience of the Basel Committee can tell us about international financial regulation and international regulation more generally. Chapter 3 argued, consistently with the theoretical points made in chapter 2, that the emerging regime for international financial regulation was more effective than one might expect based on conventional theories that look for power and effectiveness in strong states or well-defined formal organizations. It argued that this effectiveness arises from the pragmatic orientation and informal coordination of the various bodies concerned with international regulatory matters. This section returns to the idea that *practices* play a key role in the governance of global finance.

The first Concordat agreed by the Basel Committee in 1975 was a very minimal accomplishment that did not deviate much from conventional state-centric ways of addressing problems in world politics: it simply established that home-country regulators would seek to regulate head offices of banks and host-country regulators would seek to regulate the offices of foreign banks in their jurisdictions. It was a first step in reasserting the power of states that was being eroded by banks taking advantage of the lack of clear divisions of regulatory responsibility to avoid regulatory scrutiny. However, it did this by simply stating formally that states had the responsibility for regulation in their own territory that one would expect them to have in traditional international law. This Concordat failed to address the complexity of an industry in which competitive jurisdictions would be tempted to allow sophisticated international banks to take advantage of their light regulation in order to shift activities away from more heavily regulated jurisdictions, thereby putting downward pressure on regulatory standards worldwide.

The revised Concordat of 1983 addressed this deficiency by beginning to extend the engagement of regulators with the internal operations of multinational banks – a trend that would continue to grow through subsequent Basel Committee initiatives. With the 1983 Concordat, the Basel Committee agreed that the primary form of supervision of multinational banks would be home-country consolidated supervision. Henceforth banks would be required to supply data on their worldwide operations to their home regulator, thereby constricting their ability to play one jurisdiction off against another. Since the home regulators of most of the international banks were in the wealthy member states of the Basel Committee, this regulatory initiative continued to rely on key features of world politics long recognized by state-centric theorists – the dominance of the international system by a few powerful states (Kapstein, 1994). Nevertheless, the idea of consolidated supervision, which marked a shift to requiring multinational banks to provide internal data instead of individual states scrambling to obtain information from banks in their jurisdiction and then having to find ways of aggregating and sharing that information, was also new in the way in which it involved regulators relying on their capacity to modify and draw on the internal business practices of banks. It also involved a new level of cooperation among regulators.

A logical next step after agreeing to the 1983 Concordat was to go beyond clarifying who was responsible for regulating international banks to establish minimum standards for that regulation. In the mid-1980s regulators became alarmed at the growing threat of systemic instability in the international banking industry. In part this was in response to the debt crisis, which had left many large international banks with heavy exposure to countries that were having difficulty covering their borrowing costs. However, it also was due to banks taking on new and poorly understood risks as they searched for new sources of revenue.

In part this risky activity involved new types of products, such as guarantees for commercial paper issued by non-financial firms. The risky activities also involved the rapid expansion of lending, which was funded not just by traditional deposits, but also by new and volatile sources of funds, such as borrowing from other banks. This meant that assets and liabilities were expanding much faster than bank capital, a problem, since, as noted in chapter 3, bank capital is important in offsetting risks of this type. Bank capital does this in part because it is the difference between assets and liabilities, and can be used to cover liabilities, and thus it acts as a cushion against bankruptcy. Owners of capital, mostly held in the form of shares, have the last claim on bank assets – after depositors – when a bank fails. In normal times owners of bank capital earn higher returns than depositors, in compensation for this risk, and this higher cost of bank capital relative to deposits acts as a brake on expansion of bank lending. Owners of bank capital have a greater incentive and capacity to monitor the riskiness of activities taken on by bank managers. Thus bank capital plays an important role in controlling risk, and regulators became increasingly concerned as levels of bank capital dropped around the world through the 1980s.

In response to these problems, the Basel Committee negotiated the Basel Accord on capital adequacy of 1988. The Accord called for banks to hold capital equivalent to 8 percent of their assets such as loans. However, in calculating this 8 percent capital–asset ratio, assets were weighted so that riskier assets required the full 8 percent, while less risky ones could be half as much, a quarter as much, or even zero capital. For instance, loans to corporations were weighted at 100 percent, while loans to OECD governments were weighted at 0 percent. The Basel Accord was remarkably successful, as it was implemented within a few years not just in the member states of the Basel Committee, but in most banking markets around the world as well. Capital levels reversed their decline, and the rapid expansion of bank lending slowed so dramatically that some observers blamed the Accord for creating a "capital crunch."

The Basel Accord, like the Concordats, drew on both traditional state-centric mechanisms for addressing international problems and newer techniques involving closer engagement with market practices. The state-centrism was evident in the fact that implementation of the Accord depended on national regulators changing national rules. The Accord was ostensibly simply a set of voluntary standards for regulators, and the Basel Committee had little formal independent authority from states. In addition there was considerable bargaining for competitive advantage among the Basel Committee's member states. Most important was the tension between the USA and Japan. Japanese banks had been shooting to the top of the tables of the biggest international banks, displacing US banks from their leading positions. Mixed in with the US interest in better regulation of global finance in general was its desire to alter the conditions that had allowed Japanese banks to overtake US banks.

Traditional aspects of the inter-state system were also evident in the exclusive control exercised by the wealthy member states of the Basel Committee over the standard-setting process, creating an agreement that was not as sensitive to the needs of other countries as it might have been. For instance, supporters of developing countries criticized the arbitrarily simplistic difference between the 100 percent risk weight for loans to their governments as compared to the 0 percent risk weight for loans to the wealthy member states of the OECD, and pointed out that this would make the financing of development projects more difficult.

Traditional power politics evident in the Basel Accord was the role played by the USA and the UK in the final stages of the negotiations (Kapstein, 1994). It appeared to many that the negotiations were moving too slowly. In 1987 the USA and the UK announced a surprise bilateral accord that had most of the features of Accord that was agreed by the full Basel Committee in 1988, but that had been agreed by these two countries outside the Basel process. To some observers this seemed to be an example of the type of leadership by powerful states that was needed to get anything done in the anarchic international system. On the other hand, most of the details of the Accord had already been worked out multilaterally by the Basel Committee, and it would be the Committee that managed the final Accord (Porter, 1993). It is also not clear that members of the Basel Committee other than the USA and the UK signed on only because of their fear of the combined power of these two states, perhaps involving the threat of having their banks excluded from these crucial markets. Other countries also saw merit in the Basel standards, a consensus that most likely owed more to their long years of working together in the Basel Committee than to the US and UK action.

Along with these traditional state-centric features of the Basel Accord came a stepped-up interaction between the Committee and the internal operations and business practices involved in international banking. This is evident in the degree to which the Accord relied on expanding the role of bank capital, which was aimed at expanding the quality of the monitoring and control by holders of capital over excessively risky activities of managers. The implementation of the Accord forced large banks to begin paying attention to variations in the riskiness of their assets, a change requiring them to alter their internal planning and reporting procedures. A bank's capital adequacy also became a much more important indicator of its performance for market actors, including investors and depositors. For instance, the yearly tables ranking the world's top banks in *The Banker* and the *Institutional Investor* began putting greater emphasis on capital in addition to their existing measures based on bank assets.

During the late 1980s and the 1990s it became apparent that the exclusiveness of the Basel Committee's membership was a problem. When it was formed in 1975, it could be argued that the restriction of its members to a dozen of the world's wealthiest countries was not unreasonable, since most international banks were headquartered in these countries and carried on their activities there. However two decades later things had changed: the number of international banks headquartered outside the Basel Committee member states had increased dramatically, and the most severe international banking crises had involved developing countries not represented in the Basel Committee. The Euromarkets had expanded beyond their original London base to include a wide variety of offshore centers, such as Vanuatu and the Cayman Islands, and indeed some of the products that were originally available only in the Euromarkets, such as bank accounts denominated in a foreign currency, were now routinely available in most banking markets. The Basel Committee took a number of initiatives to address its lack of representativeness, such as developing links with groups of regional bank supervisors. These initiatives are discussed in chapter 8.

By the mid-1990s a consensus had developed among regulators and bankers that while the Capital Accord had been successful, it had become outdated. The most serious criticism was that its simple risk weight categories were too blunt a regulatory instrument, since they failed to capture adequately the complexity of the risks involved in international banking. For instance, the weights failed to capture differences between stable, prudently run firms or developing country governments and those that engaged in reckless activity. Many large banks were increasingly relying on new techniques for managing risk, including more sophisticated models and techniques for offsetting one risk against another risk (for instance, holding assets at risk of declining in value if event x should occur together with assets that would increase in value should that same event occur). Regulators were concerned that although some refinements had been made in the original Accord to include new types of risk in addition to its original focus on *credit* risk (risks associated with the credit-worthiness of borrowers), including *market* risk (the risk that changes in the market as a whole would affect the value of bank assets) (BCBS, 1996), there were other new risks that were not included, such as *operational* risk (the risk of a failure in a bank's operating systems). Regulators were also worried that banks had tried to find ways around the original standards, including transforming and bundling mortgage and credit card debt into *asset-backed* securities that could be traded in markets and held without incurring the capital charge that the untransformed debt would have. The reduced risk weight on short-term lending was also blamed for the destructive role of volatile short-term inter-bank lending in the East Asian crisis of 1997.

Beginning in 1997 the Basel Committee launched a major revision of its Capital Accord, labeled Basel II. The standard-setting process was far more complex than for the first Accord. In part this was due to the greater complexity of the rules needed if the short-comings of the original approach were to be addressed. Concern about the capacity of smaller banks and developing country regulators to handle the complexity led the Committee to include the old simpler standards in the new package as an option. The consultation process was far more extensive as well. Drafts were issued, thousands of pages of comments were received from public-sector and private-sector actors, many made available on the Committee's website, and significant changes were made in response to these comments. By 2003 most of the provisions of the new agreement had crystallized, although some influential critics, including Jerry Hawke, US Comptroller of the Currency, who sat on the Basel Committee, had begun to express serious concerns about its complexity, casting some doubt on whether it would be successful. Critics also suggested that it could exacerbate cyclical downturns, since these downturns raise risks for banks, and this in turn may require them to restrict lending.

The main new feature of Basel II is its much greater reliance on private-sector practices as compared to the first Accord. The standards are divided into three "pillars." The first pillar consists of the formal rules regarding capital adequacy. In this first pillar, the two main innovations are, first, to allow much greater reliance on the internal risk models of banks and the assessments of private-sector ratings agencies in calculating the amount of capital needed, and second, in strongly introducing a new set of requirements to hold capital against operational risk. The second pillar is supervision of banks by regulators. This includes, very importantly, assessing whether a bank's internal risk models are reliable enough to be used under the first pillar. The third pillar is enhancing market pressures on banks to behave prudently. The least developed of the pillars, this would primarily involve efforts to promote the dissemination of information about bank performance in risk management to potential investors and depositors.

A key question in analyzing Basel II concerns the implications of its increased reliance on private-sector practices for its effectiveness, legitimacy, and fairness. The idea of relying on banks' own internal risk models was justified by the supporters of Basel II by arguing that these models better capture the complexity of the risks with which banks are involved. This brings the regulatory standards for the distribution of capital across various assets closer to a bank's own assessment of risks to which the bank is exposed. By using their own models, it is argued, banks can reduce the waste involved in keeping two sets of statistics and reporting systems.

However, questions remain about this optimistic assessment. Any regulatory arrangement that relies heavily on the regulated firms' own rules provokes skepticism about whether the firms can be trusted, a particularly salient concern after the Enron and other accounting scandals of 2001–2. In the case of Basel II an additional incentive, in the form of lower overall capital charges, is offered to firms that move from the old Accord to the use of their own models. Since the models are too complex for banks other than the largest to use, critics have argued that Basel II will confer an unfair advantage on these firms. Similarly, private-sector ratings are not as available in markets outside the USA, where the largest are headquartered, especially for smaller firms, and the lack of ratings, or perhaps a US-centric bias in the existing ratings, may disadvantage firms that are not large and USA-based. Perhaps, then, the dominant players in the industry "captured" the regulators and succeeded in getting an agreement that lightened their own regulatory obligations, but not their competitors'. The discretion that regulators have in evaluating the models has raised concerns that there will be variation in Basel II's implementation in different countries, and that regulators might be tempted to let their own firms off easy in order to give them a competitive advantage.

While there is merit to these criticisms, there are also some ways in which Basel II can be seen as strengthening the hand of regulators relative to all banks, including the biggest ones. There are some indications that the criteria used by supervisors to approve the use of internal risk models will be quite tough. For instance, once the new Accord is fully implemented, banks will be required to provide data covering seven years of transactions and to prove to regulators that their risk models assess risks accurately. This proof is supposed not just to include the model's calculations, but also to satisfy regulators that the procedures and people are in place to run and use these models properly. *US Banker* (2002) estimated that the cost of providing this data and of implementing the required risk management system could run into tens of millions of dollars for large banks, and the costs for the world's 30,000 banks of complying may be over $2.25 trillion (Bansia, 2002). Those firms whose models fail to predict risks accurately can lose their right to use these models in calculating their required capital levels. The models and the data and technology on which they rely are very expensive, and thus there is a significant incentive for firms not to lose their ability to use them after having made the investment. It is likely that the Basel Committee will work to reduce problematic variations in the way in which different national regulators implement the agreement.

The increased engagement of bank regulators at Basel with private-sector practices has been enhanced not just by the incorporation of private risk models and ratings into public-sector regulations, but also by the increased sophistication of the private-sector associations concerned with international bank regulation, a point discussed in more detail in chapter 7. During the debt crisis, the Institute of International Finance (IIF) was formed by the largest international banks, and it gathered information to help them assess sovereign risks, but it played very little role in regulatory matters. Later on, when emerging market debt began to be actively traded, the Emerging Markets Traders' Association was formed, and following some pressure from Gerald Corrigan, head of the US Federal Reserve who also served as head of the Basel Committee, it created a self-regulatory code to contribute to the governance of the market. During the development of Basel II, however, these relatively modest private-sector roles were significantly expanded, with a much more regular pattern of interaction taking place between the Basel Committee and the IIF, with the latter devoting very substantial resources to Basel II issues. A striking example of the degree of private-sector participation in the formulation of Basel II was the Quantitative Impact Study released on May 5, 2003, in which more than 350

banks in 43 countries participated in a trial run of the proposed regulations to assess their impact.

Conclusion

Banks have been at the leading edge of financial globalization,
because their organizational structure, which facilitates the monitoring and assessment of the financial flows that the banks channel
between depositors and borrowers, facilitates cross-border financial
relationships when the market infrastructure is not sufficiently developed to sustain more complex and decentralized types of financial
activity. Banking regulation has also been at the leading edge of international financial regulation more generally, not just because of regulators' concern that payments and other banking activities that are
important to the economy not be disrupted, but also because banks
became so heavily involved in international crises, including the instability signaled by the collapse of the Herstatt Bank and the Franklin
National Bank in the 1970s, the debt crisis of the 1980s, and the
taking on by banks of complex and risky new financial instruments
such as swaps, the dangers of which were not well understood
initially.

Both the private-sector developments and the regulatory developments discussed in this chapter point to the importance of the
specific institutional forms that international public-sector and
private-sector financial organizations and practices take. The power
of wealthy states and firms to shape the development of international
banking in their own interests is evident in the way that the debt crisis
was managed, in such features of international banking regulation
as the zero risk weight on lending to OECD governments, providing
those governments with a cheap source of finance, and in the potential competitive advantage that could be conferred on leading banks
with the use of internal risk models in Basel II. Nevertheless, as was
the case with the emerging regulatory regime discussed more generally in chapter 3, one cannot understand the evolution of international banking without understanding the institutions involved.
This includes the tendency of banking to lead securities in globalization because of the differences in their institutional characters, but
also the way in which regulation has evolved. The regulatory regime
imposes significant costs on international banks, and this does not fit
with the contention of some critical approaches that the development
of global finance is a simple reflection of the interests of financial

capital. Assessing who benefits from regulation requires an under-standing of the way in which regulation works with, through, or against the institutions and practices that constitute international banking.

The close links between regulators and private-sector banking practices raise concerns that regulators can be captured by those they are supposed to regulate, but also provide new ways for regulators to shape the development of international banking so that its nega-tive effects are reduced and the pursuit of private gain does not unfairly harm others or undermine the stability of the system as a whole.

5

The Governance of Global Securities and Derivatives Markets

A security is an IOU that is issued by a firm or public-sector body in exchange for financing. Generally, once they are issued in *primary* markets, securities can be traded in *secondary markets*, such as stock markets. Stocks and bonds are the most common form of securities. Stocks, also called *shares* or *equities*, involve an ownership claim on a firm: the firm is owned by its shareholders. In contrast, bonds typically involve a promise by a government or firm to provide a stream of payments as well as to return the original payment to the investor, but without the bond-holder having any formal right to control or manage the issuer of the bonds.

Securities have a very long history in international finance. For instance, when Genoa played a key role in international trade from the fourteenth to sixteenth centuries, long-distance commercial voyages were financed by selling transferable shares in the expedition, which were repaid on the ship's return (Abu-Lughod, 1989, pp. 118–19). Bonds have been a popular way for European governments to finance wars since the sixteenth century. In the nineteenth century the international bond market in London was used to finance railways, mining, and other large-scale economic projects in Russia, the Americas, the Middle East, and elsewhere.

In the post-World War II period, the globalization of securities markets, as noted in chapter 2, can be dated to the first issue of bonds in a currency other than that of the country of issue to finance the Italian Autostrade project in 1963. By 1986 international bond issues had grown to $225 billion, and had increased as a share of world output from 0.199 percent in the mid-1960s to 1.29 percent in the mid-1980s (Porter, 1993, p. 105). In 2002 international bond issues had increased to $1 trillion, 3.1 percent of world output.[1] The expansion of global securities markets has required the development of more complex social institutions and practices than is the case for international banking, and thus it is not surprising that it initially lagged behind the latter. However, global securities markets grew remarkably fast, beginning in the 1980s. This growth was evident in the markets' size, the number of currencies involved, and the growing complexity of the securities that were being bought and sold.

One jump in complexity was the addition of international equities, which are more difficult to internationalize because they involve ownership claims and are riskier. Offerings of international equities had reached $63 billion by the mid-1980s, with international trading activity constituting about 15 percent of all share trading (Porter, 1993, p. 109). In 2000, $318 billion of international equities was announced, a figure which declined to $102 billion in 2002 as a result of problems in equity markets.

A second jump in complexity was the emergence of international derivatives markets. A derivative is a promise to pay, buy, or sell, the value of which is based on the changing characteristics of an underlying asset. For instance, one type of derivative, an *option*, can involve the right to purchase a stock at an agreed price, and this right can be exercised if and when the purchaser wishes, with the market price of the unexercised option shaped by the expected future price of the underlying stock. The internationalization of derivatives is difficult to measure, but some sense can be given by outstanding foreign exchange derivatives, valued at $12.3 trillion in 2003, only a small portion of the $209 trillion of all outstanding derivatives contracts.[2] By comparison, the value of traditional international banking, as indicated by the value of external assets (loans and deposits) of BIS reporting banks, was $11 trillion in June 2003. All types of derivatives could have a large international component, as when foreigners buy single currency interest-rate derivatives. In the derivatives market average *daily* turnover was $1.4 trillion in 2001, a 10 percent increase over 1998. Many people worry that derivatives markets could have a destabilizing impact, not just on other financial markets, but on other economic activity as well. The dangers of derivatives were illustrated in 1995 by the ability of one out-of-control Barings Bank derivatives trader in Singapore, Nick Leeson, to bring about the collapse of the whole 233-year-old bank after losing $1.3 billion.

Foreign exchange trading is sometimes taken as a measure of globalization that is closely related to the globalization of securities markets in the degree to which it is carried out for speculative or investment purposes. In fact, a large share of foreign exchange trading is carried out to facilitate trade or other transactions in the real economy, functioning more as a means of payment than as a financial asset. The most recent triennial BIS-sponsored survey of foreign exchange markets estimated that average *daily* foreign exchange turnover in 2001 was $1.2 trillion, a 19 percent decline compared to 1998, but still massive. Factors contributing to the decline include reduction of trading among financial firms because of new electronic trading mechanisms and mergers among the firms, the introduction of the Euro (reducing intra-EU currency trading), and a decreased enthusiasm for international activities following the crises of 1997 and 1998.

Often global securities and derivatives markets are portrayed as the quintessential abstract market force, as involving ephemeral, speculative, non-material, and frighteningly complex transactions, more like gambling than the type of economic activity that makes a contribution to the well-being of the average person. This view has a long tradition domestically, as in the historical tension between Main Street and Wall Street in the United States. As securities markets have become more global, they have been seen by many as a threat to the slower-moving domestic economy and to the state's ability to stabilize this economy and safeguard the livelihood of those who work in it. This worry was captured in the title of Susan Strange's well-known book on the subject, *Casino Capitalism*.

While concerns about the dangers of globalized securities markets are well founded, as evident, for instance, in their role in the global financial crises of the 1990s, it is a mistake to think of these markets as ephemeral, purely speculative transactions that, like gambling, are based solely on chance. In fact, these markets are highly organized. Some of this organization takes the form of a formal international organization run by states: the International Organization of Securities Commissions (IOSCO). IOSCO is very similar in form and function to the types of international organizations that have been active since the nineteenth century, even if the type of activity it seeks to govern, securities markets, had not been the focus of such an international organization before IOSCO was formed.

Just as important as IOSCO, however, are the many informal and private-sector institutions involved in international securities markets. These include more commercially oriented institutions, such as securities exchanges that are organized as firms but also have rules that govern the securities transactions they facilitate. They also include private-sector associations that seek to produce or influence rules for the industry as a whole, such as the World Federation of Exchanges in Paris. Informal shared understandings and recognized practices among the surprisingly small number of securities firms involved in international markets have always played an important role. The contribution of the wide variety of private-sector institutions involved in the organization of international securities markets is further supplemented by the rules provided by public-sector institutions that are not themselves global, but that have sufficient control over important markets that they can influence global securities markets more generally, such as the European Union, or the main US securities regulator – the Securities and Exchange Commission (SEC).

This complex and varied array of institutions that are involved in the organization and regulation of global securities markets can be described as an emerging international securities regime, similar in form to the international banking regime analyzed in chapter 4, although, as will become clearer below, the securities regime relies more heavily on private-sector institutions than does the banking regime. By including private-sector institutions and practices in our analysis of this regime, it is possible to identify patterns and relationships that would not be visible instead if we were to focus just on states and fluid anonymous market transactions. It is also possible to better understand and manage the benefits and dangers associated with global securities markets.

The rest of the chapter is divided into three sections. The first looks more carefully at the character of securities markets and why they require strong institutions in order to function. The second looks at developments in the markets since World War II. The third looks at the development and current work of IOSCO.

Why do Securities Markets Require Institutions and Rules?

Often the role of institutions and rules in securities markets is obscured by prevailing images of them. Such prevailing images include the casino-like frenzy of trading rooms or stock exchange floors, the speed and intangibility of securities trading carried out through international electronic networks, and the sheer size and apparently uncontrollable character of cross-border flows of international securities that have challenged the capacity of governments to manage their economies. However, all these transactions rely on complex institutions and rules, and indeed their speed, volume, and intangibility require these institutions and rules to be much more developed than is the case for the cross-border trade of heavy, slower-moving products such as steel.

All markets require institutions to function, and since most global securities transactions are carried out in markets, some of the institutions they require are similar to those required by all markets. A *market* can be defined as the bringing together of a sufficient number of buyers and sellers so that the prices of goods in that market can be determined by competitive bargaining. Many international economic interactions do not have these characteristics and do not involve markets, such as when a woman working in the Persian Gulf sends money back to her family in the Philippines, when a government disburses foreign aid, when a firm sends a part to one of its plants in another country, or when a firm buys a unique complex foreign product from a foreign firm that is the sole producer of that product. However, in many international industries there are mechanisms that make it possible for large numbers of buyers and sellers to come together to compete, and in these cases international markets can be an important way of carrying out international economic transactions.

One institutional requirement of markets is some mechanism to bring buyers together at the same place and time. In previous centuries this was often achieved by having special town squares or market halls and market days. Until the creation of electronic networks, securities markets were no different. Stock exchanges were designed not just to bring traders together in a central location, but also to facilitate intense face-to-face bargaining inside the exchange building through the specialized architecture of the stock exchange floor.

Another institutional requirement of markets is a mechanism for providing information that makes it possible to assess and compare products. If there is no way to do this, then it will be impossible to focus on bargaining over price. Most markets therefore produce rules for assessing the characteristics of products and data on these products. Historically this function has been carried out in securities markets by the publication of past series of prices, by reliance on specialized traders with detailed knowledge of the securities, and with standardized formats for the dissemination of information about firms and the securities they issue, such as annual reports and prospectuses.

A third institutional requirement of markets is a mechanism for enforcing an agreement to transfer property from a seller to a buyer. Without this mechanism there would be a constant tendency of markets to collapse as traders failed to follow through on their bargains, or as traders got bogged down in disputes about what was agreed. The basic system of property rights is usually provided by the state through its legal system, but for specialized transactions such as securities trading these public-sector rules are often supplemented by private-sector rules. In international securities markets a great deal of effort has been put into the mechanics of transferring ownership claims and payments, called *clearance and settlement*. When prices are fluctuating hourly, a delay in clearance and settlement can have serious consequences. In the 1990s, a private-sector organization, the Group of Thirty (G30), on the basis of an influential 1989 report, led a concerted international campaign to speed up clearance and settlement, and more recently launched a new campaign with its 2003 report, *Global Clearing and Settlement – A Plan of Action*, pointing to the risks to clearance and settlement that had been highlighted by the September 11 terrorist attacks and to the costs of clearance and settlement, which it estimated to be well in excess of $12 billion annually.

The issuing of new securities differs in its institutional requirements from secondary trading, because there is no historical record of prices to which traders can refer. Typically, new international issues of securities are underwritten by a syndicate of securities firms. The syndicate allows securities firms to share the risks associated with underwriting and provides the organizational capacity to transmit information to investors and inspire trust in the value of the new issue among those investors. New issues rely much more on non-routine informal relationships than secondary trading, which often takes place in routine trading in stock exchanges.

Electronic alternative trading systems (ATS) that have been established as competitors to traditional exchanges, such as Instinet, Island, and Archipelago, are a rapidly growing phenomenon that will contribute to the globalization of securities markets. These ATS lend themselves easily to cross-border trading and are posing a number of challenges for regulators. Although they are seen as efficient, and may increase liquidity by drawing together participants from around the world, they don't include the self-regulatory features of traditional exchanges, and public-sector regulation is difficult when the system and investors may be in different countries. ATS may also fragment liquidity in national markets, and could be seen as free-riding on the price, information, and regulatory work of the traditional exchanges. Software algorithms are a partial substitute for the absence of regulatory capacity of exchanges, but current indications are that the growth of ATS will lead to new initiatives on the part of public-sector regulators, including renewed efforts to coordinate internationally (Collins, 2002).

Derivatives, as noted above, involve an agreement to trade or make a payment, where prices are based on the changing characteristics of a different underlying asset. Derivatives have been controversial, because there are sharp disagreements over dangers and benefits associated with them. There are three main dangers associated with derivatives. The first is their volatility. For instance, if a stock increases in value from $100 to $110, a 10 percent increase, a derivative whose value is determined by the degree to which that stock's price exceeds $90 will have increased by 200 percent. The second is their complexity. Many derivatives involve contingencies where the risks and commitments are hard for managers or regulators to understand. The third is their intangibility. The ease of trading intangible derivatives increases the speed of this trading relative to more traditional material objects, and may leave nothing of value behind for creditors, investors, or employees if a firm involved in derivatives trading collapses.

Many people see derivatives trading as speculation that can do serious damage to the real economy on which the average person depends for his or her well-being, but others argue that derivatives are beneficial, because they allow risks to be transferred from those that wish to avoid them to those who wish to take them on in exchange for the possibility of higher returns. For instance, an exporting firm that wishes to avoid risks from exchange rate fluctuations can buy foreign exchange derivatives that protect that firm much as an insurance policy would for other risks. Many firms that specialize in trading derivatives try to reduce the overall riskiness of their portfolios by offsetting one type of risk against another – for instance, by holding some derivatives that increase in value and some that decrease in value if the underlying currency on which they are based depreciates.

Despite their intangibility, derivatives, like securities more generally, require institutions. Indeed, their intangibility makes these institutions more important than would be the case for more traditional products, since it requires more complex rules to establish the value of derivatives and to enforce agreements that have been concluded to trade them. For instance, the history of the emergence of derivatives in the USA, where they have been most prominent, is closely connected to changes in laws defining what types of contracts are legally enforceable, since without such enforcement the markets could not have emerged (Stout, 1999). There are a wide variety of more informal rules that contribute to order in derivatives markets as well. It has been estimated that half of the world's derivatives trading takes place between ten leading banks (Porter, 1996, p. 683), allowing those banks to establish relations of trust and punish violators of norms by shunning them in the market. Organization of the international derivatives market is also facilitated by the rules provided by the International Swaps and Derivatives Association, such as its Master Agreement Protocols (<www.isda.org>). Well-recognized mathematical models can also help stabilize expectations in the market.

The above points about the importance of institutions for securities and derivatives markets draw our attention to the difficulty of constructing the types of institutions that support the stable operation of securities markets at the global level, the continuing importance of social relations in the operation of these markets, and the degree to which the image of fluid electronic markets that are so ephemeral that they cannot be regulated is a myth. Fast electronic markets depend on strong identifiable institutions.

Post-World War II Developments in International Securities Markets

The re-emergence of international global securities markets in London after World War II involved in part the construction of the markets on the firm base of the financial institutions in the City of London that had been built up over the preceding centuries, along with the strength, experience, and international orientation of the British state and the Bank of England. But, it also involved the confidence that was instilled by the strength of the US dollar, backed up by the power of the US government and the activities of US multinational firms. The London Eurobond and Euroequity markets emerged only after the Eurocurrency markets, which consisted of US dollar-denominated bank deposits, were well established.

Despite their reputation for being the quintessential example of unregulated markets, the Eurobond markets were heavily dependent on formal and informal institutions, which in turn were facilitated by the domination of these technically complex markets by a small number of firms. In his history of the market, Kerr (1984, p. 87) comments that its center in London was a "close-knit community, particularly among the professional market-making houses." Although these firms competed fiercely with one another for business, they were also involved in very close collaborative relations in the Eurobond syndicates that were organized to underwrite new issues of Eurobonds. The syndicate would be organized by a lead firm, which would exercise some control over other firms through its capacity to allocate portions of the new issue among them. From 1963 through the 1980s the market share of the top five such firms ranged between 30 and 50 percent, and the market share of the top ten firms ranged between 50 and 70 percent, with much higher levels of concentration in more specialized segments (Porter, 1993, pp. 130–2). The market's functioning was facilitated by a tacit agreement to work only with public-sector or blue chip private-sector issuers, thereby reducing the need for institutions to help foster knowledge about and trust in the issuers.

As the Eurobond market became larger and more complex, a need was felt among leading participants for a more formal set of rules and procedures for addressing common issues. Accordingly, the Association of International Bond Dealers was formed in 1969, incorporated in Zurich. The AIBD organized yearly meetings, and began to formalize standards for the market. In 1984 those involved primarily in the issuing of bonds felt their interests would be better served by splitting off into their own organization, and the International Primary Markets Association was founded, and those whose primary focus was secondary market trading renamed the AIBD the International Securities Markets Association. Both associations are headquartered in London, although ISMA retains its legal connection and an office in Switzerland. Both organizations create standards for their members, although ISMA has more formal self-regulatory status under British and Swiss law. In recent years both associations have devoted increasing attention to electronic systems to facilitate trading and to interacting with regulatory authorities. These associations are discussed further in chapter 7.

The Globalization of Stock Markets and Derivatives Markets

The globalization of stock markets took a somewhat different path than did the Eurobond market. The ownership rights that come with stock ownership also come with greater responsibility for losses, and the certainty of the return from stocks is less than is the case for bonds. The internationalization of stock markets therefore requires more sophisticated institutions than did the Eurobond market. The emergence of international stock markets was greatly facilitated by the growth of institutional investors such as mutual funds and pension funds, because these large institutions could carry out the type of international research and monitoring of stocks and issuers that smaller individual investors could not. The globalization of stock markets has also relied to a greater degree than bond markets on existing national markets.

There are a great many types of institutional arrangements that have been tried to foster cross-border electronic links between exchanges, but many of these have not been very successful. The first example of such a linkage was between the Chicago Mercantile Exchange and the Singapore Monetary Exchange in 1984 (Karmel, 2002, p. 417). More recently, efforts have been made to link emerging stock exchanges, such as the link envisioned between the Lusaka and Johannesburg exchanges and the Dominican Republic and Costa Rican exchanges. Another method involved the extension of electronic exchanges across borders, as was tried by the world's largest electronic exchange, NASDAQ, which created an operation in Germany, took a majority holding in Belgium-based EASDAQ, and explored the possibility of opening Canadian branches, all of which failed to live up to expectations. As noted above, new alternative trading systems are likely to contribute to create new vehicles for cross-border securities trading.

A method of global integration that is also likely to become more important is mergers and acquisitions of exchanges. This has been facilitated by a process of *demutualization*, in which stock exchanges transform themselves from non-profit clubs jointly managed by the firms with seats on the exchange, into for-profit firms whose shares may be publicly traded (Karmel, 2002). By 2002, 18 exchanges had demutualized, including the London Stock Exchange, Deutsche Börse, the Tokyo Stock Exchange, and NASDAQ, while new plans for demutualization were being announced regularly (Aggarwal, 2002). Demutualization can be seen as a response to competitive pressures in which member firms of exchanges are no longer willing to bear the cost of managing and regulating the exchange and prefer the greater flexibility that comes with being able to trade their shares in the exchange. Demutualized exchanges have tended to transfer their regulatory responsibilities to stand-alone firms selling regulatory services, such as NASD-R or Market Regulation Services Inc. in Toronto, or to public-sector regulators, as was the case with the London Stock Exchange. Demutualization has facilitated the global integration of securities markets by moving another step away from the place-based mutual commitments that had sustained traditional exchanges, creating new opportunities for distant actors to participate in ownership and trading on exchanges, and making cross-border mergers and acquisitions of exchanges easier. One high-profile example was the unsuccessful attempted hostile takeover of the venerable London Stock Exchange in 2000 by OM Gruppen, the owner of the Swedish stock exchange. A more successful example was the purchase in 2002 of the London International Financial Futures and Options Exchange and the merger with the Portuguese exchange Bolsa de Valores de Lisboa e Porto by Euronext, which itself had been created by the merger of the Paris, Amsterdam, and Brussels exchanges.

The configuration of global securities markets is also indicated by the character of the World Federation of Exchanges, located in Paris. The WFE's membership consists of 54 regulated securities exchanges from around the world, accounting for over 97 percent of world stock market capitalization. Its relatively small staff produces statistical information on these exchanges, sets standards for members to aspire to, and seeks to influence public-sector regulations. The WFE also has regional groups. The most active of these is the Federation of European Stock Exchanges, although the emerging market regional groups do play a role in providing a vehicle for sharing information and advice with these new markets. The federated structure of the WFE and its modest size are a reflection of the fact that the world's securities markets continue to be divided primarily into a series of nationally based exchanges.

This ongoing division of the world's securities markets into separate national exchanges does not mean that these exchanges are equal players. On the contrary, many important developments in international securities markets are developed in the US or British markets, and then spread from there. Many firms headquartered in other countries choose to have their stock issued and traded in the US or British markets, both because of the prestige of doing so and because of the greater access to investors that a US or British listing brings. Moreover, much of the economic activity of smaller countries is dominated by the foreign branches of US or British firms, or of other large multinational firms that choose to list on US or British exchanges, thereby reducing the pool of firms that might choose to be active on the smaller exchanges. The liquidity that comes with large numbers of listed firms and large volumes of trading activity is crucial to the success of an exchange, since it contributes to price stability and allows holders of securities to sell and exit quickly and easily from the market – a crucial protection when the holders of these securities may not have the capacity to anticipate problems or directly influence under-performing firms whose securities they hold. These factors have made it difficult for smaller exchanges to compete, and have led to an increasing degree of centralization of securities markets in New York and London: in 1990 the NYSE and the London Stock Exchange accounted for 39.8 percent of the market capitalization of world stock exchanges, a share which had increased to 47.5 percent at the end of 2002.[3]

A partial exception to this centralizing tendency was the rapid growth of emerging stock markets in the 1980s and 1990s. This trend, which is explored in more detail in chapter 8, was driven by a number of converging developments, including the fallout of the debt crisis of the early 1980s, which compromised bank loans as a form of financing and led developing and post-Communist countries to encourage local stock markets, including through the sale of shares of newly privatized state enterprises. The general enthusiasm for markets, aided by the enthusiastic promotion of markets by the IMF and World Bank, was a further boost, as was the rapid growth of mutual funds and other institutional investors seeking the higher returns that emerging markets seemed to promise. After the emerging markets crises of the 1990s, however, this rapid emerging market growth was revealed to be more fragile and temporary than it had seemed at first.

Derivatives markets tend to be less dependent on nationally based exchanges than are stocks, even though many derivatives are traded on these exchanges. As noted previously, most derivatives are traded between the ten leading banks that dominate the markets. The International Swaps and Derivatives Association (ISDA), founded in 1985, unlike the WFE, is not a federation, but rather includes more than 600 institutions, mostly firms, which trade or buy derivatives from 46 countries on six continents. Like the IPMA and ISMA, the ISDA provides guidelines and standards for the market, the most important of which is the ISDA Master Agreement providing standard documentation for a wide variety of derivatives. It also seeks to influence regulators and provides statistical information.

Hedge funds, also known as *highly leveraged institutions*, have played a prominent role in derivatives markets as well. These funds, which are restricted to very wealthy investors and are much less regulated than mutual funds, seek to make money by borrowing large sums from banks and then identifying opportunities for quick profit by, for instance, detecting and exploiting small differences in prices of financial assets in two markets, or by anticipating the change in the price of a currency (Harmes, 2002). The leverage afforded by the bank loans can allow a hedge fund to generate very high returns (for instance, if the fund borrows $99 at 5 percent for each $1 of its capital and earns 10 percent on its operations, then the return on the original $1, after paying the interest on the loans, is about $5, or 500 percent). However, if the returns fall below the interest rate of the loans, then the fund can very quickly go bankrupt and even threaten the viability of the banks from which it borrowed. This is exactly what happened with the collapse of Long-Term Capital Management in 1998. As de Goede (2001) has shown, LTCM was a quintessential case of a fund that used scientific models as a guide to its operations. While these models provide sets of recognized rules that foster trust, they can go terribly wrong, since they are not well suited to anticipating or coping with large unexpected changes that cannot be projected from past data. Because hedge funds are relatively unregulated, it is difficult to estimate their size. A Financial Stability Forum report (2000, p. 96) estimated that the capital under hedge fund management increased from $10 billion in 1990 to $121 billion in 1999, noting that the US President's Working Group Report (1999) estimated that in 1998 there were between 2,500 and 3,500 hedge funds managing approximately $800 billion to $1 trillion in total assets and $200 to $300 billion in capital.

The International Organization of Securities Commissions and Other Public-Sector Regulators

Despite a long tradition of industry self-regulation in securities markets, including international bodies such as IPMA, ISMA, ISDA, and the WFE, government regulation has played a crucial role as well. Governments play a key role in enforcing contracts, in authorizing the incorporation of firms that issue securities, in providing back-up authority to the self-regulatory operations of stock exchanges, by licensing those authorized to carry out or offer advice about the trading of securities, and in many other rules that provide the legal environment that securities markets depend upon to function.

As securities markets have spread around the world, with new exchanges opening in the emerging markets, public-sector securities market regulators have been created to regulate these markets. The tendency has been to give these securities commissions some independence from the rest of the government. Securities commissions may be financed by a special levy on securities markets. This, combined with their mandate to ensure the health of their markets, gives them an interest in promoting the markets under their jurisdiction relative to other markets, along with worrying about the problems that come with poorly regulated markets, such as fraud, that damage the confidence of local investors and may disrupt the local economy. The most influential securities commission is the US Securities and Exchange Commission, with the British Financial Services Authority, bringing together banking, securities, and insurance regulators, also very prominent. Beginning in the late 1990s an intense discussion began in the European Union aimed at determining what type of public-sector European securities arrangement should be created, and the implementation of such an arrangement was a key goal of the EU's Financial Services Action Plan, launched in 1999.

As securities markets became more international, many of the problems existing in domestic markets also became global, and became a concern especially of the US SEC. For instance, cross-border fraud, on the part of firms located in countries with secrecy laws allowing the owners' identities to be concealed, or where authorities would not cooperate with US authorities, thereby putting the firms outside the reach of US law, was seen as a particular problem. The US SEC began concluding bilateral *memoranda of understanding* with other securities regulators, to exchange information. In the 1980s it also began exploring more aggressive extraterritorial application of its laws – for instance, by considering requiring foreign firms operating in the US market to divulge information on the firm's worldwide financial operations, even if this might clash with privacy or confidentiality laws in the firms' home jurisdictions. While the enormous size and importance of US markets relative to others have always given US authorities tremendous leverage in pressuring foreign firms and regulatory authorities, this type of extraterritorial application of US law has always been controversial, and was not viewed favourably by non-US actors when it was put forward as an option for the regulation of global securities markets.

A more multilateral and successful option was the International Organization of Securities Commissions, a worldwide organization of securities regulators, which by 2003 included 181 members responsible for regulating more than 90 percent of the world's securities markets. IOSCO began as the Inter-American Association of

Securities Commissions and Similar Organizations in 1974, at which time it focused on promoting the development of stock markets in the Americas. In 1984 IOSCO took on its present name and recast itself as a global organization. Until the end of the 1990s, IOSCO was headquartered in Montreal, at which point it began to transfer its headquarters to Madrid.

One of IOSCO's priorities was the multilateralization of the types of memoranda of understanding (MOUs) that the SEC was eager to conclude with securities regulators in other countries. IOSCO agreed on a standard MOU, began promoting the value of such MOUs amongst its members, and kept a list of the many MOUs that were signed, which by 2003 involved 104 regulatory organizations, with most having signed multiple MOUs (for instance, the Monetary Authority of Singapore had signed twelve). The effect of this proliferation of MOUs was to create a network of regulators that were willing to share information and cooperate in the prosecution of cross-border securities fraud. The process took a significant step forward in 2002 when IOSCO agreed to a multilateral MOU, and as of October 2003, 24 IOSCO members had signed the MOU, and an additional 40 had applied to undergo the rigorous screening review process to become signatories. As informal agreements, the MOUs allowed regulators to avoid the scrutiny, inflexibility, and political complications that come with formal treaties that would require ratification by legislatures. The process of multilateralizing a series of bilateral agreements is similar to the strategy that was followed by the USA and leading European countries in their efforts to construct a regime to protect their firms' direct investments in foreign countries, as we shall see in chapter 6. Such a process gives greater leverage to powerful countries which negotiate with smaller countries one at a time, in contrast to fully multilateral negotiations, and combined with the lack of legislative review of the MOUs, might raise questions about democracy and accountability, although those negotiating them see them as technical agreements designed to prevent and punish crime, and therefore entirely positive.

IOSCO has also engaged in a wide variety of other projects. These include efforts to set agreed international standards of conduct for securities regulators, analysts, credit-rating agencies, collective investment schemes (mutual funds), and hedge funds; detailed reports and recommendations on new regulatory issues, including technological developments in electronic trading; training of emerging market regulators; work with the international accounting bodies on accounting standards; and efforts to facilitate the cross-border issuing of securities by creating agreed rules for disclosure for initial offerings of equity.

IOSCO's progress with these various projects has been uneven. On the one hand, IOSCO has certainly constructed a baseline set of internationally agreed norms for regulators of securities markets that can be said to constitute an international regime for securities regulation. IOSCO's technical reports and the opportunities it has provided for discussion among regulators have also greatly increased the knowledge of regulators about how best to regulate global markets, as well as fostering patterns of cooperation that can be useful in addressing joint problems. In addition, IOSCO has begun monitoring and reporting on compliance by members with some of its agreed standards, and the capacity to do this is a good measure of the strength of an international organization. On the other hand, many of IOSCO's agreements are quite vague and not very demanding, and it has focused on technical problems that, if solved, would facilitate the smoother operation of global securities markets, rather than successfully addressing the difficult and politicized questions, such as whether premature promotion of securities markets in developing countries can have negative consequences for their growth and stability. Despite considerable effort, it has not succeeded in developing capital adequacy standards comparable to those of the Basel Committee; in part this is a reflection of the greater difficulty of doing so in securities markets, but it is also due to the inability of IOSCO's members to overcome their differences.

As Pistor (2002, p. 112) has noted of one of IOSCO's major accomplishments, its Objectives and Principles of Securities Legislation: "the IOSCO Principles cannot be characterized as freestanding rules. They reference other laws and legal concepts, including domestic laws and synthetic concepts found in other IOSCO Principles. In addition they call attention to how closely related a well-functioning regime for regulating securities market is to the political system." Laws upon which the principles depend include company, commercial, contract, tax, bankruptcy, insolvency, competition, banking, and dispute resolution laws – another reminder of the dependence of global securities markets on a sufficiently strong institutional context.

Conclusion

Securities markets have become substantially more global since World War II, but, contrary to popular perception, they are not a borderless system of flowing electronic impulses for which distance and territory are irrelevant. Rather, as in all markets, securities markets require buyers and sellers to be brought together in a setting in which rules for enforcing property rights and mechanisms for dissemination of price and other information are well developed. Despite the growth of electronic networks, institutions continue to be important in fostering these preconditions for the successful operation of global securities markets. Bringing participants together in close proximity in a fixed territorially specific location, as is the case with financial districts and some floor-based stock exchanges, continues to be important. Both private- and public-sector organizations concerned with regulated exchanges, namely the WFE and IOSCO, are mainly mechanisms for assisting their relatively independent member countries in collaborating with one another on issues of common interest, and the international organizations themselves have only a modest degree of autonomy.

Despite this persistence of nationality and territory, the global aspects of securities markets have become stronger in recent decades. Derivatives, bonds, hedge funds, globally oriented mutual funds, and alternative trading systems tend to be less nationally focused than stock exchanges. The ability of these financial instruments and institutions to assist in quickly shifting financial resources from one market to another has contributed to an increasing level of cross-border price sensitivity and interdependence. The market-oriented and critical approaches examined in chapter 2 have often suggested that investors can use securities markets to move capital out of a jurisdiction quickly when they don't like the policies of the government, and that this has severely eroded the power of governments. While the globalization of securities markets certainly creates increased pressures on governments to make their markets more attractive to foreign investors, the importance of the institutions and rules that this chapter has revealed suggests that it is a mistake to imagine that the fluidity of international securities markets makes regulation impossible. The high dependence of securities markets on government rules and private-sector rules backed up by government rules makes them dependent on government regulation. The development of IOSCO and global private-sector associations has reduced the ability of participants in securities markets to play off one jurisdiction against another, or to use a lack of rules as a way to engage in fraud. This global-level regulatory capacity is uneven, and so far, as is the case in international banking, it has tended to focus on rules to make global finance work more smoothly rather than to protect citizens from the effects of global financial instability. This does not mean, however, that securities markets escape rules and regulations so easily that these limitations are inevitable. The limitations in the scope of international securities regulation reflect the choices made by governments as much as the capacities of governments. Bringing about better regulatory policies will require careful attention to the complex mix of public- and private-sector institutions that have made the growth of global securities markets possible.

6

Foreign Direct Investment

Foreign direct investment (FDI) refers to an investment by a multi-national corporation (MNC) in a country – called a *host* country – other than the country in which it is headquartered, called its *home* country. FDI, unlike bank loans, involves both ownership and control by the MNC of the foreign operation in which it has invested. FDI also differs from *portfolio investment*, which is investment in foreign stock and bonds without direct control. Portfolio investors can sell their stocks and bonds if they don't like the performance of the firm that issued them, while foreign direct investors are more likely to exercise their managerial control to try to improve the performance of the foreign operation. If the foreign operation is incorporated in the host country, with a separate legal identity, it is a *subsidiary*, and if not, it is a *branch*.

FDI has grown very rapidly in the period since World War II, and is thus an important aspect of the globalization of finance.[1] In 1980 FDI inflows were $59 billion, accounting for 2.6 percent of gross fixed capital formation (GFCF). By the first half of the 1990s annual FDI inflows were averaging $254 billion (4.4 percent of GFCF), subsequently reaching a peak of $1.4 trillion in 2000 (21 percent of GFCF) before declining to $651 billion in 2002 (12 percent of GFCF), 71 percent of which went to developed economies. FDI stock in 2002 was $7.1 trillion, up from $699 billion in 1980. Cross-border mergers and acquisitions increased from $116 billion in 1988 to $1.1 trillion in 2000, before falling back to $370 billion in 2002. Sales of foreign affiliates increased from $2.7 trillion in 1982 to $17.7 trillion in 2002, increasing from 133 percent of world exports to 226 percent. For developing countries, FDI increased as a share of GDP from 0.42 percent in 1970 to 1.6 percent in 1994, while foreign aid did not grow significantly and private-sector debt financing declined (portfolio flows increased from 0 to 1.5 percent) (Armijo, 1999, p. 6). FDI in developing countries tends to follow a bloc pattern involving outflows from North America, Europe, or Japan to the rest of the Americas, Africa, and East Asia respectively (UNCTAD, 2003, p. 23).

FDI has also grown in complexity, from the type of simple foreign offices mainly engaged in trade in the nineteenth century, to complex highly integrated global operations, where different components of a single product are made in the multiple countries in which the MNC's foreign operations are located, or involving joint ventures where two or more firms share in the ownership and management of the foreign operation, or more informal strategic alliances, in which firms agree to collaborate closely on particular research or production projects, often without constituting the project as a legally distinct firm (Mytelka, 1991).

FDI has been very controversial, but the concerns about FDI have differed from concerns about other types of cross-border financial flows. Since FDI has usually involved investment in machinery, training, customer relationships, or other assets that cannot be easily traded in markets, it is less likely that foreign direct investors will panic and liquidate their investments in the destabilizing way that portfolio investors, or banks refusing to renew short-term bank loans, can. Since FDI involves ownership and control by private firms of other private-sector enterprises, the threat that it seems to pose to sovereignty is less overt than is the case with the type of pressure on developing governments involved after the debt crisis of the early 1980s in the complementary effects of IMF conditionality and the threat by banks to stop rolling over loans to those governments.

Intense controversies associated with FDI have mostly revolved around worries about effects on national economies and cultures of having important industries owned by foreigners. Critics have seen a wide variety of negative effects flowing from this foreign control. These include economic effects, such as less robust growth and a loss of jobs, research and development, and entrepreneurial opportunities, as foreign firms displace nationally owned ones; cultural effects, as foreign products and logos displace traditional national ones; and political effects, as owners and employees of foreign firms lobby or otherwise influence host governments. Supporters of FDI, in sharp contrast, have seen them as having positive effects on employment, technology transfer, skills development, and consumer choice. These controversies about FDI are very much part of the more general controversies about globalization, even if they have their own distinct histories that predate by many years the anti-globalization movement.

The rest of the chapter examines FDI in four sections. In the first, theoretical explanations for the MNC that are consistent with the approaches to global finance discussed in chapter 2 will be set out, along with an approach consistent with the emphasis on institutions of this book. In the second section a brief history of FDI is given, drawing out the ways in which it can be seen as contributing to and being part of globalization. The third section discusses more recent efforts to create international regulations for foreign direct investment, including the high-profile failed Multilateral Agreement on Investment negotiations at the OECD, which the anti-globalization movement had a big part in defeating in 1998. The fourth, concluding section draws lessons from the experience with FDI for our understanding of the globalization of finance more generally.

Approaches to Understanding FDI

Prior to the 1970s very little scholarly attention was given to the MNC and FDI. Market-oriented approaches supportive of markets tended to assume that most international economic transactions could be explained either by trade theory, which focused on imports, exports, and comparative advantage, or by theories of international finance, which focused on the tendency of finance to flow from developed countries in which it was abundant to developing countries in which interest rates were higher due to its greater scarcity. More critical approaches had commented extensively on concentrations of economic power domestically, and on the connections of this concentration with political and economic imperialism, but not on the specific organizational form taken by the MNC.

In seeking to explain why cross-border transactions take place within the organizational structure of the MNC, which might appear to involve a wasteful, costly bureaucracy that would put those using it at a competitive disadvantage as compared to arm's-length exports and imports or portfolio financial flows, market-oriented analysis has tended to focus on the distinctive characteristics of the types of trans-actions that MNCs handle (Rugman, 1981; Dunning, 1988). These transactions are seen as ones that are not well suited to arm's-length anonymous markets, because the types of market preconditions set out in chapter 5 are not sufficiently developed relative to the complexity of these transactions. This is especially the case for knowledge-intensive products and large-scale specific products that are unique or too intangible for price-based competition to allocate effectively. For instance, specialized managerial or scientific know-ledge may be hard to transfer from the heads of those who have it to products that can be bought and sold in markets, with partial exceptions such as the sale of instruction manuals or books about management techniques.

Market-oriented analysis has argued that the organizational, hierarchical character of the MNC makes it better suited to certain complex transactions such as those mentioned in the previous para-graph. Rather than relying on prices and competition to allocate resources, an MNC can allocate resources internally through a chain of command and by providing financial incentives to its employees that could not be realized if each person involved in the production process had to try to sell their output for a profit to the people with whom they were working. For instance, rather than having a scien-tist or manager negotiate with a foreign firm to sell their expertise, an MNC can set up an operation in the foreign jurisdiction and have the scientist or manager move there, bringing their knowledge to bear in that operation in a more integrated way than would be the case in a purely market-based transaction.

From a market-oriented perspective it is then possible to treat the hierarchical structure of the MNC and the horizontal and more anonymous structure of arm's-length trade as competing institu-tional arrangements in which the most efficient arrangement in any given situation will win out over time. From this perspective MNCs are efficient responses to the difficulty of carrying out useful but complex cross-border economic transactions – for instance, trans-ferring knowledge from countries that have abundant expertise to countries that do not. This is the perspective that predominates especially in international institutions such as the IMF and World Bank and in the governments of countries in which MNCs are headquartered.

Market-oriented approaches to the MNC can be strongly chal-lenged by more critical approaches. These critics of the MNC point to the many ways in which the MNCs' enormous organizational capacity allows them to self-interestedly and arbitrarily wield power in ways that have little to do with the idealized picture painted by market-oriented analysis (Hymer, 1975). This power can be exercised over markets, over those working for the MNC, and over governments. It is useful to look briefly at each in turn.

MNCs have long been criticized for their ability to manipulate markets and unfairly undermine competitors. Many complex production processes which produce high-priced or low-cost products are difficult to learn, and a large firm may be able to dominate a market constantly by taking an initial lead and never providing potential competitors the opportunity to gain experience and drive their costs down to a level at which that firm could compete. As well, many complex products exist as parts of larger technical or marketing systems, and a firm that controls those systems can exclude competitors from markets. A prominent example was the allegations against Microsoft for using their Windows dominance of personal computer operating systems to create barriers to competing software producers. Particular concern has been expressed about the ability of MNCs to dominate small markets in developing countries.

Contrary to the optimistic market-oriented view that MNCs facilitate mutually beneficial transfers of knowledge from home to host countries, critics see the MNC's zealous control of knowledge and its use as a competitive weapon as having negative consequences for economic and social well-being. MNCs have been accused of not really transferring technology to developing countries, of failing to train host-country employees, or of importing home-country technologies ill suited to host-country conditions, displacing indigenous technologies. The MNC tends to centralize high value-added sophisticated activities at its home-country headquarters and low-skilled activities in host countries. Thus it has been criticized for reinforcing and reproducing existing global inequalities between the wealthy countries in which most MNCs are headquartered and the poorer host countries in which they locate branches and subsidiaries.

MNCs have also long been criticized for their influence over governments. Election campaign contributions, bribes, and threats to shift production to foreign jurisdictions are ways in which MNCs may seek to directly influence governments. Transfer pricing, in which MNCs may manipulate their internal accounting in order to make it appear that most of their profits are made in low-tax jurisdictions, has been an important area of concern for governments. MNCs have also been active in trying to shape international rules that constrain governments and protect their investments, such as

North American Free Trade Agreement investor protections which are discussed in more detail below. Stephen Gill (2003, ch. 7) has called this the "new constitutionalism," in which international law is used to create rights for firms at the expense of citizens.

A particularly controversial type of international law has been the World Trade Organization rules on trade-related intellectual property (TRIPS), which were put on the trade negotiation agenda mainly as a result of lobbying by large pharmaceutical MNCs (Sell, 1999). The TRIPS agreement requires countries to enforce 20-year patent protection. MNCs and industrialized country governments argued that this was needed if MNCs were to be encouraged to invest in large-scale costly research, while critics, including many developing countries, argued that such patent protection conferred an excessively long monopoly and restricted unduly the ability of developing countries to get access to technologies needed for development. In response to heavy criticism of the lack of affordable access to needed medicines of people suffering from AIDS/HIV in Africa, some loosening of the TRIPS provisions was agreed at the start of the Doha round of trade negotiations in 2001.

The market-oriented and critical approaches to the MNC and FDI present very contradictory pictures, which appear irreconcilable. In this area, both approaches take institutions more seriously than is typical in their analyses of the globalization of finance more generally. Nevertheless, they still do not pay enough attention to the characteristics of international institutions that were set out in chapter 2, especially the role of social practices, and the complex ways in which public- and private-sector rules can be entangled. Despite acknowledging the importance of institutions, market-oriented theories of the MNC still treat market transactions as the benchmark against which the MNC is analyzed. The MNC is treated as an alternative that emerges when markets fail, and the competition between the MNC and arm's-length markets can be thought of as a type of market for institutions. More importantly, the unit of analysis is the transaction, which is treated as a voluntary, rational, cost-minimizing and benefit-maximizing interaction. This completely obscures the independent role played by power. Similarly, critical approaches treat the MNC as a relatively independent power-seeking organization not unlike an army or a state, an organizational form that displays great continuity across issue areas, industries, and historical time.

It is useful to think of MNCs as constituted by practices that link the changing internal organization of the MNC to the larger organized environment within which it operates. For instance, corporation law, which varies by country but is being harmonized to some degree, defines the rights of shareholders and other stakeholders, and has a very large impact on the relationship of managers, workers, and customers, and on the performance of the MNC more generally. Similarly, increased reliance of MNCs on financial practices developed in international or foreign stock markets for assessing their performance and for managing their internal assets may orient them more towards short time horizons at the expense of longer-range planning. Variations in technical practices can account for enduring differences in the organization and performance of MNCs in different industries. Political pressure by NGOs or governments can lead MNCs to create codes of conduct that can reshape their labor relations to some degree. Human rights laws in particular countries can be used to hold corporations more accountable for violations. Organized efforts by Transparency International, a network supported by many MNCs, and the OECD's 1997 Convention on Combating Bribery of Foreign Public Officials in International Business Transactions can reduce substantially the role of bribery in MNC–host country interactions. In short, the MNC is not a fixed organizational form that inevitably manipulates markets and governments as it seeks to maximize its power; nor is it the inevitably efficient outcome of competing ways of engaging in transactions; rather, it is a type of institution that is shaped to an important degree by the domestic and international institutions and practices in which it is involved or on which it is dependent.

An emphasis on the role of social practices and public-sector institutions in constituting the MNC is useful in assessing its role in globalization. The MNC's channeling of international economic transactions through its bureaucratic structure can be a sign of either intense globalization or a lack of globalization, depending on the institutional context of these transactions. The former may be the case if the MNC brings about the type of cross-border economic relationship that is possible only in association with the cross-border structure of the MNC itself. The latter may be the case if the MNC substitutes its own bureaucratic organization for economic transactions that might otherwise be carried out either by markets, if the necessary international institutional framework for such transactions were better developed, or by nationally based firms in today's host countries that are better able to access a global store of technical knowledge or marketing networks than is the case today where MNCs often monopolize both.

A Brief History of FDI

The use of permanent representatives abroad by firms first became common in what is referred to as the "commercial revolution" of the thirteenth century, as with the Italian banks which had offices around Europe and the Mediterranean. Other early examples of foreign direct investment were the great European trading companies that explored the world from the seventeenth to the nineteenth centuries, including the Dutch East Indies Company, the British East Indies Company, and the Hudson's Bay Company. Although these companies differed from our current conceptions of MNCs, because they were more involved in trade than production, in other respects they are quite similar. They did much more in foreign jurisdictions than just trade with local actors, including making substantial fixed foreign investments in forts, warehouses, land, and administrative operations. The character of their foreign operations such as the extensive fur-trading network administered by the Hudson's Bay Company in Canada, or the involvement in cotton growing of the British East Indies Company in India, could be seen as involving the management of a production process as much as the conduct of trade. Although these companies were more closely linked to the state than today's MNCs, both through the formal chartering process and through the close relations between these companies and Dutch and British foreign policy, they also raised money from shareholders in competitive capital markets, as do today's MNCs (Neal, 1990, p. 118).

During the nineteenth century, under British hegemony, there was a proliferation of smaller British-based multinational firms with offices in various countries around the world. These were mostly trading operations, but they involved permanent offices, warehouses, and staff in foreign countries. It is now widely recognized that a high percentage of the British capital outflows of the nineteenth century were direct investments involving management control – thousands of small multinationals (Jones and Schröter, 1993, pp. 8–9). At the end of the nineteenth century and during the first decades of the twentieth century, more manufacturing-oriented MNCs began to emerge, including the operations of German chemical and electrical companies in various European countries, the creation of foreign auto production facilities by Ford, and the foreign food and agricultural activities of British firms.

During the period between World Wars I and II the cartel form of organization tended to be more prominent than MNCs in international industries (Hexner, 1946). Cartels involved agreements among leading firms to divide up world markets, and they were remarkably strong in industries such as steel, chemicals, and electrical machinery. In general these cartels tended to be more nationally based than is the case with today's MNCs, with each firm agreeing not to compete in other firms' own home markets. However, cartels in complex industries such as chemicals also involved substantial investment by European and US firms in less developed territories (Porter, 2002b).

After World War II, USA-based MNCs became especially active, in part because of the new global orientation of the USA and the strength of its economy relative to those of its war-damaged competitors, and in part because, as noted below, the cartel alternative, which had come to be associated with German and Japanese militarism, was subject to significant prohibitions. These USA-based MNCs stimulated a great deal of concern in host countries such as France, as evident in Servan-Schreiber's (1967) *Le Défi américain* or in Canada as in Kari Levitt's (1970) *Silent Surrender*.

During the 1970s and 1980s awareness of the importance of MNCs grew dramatically. In the academic literature, both business scholars, such as Raymond Vernon in *Sovereignty at Bay* (1971) and other work, and international relations scholars, drawing on dependency theory and other radical approaches, or initiating the new subfield of international political economy, began to treat the MNC as an actor that rivaled and threatened to undermine the power of states, and international relations textbooks began to include tables showing MNCs such as Exxon or GM as ranking above most states on some measures of economic size. The MNCs began vigorously expanding their operations in developing countries, and not just in the production of raw materials or to sell to local markets, but increasingly to shift lower-skilled manufacturing production such as microchips to low-wage locations. Many developing countries began to be more aggressive in their relations with MNCs, with host governments often taking over local MNC enterprises or instituting a wide variety of rules designed to make a greater proportion of economic benefits associated with MNC operations accrue to local actors. These rules included renegotiated contracts for raw material exports, requirements to transfer technology or to have local citizens sit on corporate boards, to source inputs from local suppliers, and to export and not simply to sell into the local market.

Since the 1980s attitudes on the part of host-country governments displayed a significant shift away from an earlier hostility and anxiety to an eagerness to court MNC investments. From 1991 to 2002, 95 percent of the 1,641 changes to FDI laws introduced by 165 countries were in the direction of greater liberalization (UNCTAD, 2003, p. 20). Reasons for this shift include the attractiveness of FDI as a substitute for bank financing which collapsed in the debt crisis of the early 1980s, the weak bargaining position of the heavily indebted countries, an ideological shift which de-legitimized state control of the economy, and the growth of MNCs headquartered in countries that had previously only been host countries. MNCs began to more fully plan their production on a worldwide basis, and rather than simply looking for low-wage locations or local markets, many MNCs also began locating in host countries to get access to knowledge or research and development funding. Some MNCs began carrying out white-collar work in host countries; thus foreign firms set up operations in India to provide software programming or telemarketing services for customers in the USA. This shift to more varied and complex types of activities in some host countries created new constituencies supportive of FDI in these countries.

Efforts to Create International Regulations Governing FDI

International direct investment has never been a purely private-sector activity – it has always relied on and been shaped by political and legal initiatives of public-sector authorities. Often these have taken the form of direct political or military intervention in defence of foreign investments, such as the notorious example of the CIA intervention which overthrew the Guatemalan government in 1954 after that government nationalized some of the holdings of the USA-based United Fruit Company which the Dulles brothers, heading the CIA and State Department, had stock in and had provided legal services for (McWilliams and Piotrowski, 1993, p. 90). Since World War II there has also been an increasing tendency to try to build international laws and norms to regulate investment, rather than simply mobilizing political and military power. This has been the case both for those who wished to restrict FDI and those who wished to encourage it.

Immediately following World War II the most prominent international legal effort relevant to FDI was the effort, led by the US government, to ban international cartels. Ostensibly this was due to the association of the cartels of the inter-war period with German and Japanese militarism. The fact that Standard Oil's provision of strategically important synthetic rubber patents to German firm IG Farben was seen as hurting the US war effort was also a factor. The anti-cartel campaign also resonated with the strong anti-trust tradition in the USA, which prohibited horizontal collaboration between firms, dating from the widespread popular anger with the gigantic trusts of the late nineteenth century (Porter, 1999). However, the campaign also was an ideal fit with US post-World War II interests, since it restricted the form of industrial organization that had characterized its key competitors and left the field open for its own oligopolistic form of industrial organization, in which a few large firms could dominate an industry by acquiring and merging with competitors. The campaign was pursued vigorously in the UN and the European Community, but abated when other countries began talking about developing anti-trust rules to restrict the operations of US MNCs in small developing country markets. When US firms began to get anxious in the 1970s and 1980s about the collaborative arrangements between Japanese firms, which they blamed for the declining US competitive position at the time, anti-trust or *competition policy* was revived as an issue, and attempts were made to incorporate it into discussions at the World Trade Organization in the 1990s.

In 1961 the Code of Liberalization of Capital Movements was agreed at the OECD, and this remains the main multilateral agreement enhancing the rights of MNCs to engage in FDI. As an OECD official remarked (Schuijer, 2002), the code is "soft law," and if a member fails to comply, "there will be consultations in the relevant OECD Committees, peer pressure from the other members, and eventually a recommendation by the OECD Council. This system does work, but the process is sometimes drawn-out and arduous." As new members have joined the OECD, such as Mexico, the Czech Republic, Hungary, Poland, South Korea, and Slovakia, they have had to agree to the provisions of this Code and its subsequent revisions. Critics have pointed to this as a factor in the financial crises in Mexico in 1994 and Korea in 1997.

During the 1960s and 1970s there was an intense debate at the UN between host countries which wished to assert their right to expropriate the assets of MNCs and the United States and other industrialized countries which argued that the rights of foreign investors should be paramount, with the former making some important gains in putting forward their case, such as with the adoption of the Charter of Economic Rights and Duties of States adopted by the

UN General Assembly in 1974 (Dell, 1990, p. 48). The widespread nationalization of assets of the oil MNCs, first by Libya and then by other oil exporters, was an inspiration to many host countries, especially after the oil price increases of 1973 brought immense revenues to these countries. The UN Commission on Transnational Corporations and a Center on Transnational Corporations (CTC) were established in 1974 to provide information on MNCs, to give assistance to host countries in negotiating with them, and to control their negative effects (Dell, 1990, p. 74). The CTC became the agency responsible for a Code of Conduct for MNCs that sought to regulate perceived abuses by MNCs in host countries. All these developments took place in the context of the decade-long and ultimately unsuccessful struggle for a New International Economic Order (NIEO) by developing countries, which hoped that organized demands directed at the wealthy countries could bring about fundamental structural change in the international system.

As noted, attitudes towards FDI began to change dramatically in the 1980s following the debt crisis. The NIEO coalition broke up. The UN CTC was closed down in response to US pressure in 1992 and 1993, and in its place UNCTAD's Division on Investment, Technology, and Enterprise Development began producing research much more favorable to the benefits of FDI. A series of initiatives was launched to create strong new international rules protecting investors. These have taken the form mainly of *bilateral investment treaties* (BITs), the first of which was signed in 1959. By 1989 this number had increased to 385, and by 2002 to 2,181. Initially, these were mostly between either the USA or a European country and a developing country, but by 2003, 45 percent of BITs did not include a developed country. BITs covered 27 percent of FDI stock in developing and transition countries in 2000 (UNCTAD, 2003, p. 89).

DeLuca (1994) has argued that the US goal in creating these treaties was to lay the groundwork in international law for a multilateral investment treaty. A similar point can be made about the investment provisions of the Canada–US Free Trade Agreement (CUFTA) and NAFTA, each of were unusually strong and were well timed for influencing the Uruguay Round of trade negotiations which concluded in 1994. The BITs and NAFTA provided investors with the right to bring complaints against states to a process of binding arbitration, the first time in international law that states had been held accountable to private actors in this way. The implementation of the NAFTA provisions has been especially controversial, because foreign investors were able to overturn environmental initiatives of governments and collect damages on the grounds that these environmental initiatives represented an expropriation of profits that the firms would have earned. Activists castigated the NAFTA investment provisions as providing a set of special rules for investors at the expense of citizens' welfare. The three NAFTA member states restricted the scope of the investor protection provisions of NAFTA in 2001 as alarm about their use by firms to undermine regulations grew, but concerns remained, and in 2002 the Canadian government indicated that it would seek further restrictions.[2]

Fresh from their success at having investor rights strengthened dramatically in the BITs, CUFTA, and NAFTA, the US and other governments began to work on more ambitious efforts to create a multilateral investment agreement. They had initially placed considerable hope in moving this project forward with the Uruguay Round negotiations. The Trade-Related Investment Measures (TRIMs) agreement did indeed prohibit some of the key measures used by developing host countries to regulate MNCs, such as rules requiring local sourcing or trade balancing, but the TRIMs agreement was far weaker than the BITs, CUFTA, or NAFTA provisions (Sell, 2000). The focus then shifted to the OECD, where negotiations began on a Multilateral Agreement on Investment (MAI). The hope was that a strong agreement could be concluded among the wealthy member states of that organization, building on the OECD's history of creating rules to facilitate cross-border investment, and then that this agreement could be extended to countries not in the OECD.

In the end, the MAI negotiations became a fiasco for the OECD. Initially started in secrecy, opposition to the agreement mushroomed after a draft was leaked by a Canadian non-governmental organization, the Council of Canadians. The lack of public consultation added further concern to worries about excessive rights for investors (Smythe, 1998). After an impressive worldwide lobbying effort by NGOs, together with the increasingly cold feet of many OECD member states, the OECD abandoned the MAI in 1999.

One final set of international rules with significance for FDI is the Financial Services Agreement (FSA) established at the WTO in 1997. The FSA was designed primarily to create easier cross-border access for banks and other firms selling financial services. By making it easier for multinational financial firms to open offices in foreign jurisdictions, it facilitates FDI in the financial sector itself, and to the degree that such FDI facilitates cross-border investment in other industries (for instance, by offering non-financial MNCs access in host markets to banks with which they are used to doing business), it facilitates FDI in general. Countries signing the FSA were allowed to restrict their commitments, and not all WTO members signed – thus the FSA is not as strong as other WTO agreements. Moreover, the FSA included a *prudential carve-out* which allows commitments made by a state to be pre-empted if compliance with such commitments would create dangerous financial instability

Conclusion: FDI and the Globalization of Finance

Foreign direct investment involves a form of financial relationship that is a defining feature of one of the most prominent symbols of globalization, the multinational corporation. The distinctive history and controversies associated with FDI reinforce the importance of paying attention to the varied institutional fabric of global finance rather than thinking of it as an ocean of undifferentiated flows. As the theories of the MNC discussed in this chapter show, the MNC is much more about organization and control than about a transfer of financial resources. This highlights a more general feature of finance that is important for understanding its role in globalization, since a great variety of other financial practices, including accounting, financial planning, and derivatives contracts, are as much about various aspects of organization and control, including monitoring behavior, specifying commitments, and coordinating expectations, as about resource transfers. It is easy to overlook the contribution of finance to organization and control, because the mechanisms involved are often decentralized and discursive, rather than the centralized deployment of material resources that we often associate with organization and control. In a globalizing world these forms of decentralized and discursive organization – social practices – are becoming increasingly important.

In the case of FDI, the property rights in the host country that are conferred on the MNC by its ownership of its investment are not at all self-evident and unchanging. On the contrary, these rights have been constituted not just by the act of investing, but simultaneously by the frequently contested domestic and international legal context in which the relationship between these rights and other rights, such as those of sovereign states or employees, are adjudicated. The significance of these rights for the MNC also varies greatly, depending on variations in the scientific and technical practices of the activity involved, as evident in the leading role played by pharmaceutical MNCs in pressing for an expansion of intellectual property rights. Sometimes the exercise of these rights is shaped by ethical standards that are not formally part of the legal system, such as the commitments against bribery fostered by Transparency International and the codes of conduct adopted by some MNCs in response to criticisms by civil society of MNC environmental or labor practices. Thus the MNC is not a fixed autonomous organizational form, but rather a contested and changing organizational arrangement that is heavily shaped not just by its internal structure, but by the intersecting legal, political, technical, scientific, and financial institutions and practices in which it is engaged and on which it is dependent.

Part III

New Actors and New Frontiers in Global Finance

7

Business Institutions and Private-Sector Norms

Often the globalization of finance is seen as a quintessential example of the central role of the private sector in globalization. As noted previously, in market-oriented approaches the private-sector influence is usually portrayed as occurring through the impact of inexorably expanding fluid anonymous financial markets and the constraints these markets impose on states. In critical approaches, the private-sector influence is often portrayed as involving close links between powerful individual financial firms that use their financial and political influence to exploit others, or to create rules to reinforce their dominance. Alternatively, in some critical approaches, private-sector financial actors are seen as exercising their power as a leading fraction of the dominant class, using their control over finance to control other businesses and governments.

These analyses of the role of the private sector in global finance seriously underestimate the complexity of the private-sector institutions involved. As noted in chapter 5, markets need rules to function, and these are often provided by private-sector associations or business practices rather than by states. As well, public-sector regulators, which often have great difficulties in keeping up with the pace of change and growth in financial markets, have increasingly relied upon private-sector institutions in the formulation and implementation of policies. The institutional landscape within which global finance operates involves an enormously complex variety of private-sector institutions, but, as will be shown in more detail below, the most significant of these are integrated in complementary ways with public-sector institutions. Whether the public sector or private sector is dominant in these complex relationships cannot be deduced from grand statements about states and markets or states and multinational financial firms, but must instead be assessed with regard to each specific case. Despite this complexity and variation, the overall pattern of strengthened organizational capacity involving integrated international public and private institutions is strikingly consistent across financial industries and issue areas.

The chapter begins by identifying types of private-sector institutions. It then comments on the many ways in which public- and private-sector institutions complement one another. Finally, it provides more detailed analysis of some of the most important of these institutions.

Varieties of Private-Sector Institutions in Global Finance

Business institutions and rules in global finance, as in other industries, range from very micro-level informal business or professional practices on the one hand, such as informal norms for allocating shares of a large bond issue among the members of a bond-underwriting syndicate, to large formal organizations, such Citibank. Private-sector financial institutions also vary greatly in the character of their relationship to public-sector institutions, ranging from a relatively small private-sector component, such as the use of private-sector debt ratings in strong public regulatory regimes, to impressively autonomous and strong private-sector rule-making institutions, such as the International Accounting Standards Board. Fully differentiating private-sector institutions along all of these axes – degree of formality, size, and relationship to the public sector – is not feasible in a chapter of this size. However, it is useful to note some of the key types of private-sector institutions, ordered from the smallest and least formal to the largest and most formal.

(1) *Business practices*: A great deal of order and regularity in global finance is provided by recognized business practices that are not necessarily tied to any particular formal organization. For instance, many new financial products, such as a derivative whose value depends on future exchange rate movements, start from a unique mathematical risk model but over time become widely recognized in the market as a standard product with well-established

features, rules, and expectations. Sometimes the rules and norms associated with the product will eventually be written down, as is the case with the International Primary Market Association's book of recommendations. Where these practices are linked to a professional association in the form of a code, then their capacity to inspire compliance may increase greatly, as such compliance may be a condition of maintaining one's accreditation and ability to work and to avoid costly legal damages from suits brought by those harmed by non-compliance.

(2) *Professional associations*: Global finance has a number of characteristics that make professional associations important in its governance. First, it is highly knowledge-intensive, and professional associations devote much effort to ensuring that their members are adequately trained. Second, it relies to a very important degree on trust, because of the large, intangible, complex transactions involved, where the purchaser often has difficulty understanding or controlling the risks associated with the transaction. Professional associations can function to certify their members as trustworthy. Third, as global financial markets have expanded, professionalization, accreditation, and licensing have become more important relative to alternative forms of organizing knowledge or to risk-management activities such as relying on old-boys' networks or the informal in-house knowledge that many large banks possess. The CFA Institute, with its Chartered Financial Analyst accreditation, is an example of an important internationally active professional association.

(3) *Financial exchanges and clearinghouses*: As noted in chapter 5, stock exchanges have a long history of self-regulation in securities markets, and as financial markets have become global, the regulatory functions of stock exchanges have been modified in response. This has occurred in part through the cross-border regulation which a large exchange like the New York Stock Exchange can provide when subjecting foreign stocks traded on it to the NYSE rules; in part by the involvement in international public- and private-sector collaborative efforts, such as the World Federation of Exchanges or the International Organization of Securities Commissions; and in part through the transformation of exchanges from mutually owned clubs dependent on informal local relationships to a more corporate, for-profit form of organization which can regulate local and foreign participants equally well. A clearinghouse, such as the Clearing House Inter-Bank Payments System of New York, which handles 95 percent of worldwide US dollar transactions, can contribute to regulation and

governance by requiring users to be in compliance with its own rules as well as those of public-sector regulators.

(4) *Trade associations and lobby groups*: All industries, including finance, have associations that defend their interests and address common problems, and with globalization these have become increasingly internationalized, whether by the construction of international industry associations or through the increased prominence of foreign members and issues in the work of national industry associations. These associations often engage both in lobbying and in providing services or standards for their members. Research and statistical work can be important for all three of these.

Like other complex industries, global finance relies to an important degree on informal groupings composed of very high-level executives, such as the Financial Leaders' Group, which plays a key role in pushing for the liberalization of financial services at the World Trade Organization. In part this is because traditional nationally based industry associations are too bureaucratic, or have to serve all their members, including typically a very large proportion of small firms with little interest in international activities. As well, many problems in global finance cut across more than one industry sector (such as banking and securities), and traditional associations may not be as well suited to addressing these problems as is an informal group drawing high-level members with the expertise needed to address the particular problem. A third reason is that informal groupings have the flexibility to match the rapid pace of change in global finance, such that high-profile issues can come and go within one or two years. Often the public-sector bodies working on international financial regulation are relatively small informal high-level groups, and adopting a similar form of organization can facilitate the private sector's interactions with these bodies.

(5) *Individual financial and coordination services firms*: A significant degree of order in global finance is provided by the internal rules and practices of large firms that extend beyond their own organizational boundaries to influence global finance as a whole. *Coordination services* refers to firms that sell services that contribute to rule making or rule implementation in global finance.[1] Debt-rating agencies, law firms, accounting and auditing firms, consulting firms, re-insurers, and risk management firms are examples. All of these can be important in helping bring financial market actors into compliance with a set of rules, even if the character of these rules differs considerably. For instance, debt-rating agencies judge the

performance of firms and governments against a set of internal criteria and models, and their ratings put pressure on rated actors to comply with the ratings agencies' expectations (Sinclair, 1994). Re-insurers similarly establish formal and informal rules that guide their decisions about whether to take on the risk involved in underwriting the policies of insurance firms and thereby put pressure on insurance firms to seek to comply with those rules (Haufler, 1997). Some large *individual financial services firms* can contribute to order and rule implementation in the market as a whole by providing sets of rules governing the transactions that take place within these firms. Lloyds Insurance in London is a firm, but also a worldwide market, with an extensive set of internal rules governing the interactions of brokers and clients in that market. As noted in chapter 4, the internal risk management systems of banks, which involve extensive sets of rules and procedures, are becoming very prominent in the current reform of the regime for international bank regulation.

(6) *Think tanks and research institutes*: In a knowledge-intensive industry such as global finance, behavior can be heavily shaped by best practices that are developed in technical reports produced by private-sector think tanks and research institutes. The Group of Thirty, which includes 30 high-profile individuals from the public, private, and academic worlds, and issues influential reports on international banking policy, is an example. As noted in chapter 5, the G30's policy recommendations have been especially influential in the effort to shorten the time it takes for the clearance and settlement of securities internationally. The Institute of International Finance is another prominent organization whose members are mostly multinational banks, that produces influential reports, along with efforts to influence international bank regulation that are more like conventional lobbying, but at the global level, since it is targeted at the work of the Basel Committee on Banking Supervision.

(7) *Standards-setting bodies*: Many standards are produced by trade and professional associations in the course of these associations' other activities, but in some cases standard setting is a sufficiently well-developed activity that it takes place in bodies specifically devoted to standard setting. The best example of this in global finance is the International Accounting Standards Board, which is entirely devoted to the production of accounting standards and deliberately maintains its autonomy from other organizations. The Commission on Banking Technique and Practice within the International Chamber

of Commerce that produces highly technical standards also fits within this category.

(8)   *Private regimes*: As noted in chapter 2, an *international regime* is a set of formal and informal rules and norms that govern a particular international issue area or industry. It is a large-scale institution that can include many other institutions. Although the word *regime* is increasingly used in practical discussions of international affairs, it remains much more abstract than *organization*. Identifying regimes requires the exercise of analytical judgment about whether sufficient coherence and integration exist in the institutions governing an issue area to warrant the label, whereas organizations can be identified by such concrete indicators as the presence of a founding charter, the size of the budget, and the number of personnel. In the governance of insurance and in securities markets, private institutions have been sufficiently important relative to public-sector ones at some historical periods that using the *regime* label to describe them is useful. This is the case, for instance, with international insurance before the creation of the public-sector International Association of Insurance Supervisors in 1992 (Haufler, 1997) and the Eurobond market during the 1960s.

The Relationship between Public-Sector and Private-Sector Institutions in Global Finance

Contrary to what one might expect, given the prominent role of private-sector actors and institutions in global finance, there are almost no cases of meaningful self-regulation that exist entirely independent of public-sector institutions. There are some types of rules that are important in guiding the operations of firms, such as the rules involving mathematical models for calculating risks and prices, or internal administrative procedures for controlling risk, which have at times been entirely initiated and controlled by the firms, but even these have become increasingly integrated with public-sector rules as the international regulatory regime has developed, as noted in chapter 3. Often the wide variety of ways in which public- and private-sector rules work together is not recognized, and thus it is useful to specify some of the more important ones.

(1)   *The use of courts to enforce private-sector rules.* Often self-regulatory arrangements can rely on legal action or the threat of legal

action to take care of instances in which self-regulation by itself would fail. For instance, Section 13 of the International Swaps and Derivatives Association 2002 Master Agreement, entitled "Governing Law and Jurisdiction," commits the parties to irrevocably waive "all immunity on the grounds of sovereignty" and to submit to English law, US law, or other mutually agreed and specified law. Sometimes private legal action can be brought against a private-sector association to hold it accountable to recognized legal standards of conduct, as with the awarding of $1.027 billion in a class action suit brought against NASDAQ for price fixing (Kaplan, 2002). This type of legal action is most common in the United States, because of its common law tradition and active consumer associations, but it has international significance both because of the importance of the US market in international affairs and because of the interest in other jurisdictions in relying more than previously on such mechanisms (Lex Fori, n.d.).

(2) *The requirement that private-sector actors be in compliance with public-sector regulation as a condition of associational membership.* The International Securities Markets Association, for instance, accepts as members only firms that are in good standing with their home-country regulator. The Clearing House Inter-Bank Payments System accepts only members that are regulated by the public-sector Federal Reserve. Such mutually beneficial relationships give firms a greater incentive to comply with public-sector regulations, and give associations more confidence that their members will uphold the association's private-sector standards.

(3) *The use of the threat of public-sector regulation to strengthen private-sector regulation.* Public-sector actors may call on private-sector actors to create rules, and motivate them to do so by threatening to implement public-sector rules if they do not. Examples are threats on the part of regulators at the Bank for International Settlements (1996, p. 31) to take initiatives on foreign exchange settlement risk if the private sector fails to do so. Similarly, the Emerging Markets Traders Association moved to create a code of conduct for member firms only after E. Gerald Corrigan, then head of the New York Federal Reserve and the Basel Committee on Banking Supervision, thumped his fist on the table in a meeting with the traders and made it clear that if they did not move to regulate the market, governments would (Buckley, 2000).

(4) *The incorporation of private-sector rules into public-sector regulation.* Increasingly regulators do not have the financial or

technical resources to monitor all firms as extensively as they may have in the past and are therefore relying more heavily on private-sector rules in public-sector regulations. A key example in global finance is the emphasis of the revisions of the Basel Committee on Banking Supervision's international standards on capital adequacy, in which regulators will increase their focus on examining banks' procedures for assessing and controlling risk rather than trying to examine and control their risks more directly.

(5) *The use of private-sector pressures to enforce public-sector regulations.* A cost-effective way for public-sector regulators to foster compliance is to require firms to divulge information about their performance that market actors will reward or punish. For instance, one of the priorities of the public-sector Financial Stability Forum in its efforts to reduce the danger of global financial crisis has been to survey market actors to determine what type of information about compliance with standards would be most likely to be incorporated into their risk models. If market actors punish firms or governments that exceed the standard for risky behavior by refusing to provide financing to them, then the incentives for compliance with those standards are greatly increased.

(6) *Reliance on private-sector associations in the formulation of regulations.* Private-sector associations are increasingly brought into the process of international policy formulation in global finance. For instance, the private-sector members of both the International Organization of Securities Commissions and the International Association of Insurance Supervisors, while not enjoying the rights of the public-sector members, have played an increasingly important role.

Some Examples of Private-Sector Institutions that Play an Important Role in the Governance of Global Finance

This section briefly examines the most prominent private-sector associations active in global finance.[2] It starts with those that engage primarily in influencing governments, looks at two involved primarily in standard setting, and turns finally to one concerned primarily with an aspect of the infrastructure of markets, the transfer of dollar payments between banks.

1. Associations seeking to influence public-sector actors: the Institute of International Finance (IIF) and the Financial Leaders Group (FLG)

The IIF was created originally by the world's largest commercial banks in connection with the developing country debt crisis of the early 1980s. In its first years the IIF mainly assembled information that would assist banks in managing their loans to developing country governments, such as statistics on government indebtedness. It played little role in regulatory matters at the time, providing little input into the development of the Basel Capital Adequacy Accord of 1988, the most important set of international rules for banking. However, by the first years of the twenty-first century, it had greatly increased its involvement in regulatory issues, becoming the main private-sector interlocutor for public-sector actors involved in bank regulation at the Basel Committee and in the debate over the post-Asia crisis reform of the international financial architecture. In the latter case, for instance, it has strongly opposed the idea of "private-sector burden sharing" – the effort to get private-sector actors to bear a greater share of the cost of international financial crises by, perhaps, imposing an IMF-authorized standstill on funds that seek to flee a country in the midst of a crisis. The IIF draws members from around the world – more than 320 members headquartered in more than 60 countries – and it has expanded its membership beyond commercial banks to include other types of financial firms. Its institutional capacity is evident in the number of active working committees it is able to sustain, in its expenditures in 2002 of $15.9 million, and in the publications it produces. As noted in chapter 4, despite this impressive organizational capacity the IIF has influenced international banking regulation but has not controlled it, and regulatory initiatives remain in the hands of public-sector bodies.

The FLG consists of chief executive officers (CEOs) from leading international financial firms, mostly from the USA, the UK, continental Europe, and Japan, and its main goal is to bring about the liberalization of financial service trade at the World Trade Organization. It was established during the Uruguay Round of negotiations to provide a channel for public-sector negotiators to interact with private-sector actors, and since then it has continued to work on financial services issues that are being considered at the WTO, such as efforts to set guidelines for domestic regulation. It is assisted by a lower-level, more technically focused group that is better suited to working on the details of regulatory matters than are CEOs. It aspires to create a global network in which member financial firms with complaints about host countries can raise their concerns with the FLG, which can in turn raise concerns with home-country governments. These governments can then raise the concerns with the host governments or at the WTO. Once established this arrangement will give the financial sector a strong organized capacity to bring issues to the attention of governments. However, as with the IIF, the initiative on the development of regulations in this area remains with the WTO member governments, and proceeds very slowly despite the efforts of the FLG.

2. Associations concerned with governance in securities markets: the World Federation of Exchanges (WFE), the International Securities Markets Association (ISMA), and the International Primary Markets Association (IPMA)

The Paris-based WFE is entirely oriented towards global issues, and with 56 member exchanges from around the world it draws widely from different regions. Membership restrictions are oriented primarily towards ensuring that new members meet exacting standards, rather than promoting the interests of some regions' exchanges over others. WFE membership helps foster confidence in the integrity of an exchange, especially if it is a new exchange that does not already have a strong reputation. The WFE works in conjunction with regional exchanges such as the Federation of European Securities Exchanges. The WFE's institutional capacity is evident in the statistics, standards, conferences, training, and publications that it manages, as well as in its revenues – in 2001, of 2.7 million Euros. In its interactions with the public-sector International Organization of Securities Commissions, the WFE sees itself as promoting private-sector solutions to problems in securities markets.

As noted in chapter 5, the roots of both ISMA and IPMA go back to the Association of International Bond Dealers, created in 1969 to establish rules for the Eurobond market, and although facilitating interactions among private-sector participants remains the primary focus of both organizations, they have become increasingly involved in seeking to shape public-sector regulations in recent years. ISMA focuses on secondary trading of international bonds once they have been issued, and IPMA focuses on the process by which new bonds are first distributed and sold. ISMA has established TRAX, and now

COREDEAL, electronic systems to facilitate international bond trading. Its standards are reinforced by its status in the UK as a recognized exchange and self-regulatory organization, and its recognition in Switzerland as an "institution similar to an exchange." In 2001 its income was 17 million Swiss francs. IPMA describes its core purpose as "to organise the market from the inside, helping the market to define itself in the context of the overall regulatory environment by codifying and harmonising international market practises" and to act as a representative body in dealing with political and regulatory authorities (<www.ipma.org.uk>). IPMA has established a well-recognized set of recommendations that function as voluntary standards, helps to resolve conflicts among member firms informally, and represents members' interests in international regulatory matters. In recent years the size of the market, new market practices from the USA, and the development of proprietary computer systems to facilitate the work of primary markets led IPMA to create a member-owned electronic communications system that will facilitate trading, and which IPMA will regulate.

3. Standard-setting associations: the International Accounting Standards Board (IASB) and the International Certified Financial Planner Council

As global securities markets have become more important, the need for accounting standards that are recognized across borders has become more pressing. Accounting is supposed to produce trustworthy financial data about the performance of firms and governments, and such data are crucial for investors to be able to make informed decisions about how to allocate their investments and for borrowers to instil confidence in investors. The Enron and Worldcom scandals of 2001 demonstrated how faulty accounting can contribute not just to the collapse of huge firms, but also to creating serious damage to confidence in securities markets as a whole. These companies were primarily USA-based, and the problems that can be associated with accounting can be even more severe internationally, where standardized measurement and judgment can be complicated by differing accounting traditions.

Two main competing solutions to this problem have been important. The first is the use of US Generally Accepted Accounting Principles (GAAP) which has been extended to many non-US firms because of their desire to participate in the US financial markets as the world's largest and most important. The second have been the International Accounting Standards (IAS) produced by the International Accounting Standards Board (IASB). The IASB is a private-sector international standard-setting association. It is funded from a variety of public-sector and private-sector sources, but it maintains a separation between those who finance it and those who set standards. After 25 years of work, the IASB took a very large step forward with the EU's and Australia's decisions to adopt IAS by 2005. The IASB's stature was also enhanced by the damage done to the credibility of US GAAP by Enron and other scandals and the ensuing strengthening of US authorities' interest in harmonizing with the IAS. The IASB and the International Federation of Accountants, with which it is associated, are the only two private-sector associations in the Financial Stability Forum's list of 12 key sets of international financial standards and codes. The IASB's budget has increased dramatically in recent years to £11.3 million in 2003.

Individual financial planning has become more important with the expansion of global securities markets. Where previously non-experts might have deposited their money in bank accounts and left the management of that money to the bank, now there is an increased tendency to put the money in mutual funds or directly in securities markets, and to rely on the advice of financial planners and analysts in doing so. Some countries have experienced problems with the training or integrity of these planners and analysts, including incentives provided by the funds or companies they were promoting that may not have been transparent to clients relying on their advice. Initially, international financial planning standards relied on US standards, with national financial planning associations making use of the Certified Financial Planner designation managed by the US CFP Board of Standards. These associations were grouped into the International CFP Council, which is in the process of converting itself from a consultative body of the US-based CFP Board of Standards to an international governing body to which the latter body will be affiliated. As of 2002, the association included member associations from 17 countries.

4.   The organization of infrastructure: the Clearing House Inter-Bank Payments System (CHIPS)

CHIPS describes itself as "the #1 bank-owned privately operated real-time final payments system for business-to-business transactions . . .

the international standard for clearing and settling transactions in US dollars," transferring $1.2 trillion daily. A failure in such an inter-connected system, even of one large participant, could do serious damage to global finance as a whole. CHIPS transactions are chan-neled through a New York-based computer system, and are subject to a variety of rules designed to ensure the stability and integrity of the system. One important private-sector rule is a real-time comput-erized mechanism for preventing the use of the system by members who have exceeded limits on financial exposures. CHIPS has also strengthened its integrity by requiring members to be regulated by the Federal Reserve, and to maintain a physical presence in the United States. Because of the importance of US dollar transactions in global finance, CHIPS plays an important role in stabilizing the system as a whole, not just by ensuring that the transactions it manages are carried out prudently, but also by excluding questionable actors from participation in transactions that are crucial for any firm that aspires to be globally active.

Conclusion

There are, then, a wide variety of private-sector institutions in-volved in global finance, ranging from routine business practices through more formal trade associations (for more examples see <www.paif.ca>). These institutions vary by function and by industry. Thus the common images of the private sector in global finance as involving either fluid undifferentiated financial flows or a coherent and integrated elite are inadequate. Private-sector institutions in global finance are fragmented, uneven, and surprisingly weak, but they are important nevertheless, especially when their interactions with public-sector rules are considered.

The types of institutions discussed above are not the only ways in which leading financial firms are able to influence global finance. An additional important influence is when leading figures in the finan-cial world take up positions in government, and vice versa. An example is Robert Rubin, who had a long career with Goldman Sachs on Wall Street before becoming US Treasury Secretary and working very aggressively to open foreign financial markets to US firms under US President Bill Clinton. After leaving government, he took up a senior post at Citigroup, the largest US bank. E. Gerald Corrigan, who served as head of the New York Federal Reserve and of the Basel Committee on Banking Supervision, subsequently took a senior position at Goldman Sachs, and in that capacity lobbied the US government about the regulation of hedge funds on behalf of large banks.[3] Bhagwati (1998, p. 12) has called this close relationship between Wall Street and the US government the "Wall Street–Treasury complex." The financial industry has also been an important source of campaign contributions to key US lawmakers.[4]

This close relationship lends support to critical approaches to the globalization of finance that see Wall Street and Washington working together to promote the interests of finance capital at the expense of everyone else. However, while there is no doubt that this is a serious problem in global finance, it would be a mistake to overstate the organizational capacity of the private sector. If financial capitalists were as all-powerful as some critics fear, then one would expect them to be much more effective at creating private-sector institutions to strengthen their role in the governance of global finance. Instead, the IIF was slow to involve itself in regulatory issues, despite their importance, and the FLG, despite its high-level participants, has not been very successful in its primary goal of maintaining momentum on financial services liberalization at the World Trade Organization. While it is important, the WFE plays a secondary role in the governance of global securities markets as compared to the public-sector regulators at IOSCO. As has been noted in other chapters, even wealthy private-sector actors must work through institutions to achieve their goals, and in global finance the patchy quality of private-sector institutions and the ongoing importance of public-sector institutions limits the power of financial elites in significant ways, even if the capacity of these private-sector institutions to participate in making and implementing rules has increased substantially in recent years.

8

Developing and Transition Countries

A key feature of past and present processes of international integration has been the relationship between a wealthier political and economic international center at which the most complex forms of economic activity take place and a less well-off periphery in which simpler economic activity predominates, as was the case when the periphery consisted mostly of European colonies, or today when it may include impoverished but sovereign countries. There are a great number of theoretical approaches that have been used to understand this relationship. Some, such as world systems analysis, have especially stressed the degree to which the periphery's integration into the world capitalist economy has been a cause of the inequality between center and periphery. Other approaches, including modernization theory, have blamed a *lack* of integration for the gap in wealth and power between the world's center and periphery. Thus the frontier between world centers and world peripheries has been interpreted both as a shifting point in an integrated exploitative relationship and as a boundary between the modern capitalist world and other regions of the world not yet incorporated into the capitalist world economy.

Financial relations have always been important in the relationship between the world's core and periphery, and have often been seen as playing a leading role both in drawing previously unintegrated regions into the world system and in exacerbating differentials of wealth and power once they are incorporated. For instance, the gold accumulated by Europeans in their conquest of the Americas helped to sustain the financial circuits that contributed to the growth of the market economy in Europe and the links of that economy to the Asian trade routes (Braudel, 1984, p. 166). The wealth, and the exceptionally high level of development of financial markets in the thirteenth-century Italian city-states, seventeenth-century Amsterdam, nineteenth-century London, and twentieth-century New York, were all connected to the location of those cities at the center of world trade routes, and to the function they played in financing the trade and production linkages between that center and the periphery (Arrighi, 1994; Porter, 1995).

As integration between core and periphery has become tighter and more complex, so have financial relations. Suter (1992), for instance, notes a remarkable pattern of system-threatening financial crises that broke out in the periphery roughly every 50 years, peaking in the years around 1830, 1880, 1940, and 1985. He argues that these were provoked by recurrent patterns in which a rapid economic expansion based on a particular set of new industries lost steam at the core, leading to a rapid outflow of financial assets, generated during the boom, to the periphery, generating an initial expansion there, which subsequently outran the economic fundamentals, including unanticipated diminished opportunities for exports from the periphery back into core markets.

In the first three decades after World War II core–periphery financial relations were primarily characterized by foreign direct investment, discussed in chapter 6, and bank loans, discussed in chapters 3 and 4. There was important variation across regions in the relative importance of these two types of financial relations. For instance, in 1970 net resource flows as a share of GNP for Brazil were 0.39 percent for foreign aid, 1.2 percent for FDI, 1.27 percent debt to government, and 2 percent debt to the private sector, while the comparable figures for Korea were 2.3 percent, 0.73 percent, 1.1 percent, and 0.28 percent, and the figures were zero in all cases for China (Armijo, 1999, p. 5). All peripheral regions included countries that relied heavily on foreign bank loans during the 1970s, and were subsequently seriously hurt by the debt crisis of the early 1980s, including socialist countries such as Poland and Hungary. However, some countries were especially hard hit, such as Mexico and Argentina, and some had very large state-run economies that borrowed very little in proportion to their economic capacity, such as China and the Soviet Union.

The debt crisis of the early 1980s marked a key turning point in the financial relations linking the core and the periphery of the world economy. As noted previously, the period before the crisis had been marked by high levels of state control in developing and socialist countries, and the prevailing inclination among these countries' governments was to obtain more autonomy from MNCs by state interventions in the economy, including expropriations of MNC operations, and also by relying on bank loans rather than FDI, since the former seemed to come with fewer strings attached. In 1980 in developing countries as a whole, government borrowing accounted for 1.47 percent of GDP, while FDI accounted for 0.21 percent.[1] Following the debt crisis, there was an economic sea change in these countries' levels of commitment to market-oriented financial policies in three main related respects. First, governments became more enthusiastic about FDI, as discussed in chapter 6, and by 1994 FDI inflows amounted to 1.57 percent of GDP, while debt to government inflows accounted for only 0.08 percent. Second, state intervention in the economy was dramatically reduced, including in the countries that embarked on a rapid transition from socialism to capitalism, thereby providing more opportunity for financial markets to allocate capital, such as when large enterprises were converted from state ownership into private firms with shares traded in stock markets. Finally, there was a major shift away from bank lending to securities markets in private-sector financing of developing countries and countries in transition – which together came to be labelled *emerging markets* by the World Bank and others. Inflows of portfolio capital to developing countries was 1.5 percent of GDP in 1994.

The period after the 1980s debt crisis was accompanied by major political changes in the relationship of these emerging markets to the global financial system. Initially a daunting agglomeration of US political power, IMF and World Bank technical and economic power, and neoliberal ideology fused into a set of dominant pro-market policies labeled "the Washington consensus," to which there seemed no feasible alternative. However, as we shall see below, this consensus began to crumble following the crises of the 1990s, and developing countries began to play a larger role in the governance of global finance.

Looking at these historical developments and changes as a whole, it is clear that financial relations have always been an important aspect of core–periphery relations, and these have become more complex and volatile over time. The rest of this chapter examines developments since the early 1990s in three sections. In the first, the significance of the greater reliance of developing and transition countries on securities markets, including the Mexican, East Asian, and other financial crises that have been associated with this reliance, will be discussed. The second section focuses more directly on the integration of two of the world's largest, previously financially autonomous countries into global finance – China and Russia. Together these countries accounted for 23 percent of the world's population in 2003, and both are major powers. The third section examines the ways in which developing and transition countries have begun to take a more active role in the governance of global finance, rather than simply being the recipients of policies developed in Washington.

Emerging Markets and the Global Financial Crises of the 1990s

One of the most distinctive features of global finance during the 1990s was the huge volume of portfolio finance that flowed into the developing and transition countries. Portfolio investment flows to developing countries increased from $33 million in 1984 to almost $89 *billion* in 1993, at which point it constituted 31 percent of net resource flows to developing countries (Haley, 1999, p. 75). Initially this seemed to many to be cause for celebration, ending the virtual exclusion since the 1980s debt crisis of many heavily indebted countries from global financial markets, and promising to finance desperately needed investments in new infrastructure and manufacturing. Unfortunately, by the end of the decade, following near catastrophic financial crises in Mexico, East Asia, and Russia, the dangerous side of these flows had become glaringly obvious, even to their proponents.

There are a number of reasons for this boom in portfolio investment that help reveal both its positive and negative aspects. As noted in chapter 5, portfolio investment, which does not involve managerial control over the project that is being financed, differs from other types of financing in relying on the capacity of the investor to exercise control by selling his or her holdings in a financial market, rather than by seeking to directly shape the management of the project. This requires the types of institutions that are preconditions for markets that were also discussed in chapter 5, including mechanisms, such as a well-developed financial press, for distributing information on investment conditions and performance to widely dispersed investors.

The positive features of portfolio investment relative to bank lending, state-controlled financing, or direct foreign investment, include its flexibility, its sensitivity to price signals, and if financial markets are well regulated, large, and stable, its potential to reduce costs, since it replaces the analytical and organizational functions of bank or government bureaucracies with decentralized flows of information and patterns of buying and selling.

The negative features of portfolio investment relative to other forms of financing include its greater volatility, its tendency to encourage decisions based on short-term factors or market psychology rather than careful assessment of the long-range prospects of an investment, and its tendency to involve exuberant bubbles and panics. These can be linked to characteristics inherent in the markets in which such investment takes place. With a bank loan or an investment managed by the public sector there is an organization that can engage in serious sustained analysis of the project, and there is an incentive to do so, because the cost of the project's failure will tend to be borne by the organization doing the analysis. By contrast, with portfolio investment, each investor can choose between doing his or her own research or relying on the mood of the market as revealed by trends in the investment target's prices. The latter is much cheaper, especially since a portfolio investor may keep their holdings in a project only for a short time. To some degree the prices of investment targets in financial markets reflect an aggregated assessment of useful information about those investment targets, perhaps as a result of the purchase and dissemination of analysis produced by firms specializing in financial analysis. However, there is an inherent tendency to free-ride on the information produced by others, and therefore for inadequate levels of reliable information to be produced. Moreover, since the future performance of one's asset can be shaped as much by the impact of the market's perceptions of that asset's price, judging those perceptions can become more important than assessment of the real performance of the project of which that asset is a part. Taken together, these features of securities markets contribute to their frequent tendency to involve "manias, panics and crashes" (Kindleberger, 1989).

Both the positive and the negative factors above were at play in the upsurge of portfolio investment in developing countries in the 1990s. Across the industrialized and industrializing world there was a major shift in the types of financial assets in which savings were held, from bank deposits to mutual funds and pension funds. Part of this was due to the greater efficiency of securities markets in channeling funds from savers to borrowers. The efficiency was associated with the growth in the types of institutions needed to sustain market transactions in developing, transition, and industrialized countries, a growth supported by the encouragement of the creation of stock markets in the developing and transition countries by the World Bank and others, as well as by technology-driven reductions in costs of information processing. The shift towards portfolio investment was in part due to the problem loans associated with the debt crisis, which had made bank-intermediated financing a less attractive alternative. However, the boom in emerging markets also involved inadequate assessment of the underlying real performance of the projects into which portfolio investment was flowing. For a while the boom was self-sustaining, as the value of investors' holdings was driven up by subsequent inflows; but once confidence began disappearing, panic and collapse could follow, as the last to sell their holdings would lose the most. This pattern occurred in Mexico in 1994, in East Asia in 1997, and in Russia in 1998.

Great volumes have been written about the causes and consequences of these global financial crises of the 1990s.[2] As with any complex event, a great many explanatory factors have been identified. These include the following.

1 *Inadequate transparency in emerging markets.* This explanation tends to place responsibility for the crises on the emerging markets for not providing the information that would allow foreign portfolio investors and lenders to assess the risks they were taking on accurately. Both public- and private-sector emerging market actors were criticized. For instance, in Thailand, where the 1997 crisis began, the Thai central bank did not reveal the full extent of the country's financial obligations. On the private-sector side, companies in East Asia were criticized for "crony capitalism" – the informal arrangements between and within companies. A number of questions about the adequacy of transparency problems as an explanation have been raised, including their inability to explain the simultaneity of the crisis across countries, the fact that these same countries were lauded for their economic performance prior to the crisis, and concerns about whether greater transparency might have exacerbated the crisis as the panic might have accelerated.

2 *Inadequate regulation of global financial firms and home jurisdictions.* These explanations tend to place responsibility on actors from the industrialized countries. Critics have pointed to the role of relatively unregulated hedge funds that made money by speculating massively on short-term changes in currencies, thereby contributing to the collapse of some currencies. Critics have also blamed the low risk weights assigned to short-term bank loans by regulators at the Basel Committee on Banking Supervision. These were initially assigned because short-term loans seemed to pose fewer risks for lending banks, but short-term inter-bank lending played an important role in the East Asian crisis. Much blame was also placed on the

USA and other home jurisdictions of multinational financial firms, along with the IMF and World Bank, for aggressively pressing developing and transition countries to liberalize the access of these firms to them rapidly and prematurely.

3 *Errors in the management of exchange rates.* Both the 1994 and the 1997 crises began with a currency collapse, in Mexico and Thailand respectively. In both cases the governments initially tried to maintain a commitment to peg their currencies to the US dollar and also allowed heavy borrowing in US dollars. The peg allowed foreign investors to benefit from the higher rate of return of Mexican- and Thai-denominated assets without incurring the risk that the local currency would decline relative to the US dollar. The US dollar borrowing allowed domestic actors to benefit from lower foreign interest rates, and with the peg they could be guaranteed that their local currency revenues could be used to repay the US dollar loans at a fixed rate. Unfortunately, when doubts set in about these economies, and foreign actors began to convert their local assets to dollars, the central banks rapidly ran out of dollars and were unable to defend their peg, and the currency then collapsed. Many critics suggested, therefore, that the peg was the problem, and consequently they advocated either greater exchange rate flexibility or zero flexibility (for instance, replacing the local currency with the dollar). Other commentators on exchange rates criticized the lack of coordination between the US, European, and Japanese currencies as a source of currency instability in emerging markets.

What do these explanations for the emerging market crises of the 1990s tell us about globalization and finance? Three implications stand out. First, the crises revealed a higher level of global integration than had been the case in the 1980s debt crisis, as evident in the speed with which events occurred and in the more complex and extensive cross-border and emerging market institutions that sustained the markets. Second, they revealed the increasingly important role played by knowledge systems and socially constructed risks in core–periphery relations. In previous periods these relations were characterized by the export of raw materials or labor-intensive manufactures; but the crises of the 1990s signified the importance of expectations, systems of rules, patterns of information flows, and intangible financial assets, rather than the production and exchange of traditional products. Third, and relatedly, they revealed the increased need for effective global governance with regard to the rules and risks associated with the incorporation of emerging markets into global finance. We shall see later in this chapter that some important steps were taken in this regard following the crises.

Two Restructuring Giants and Global Finance: China and Russia

China and Russia warrant specific consideration in analyzing emerging and transition economies and global finance, because they are the largest and most dramatic cases of rapid integration of state-controlled economies into global finance, and because the contrast between Russia's disastrous experience and China's successes highlights the importance of taking seriously the role of institutions and practices in this process.

Under the Soviet system, as in other centrally planned economies, the financial system played little independent part, acting mainly as an accounting system to channel money in accordance with the government's plan. The central bank, Gosbank, was the only bank. This role was consistent with the centralized control exercised by the government over the system, and also with the historical tendency of Marxism to see finance as serving no useful function as compared to the real industrial and agricultural economies.

Ironically, after the fall of Soviet communism, Russian reformers and their public- and private-sector Western advisors also failed to take seriously enough the distinctive role played by the financial system in the economy. They assumed that Russia could move quickly towards a market system by rapidly privatizing, and by transforming Gosbank into an independent central bank and many privately owned commercial banks. They expected that once unleashed, market forces would transform the economy into a competitive, efficient one. Unfortunately, little attention was given to the deficiencies of Russian financial practices.[3]

Four main unanticipated political and institutional factors led to the failure of Russian financial reform. First, the financial system became a conduit for a massive private appropriation of the assets that had been public property, mostly by an elite, often abusing their privileged position in the old system in ways that came to be hated by the general population. For instance, private banks were often started by party and state officials using public funds under their control, and were often used to transfer former public-sector assets to offshore accounts outside Russia. Similarly, some of the Russian state's most valuable industries were sold to private banks at fire-sale prices in corrupt and non-transparent auctions. Second, lack of financial expertise and technological capacity led to impossibly slow transactions between Russian financial actors, often taking weeks instead of the hours they would take in more developed financial systems.

Third, the lack of strong enforceable laws and regulations led to rampant fraud and criminality, a collapse of trust in the Russian financial system, and violent intimidation of bankers and other financial actors, including assassinations. Fourth, past practices of using political influence to channel credit changed very slowly, and the financial system did little to mobilize new savings or to stimulate new private-sector activity.

Globalization was implicated in the above problems in the degree to which the reform was modeled on a market ideal from beyond Russia's borders that was being aggressively promoted by Western governments, academics, and international institutions such as the World Bank, the European Bank for Reconstruction and Development, and the International Monetary Fund. It was also implicated in the huge transfer of Russian assets, often secretly, to offshore centers such as Cyprus or the Isle of Man.

However, by far the most dramatic global dimension of the Russian disaster was the collapse of the ruble and the Russian banking system in August 1998. The proximate cause of the Russian collapse was the instability of the East Asian crisis, which led to a sudden withdrawal of East Asian assets from the Russian financial system and a downturn in the natural resource exports on which the Russian economy depended. But a more fundamental problem was the government attempt to fund its debt by the sale of bonds with punishingly high interest rates, often to foreign investors or to domestic banks using foreign funds. Unfortunately, the money borrowed by the government generated almost no growth, and thus the financial transactions served only to enrich the banks and investors, with one set of lenders being repaid by borrowing more money from the next set. Massive infusions of dollars from the IMF were rapidly exchanged for rubles held by elites, who then moved their dollars offshore. Just as in Mexico and Thailand, the inflow of money was sustained by the government's promise to maintain a relatively stable exchange rate with the dollar; but this became impossible to sustain as domestic and foreign actors lost their confidence in the system and deserted the ruble in droves.

After the Communist revolution, China's banking system was organized in a similar fashion to that of the Soviet Union and other centrally planned economies, in which a dominant bank, the People's Bank of China (PBC), channeled resources in order to implement the plan. China remained almost entirely outside the evolving global financial system through the 1970s. When the People's Republic of China was recognized by the UN in place of Taiwan in 1971, it could have moved to take up the seat that had been reserved for China at the IMF and World Bank since the founding of these organizations, and which had been held by Taiwan; but for many years it chose not to take its place there (Pascual, 1995).

China embarked on a reform of its centrally planned economy in 1978, and since then it has dramatically increased its reliance on markets, with massive increases in foreign trade, inward and outward direct foreign investment, and private ownership. For instance, trade increased from about $20 billion in the late 1970s to $475 billion in 2000, and for most of the 1990s China was the second largest recipient of foreign investment after the United States (Lardy, 2002, p. 4). It took up its position at the World Bank and the IMF in 1980, and drew very heavily and successfully on the former's financing and technical assistance, borrowing $16.5 billion for 127 projects between 1980 and 1993 (Pascual, 1995, p. 62).[4]

Financial reforms came along with other economic reforms. In 1984 the PBC became a central bank, and a second set of state-owned banks and other financial institutions was created. Securities exchanges were opened in Shanghai in 1990, and Shenzhen in 1991. By the end of 1993 there were 13 banks, 12 insurance companies, 87 securities companies, 387 financial trust and investment companies, 11 financial leasing companies, 29 finance companies, and 62,900 credit cooperatives (DaCosta and Foo, 2002, p. 4). Beginning in 1997 the government began licensing a small but increasing number of foreign banks to conduct a restricted set of financial transactions, and by 2000 more than 150 foreign branch banks were operating in China (Lardy, 2002, pp. 3, 68–9). When China joined the World Trade Organization in 2001, it made dramatic concessions on financial services, promising to remove within five years limits on foreign bank licenses, prohibitions on involvement in domestic currency transactions, and geographic restrictions – and in general to give foreign banks the same treatment as domestic banks. The Chinese insurance market was also greatly opened to foreign firms, and more modest concessions on foreign access were promised in the securities industry. In short, in the quarter-century since its economic reform began, China had transformed its financial policy from one in which the financial system was a passive administrative link in the centrally planned distribution of financial resources to a market-driven policy in which foreign financial firms would play a prominent role.

Considering the similarities between the Russian and Chinese transition, the differences are striking: over the 1990s China's GDP almost doubled, while Russia's was almost halved (Stiglitz, 1999, p. 2). Russia suffered a catastrophic collapse in the wake of the East Asian financial crisis, while China was relatively unaffected. The major factor explaining the difference is the greater care taken in China to ensure that the institutional preconditions for the successful operation of markets were in place before markets were allowed to expand. For instance, controls over the operations of foreign banks, the reliance on foreign investment rather than more volatile portfolio investment, the initial geographic restrictions on foreign financial and non-financial firms, and ongoing restrictions on the trading of Chinese currency and on foreign participation in Chinese securities markets all helped to maintain economic stability within China. Similarly China has moved rapidly to adopt accounting standards and practices in line with those of the International Accounting Standards Board (Lin, 2000), and this should help to avoid the looting of public assets through questionable financial transfers and valuations that was characteristic of privatization in Russia.

This does not mean that China is free of problems. On the contrary, like other countries in transition, its banking system is burdened with dangerous levels of non-performing loans due to the legacy of pressures from government officials and state-owned enterprises for banks to keep lending to unprofitable state enterprises and to lack of expertise in the assessment of creditworthiness on the part of banks (Lague, 2002; OECD, 2002). Although state-owned enterprises have displayed remarkable increases in efficiency in the past decade and are more profitable than is often recognized (Holz, 2002; Lardy, 2002, pp. 22–8), and although the government has taken significant steps to take care of the non-performing loan problem, the banking system continues to constitute a major risk for the Chinese economy. Problems with securities fraud have also been serious.

There are signs that China will begin taking more initiative in shaping and strengthening global financial governance as it becomes more integrated with it. Chinese scholars and officials have been interested in strengthening multilateral control over some of the more destructive aspects of global finance and in increasing the scope of IMF assistance, and have been concerned at what they see as the excessively narrow focus of the Basel Committee on Banking Supervision. For instance, in 2003 the China Banking Regulatory Commission stated that it would not be implementing Basel II because it was poorly suited to Chinese conditions. Chinese scholars and officials have emphasized the need for the international financial architecture to be sensitive to the particular needs of countries outside the wealthy membership of the G10 and not to be biased against these countries in favor of creditors, as was seen to be the case for the IMF role in the East Asian crisis. They have expressed their support for initiatives to have the private sector carry a greater share of the burden of financial crises.[5]

China has taken initiatives in a variety of ways to strengthen its links with international institutions concerned with the regulation and integration of global finance, and with international financial regulatory practices. China established links with the Bank for International Settlements in 1984, and became a member in 1996. It signed on to the IMF's General Data Dissemination System in 2002, reversing its earlier view that the IMF's demands for data were unnecessary and burdensome. Since taking back control of Hong Kong, which is noted for its relatively high legal and regulatory standards relative to other offshore financial centers, China has allowed Hong Kong regulators to play a prominent role in international securities regulation and banking regulation. China has encouraged training of mainland regulators by Hong Kong regulators, and it has appointed Anthony Neoh, former chair of the Hong Kong Securities and Futures Commission and former chair of the International Organization of Securities Commissions' powerful Technical Committee, as chief advisor to the China Securities Regulatory Commission. Hong Kong hosted the first foreign office of the Bank for International Settlements, and an IMF sub-office was established in Hong Kong in 2001. Like Russia, China has become a member of the G20. The People's Bank of China established foreign offices in Tokyo, London, and New York in the 1990s, and then in Frankfurt in 2002, to interact with the European Central Bank.

China has been very actively involved in efforts to construct a regional capacity to respond to financial crisis in the wake of the East Asian central crisis of 1997, in which the IMF role was widely seen as deficient. A centerpiece of this effort was a series of bilateral swap agreements under the Ching Mai initiative of the ASEAN + 3 grouping (ten ASEAN countries plus China, Japan, and South Korea), in which countries agree to make convertible currency available to one another in the event of crisis. By 2003 China had signed swap agreements with Thailand, Japan, South Korea, and Malaysia. China was also a participant in the $1 billion Asian Bond Fund (ABF), created in 2003 under the sponsorship of the primary East Asian–bank association, the Executives' Meeting of East Asia–Pacific Central Banks (EMEAP) group, which it had joined a year after it was founded, in 1992. The ABF was designed to strengthen the East Asian bond market, which was seen as a potentially stable regional source of long-range financing. China has also been a supporter of and participant in the Boao Forum of Asia, proposed in 1998 as an East Asian counterpart to the high-level World Economic Forum in which senior government and business leaders discuss strategic economic questions. China's efforts to establish closer links with ASEAN nations is in part to promote opportunities for Chinese banks and other Chinese firms to expand and invest in the region.

As China increases its technical capacity to participate in policy and regulatory debates, and as its economic clout continues to increase, it is likely to play a significant role in strengthening the arrangements for the governance of global finance, but in a way that expands the focus of these arrangements beyond the interests of the G10 with which they have been concerned traditionally, and in a way that builds regional cooperation in East Asia, where it is likely to play a leading role. Jacobson and Oksenberg (1990, p. 132) have argued that China's size and enthusiasm for market-oriented reforms and its very active involvement with the World Bank in the 1980s and 1990s were a major factor in the World Bank's ascendancy relative to the UN Conference on Trade and Development and other international institutions, since the World Bank could claim to be global. It is likely that China will give a similar boost to the regime for international financial regulation as it becomes more actively involved in it.

The differing experiences of Russia and China with global finance reinforce the importance of institutions, practices, and rules in determining whether integration has negative or positive consequences for a country and its citizens. In Russia fast integration was attempted without adequate consideration of these, and the consequences were disastrous for the living standards of citizens and the health of the economy. Newly wealthy bankers and their Western advisors, by manipulating the political system, discredited democracy, along with the global political and economic institutions with which they were associated. In contrast, China's better-regulated engagement with global finance has been accompanied by rapid stable growth, and China has become an increasingly active supporter of strengthened arrangements for governing global finance.

The Increasingly Active Role of Developing and Transition Countries in Global Financial Governance

Before World War II the governance of international finance was controlled by informal elite networks in the home jurisdiction of international banks, especially the City of London and New York. These networks would include leading figures from private-sector international banks as well as from central banks and finance ministries. Often relationships would be cemented by shared class backgrounds, styles of attire, and club memberships. Because most of the cross-border banking activity could be organized by the banks themselves, there was little need for multilateral public-sector interactions, with the exception of monetary and exchange rate policy and in the management of German reparations between the two World Wars, which led to the creation of the Bank for International Settlements in 1930. In none of these cases did countries other than the wealthiest play any significant role in the governance of international finance.

After World War II developing countries began slowly to be incorporated into the governance of global finance, with the creation of the International Monetary Fund, the World Bank, and the regional development banks, each of which included developed countries as members. The 1944 Bretton Woods conference at which the IMF and the World Bank were set up included all the Latin American countries, along with India, Iraq, Iran, China, Egypt, Ethiopia, and the Philippines, and these countries were responsible for having *development* added to the World Bank's *reconstruction* mandate (Dávila, 1999, pp. 4–5). The IMF's focus was exchange rate management, and the World Bank's and regional development banks' focus would become development financing. For their first two decades these multilateral organizations devoted no attention to financial regulation.

Despite the IMF's and the World Bank's inclusion of developing country members, many criticisms have been made of the lack of influence of these countries on decision making in these organizations (Woods, 2000). Critics point to the weighting of the voting system by the size of a country's financial contribution, which gives the USA and other wealthy creditor countries control; to the constituency system, which leaves most developing countries to be represented by other countries on the Executive Boards; to the organizations' location in Washington; and to the staff recruitment policies, which have been accused of producing a narrowly focused professional elite with little connection to the citizens of the countries their policies affect.

The regional development banks have provided an alternative vehicle for developing country participation, although tension between the desire for control both by countries providing funds and by the borrowers affected by the banks' programs has been evident as well (Culpeper, 1997). The Asian Development Bank has been heavily influenced by Japan's leading role and by the eclectic character of its member countries. The rules establishing the African Development Bank ensured that it was controlled by its developing country African members, but it has been subject to many conflicts with countries providing funding, and relatively lower levels of funding as a result. The Inter-American Development Bank has been influenced by the long-standing tradition of regionalism in the Americas, and the tendency of the USA to incorporate this regionalism into its strategy for combating communism, anti-US sentiment, and social unrest. The European Development Bank was specifically set up to support the transition in the European post-Communist countries.

The collapse of the Bretton Woods system in the early 1970s triggered a re-examination of the IMF's governance by the G7 and other actors. The main innovation to come out of this was the creation of an advisory "Interim Committee," consisting of a subset of finance ministers from the IMF's developed and developing country members who represent constituencies, as in the lower-level and more operational Executive Board. The Interim Committee, renamed the International Monetary and Financial Committee in 1999, was a compromise between the representative but unwieldy meetings of the full membership and smaller unrepresentative bodies such as the G10. Developing countries were dissatisfied with their level of input into the reform discussions of the 1970s, especially when the G7 was created and began to play a leading role. In response to their lack of influence, and with the sponsorship of the Group of 77 non-aligned bloc, developing countries formed the Group of 24 in 1972.

For most of its existence the G24's activity has mainly involved a meeting before the IMF and World Bank annual meetings and the issuing of periodic communiqués and reports. The G24 made some important contributions in highlighting differences in the interests of the developing and industrialized countries, including taking more seriously the systemic roots of global financial problems and the need for more equity between the treatment of developed and developing countries in IMF surveillance and decision making (Dávila, 1999, and Mohammed, 1999). The G24 has tried to work with the G9, the nine developing country Executive Directors at the IMF and World Bank. In the 1990s the G24 was strengthened by the decision to fund a modest permanent staff in Washington and to commission a series of detailed research reports on aspects of common concern. On the other hand, its distinctiveness and coherence were challenged by the emergence of competing groupings, such as the G15 developing countries established in 1989 (<www.miti.gov.my/g15-background.html>), which included members from East Asia not included in the G24, or the G20, which included the G7 countries along with significant emerging market countries.

As discussed in chapter 3, it was only in the 1970s that multilateral arrangements for collaborating in the regulation of global private-sector finance began to emerge. With the exception of the Inter-American Association of Securities Commissions and Similar Organizations, which sought to promote the expansion of securities markets in the Americas and involved Latin American regulators for that reason, there was initially no involvement from developing countries in these new arrangements for the governance of global finance.[6] Neither the BIS, which provided the secretariats for key regulatory bodies, nor the G10, which provided mandates, included any developing country representation. During the debt crisis of the early 1980s the international banks, their home states, and the IMF worked assiduously to prevent the emergence of a debtors' cartel and to deal with indebted countries on an individual basis, thereby helping to avoid the emergence of a unified strong developing government voice in the financial crisis and ensuring that the existing dominant actors in the governance of global finance retained their control. The structural adjustment policies and the other aspects of the neoliberal Washington consensus that were developed to address the debt crisis involved very little input from developing countries.

The 1990s were striking for the changes that began in this one-way process in which developing countries simply implemented or experienced the effects of financial policies developed by wealthy countries and private-sector actors. One might have expected that such change would occur because developing countries demanded a greater role. This was not generally the case, however. Developing country criticism of their lack of representation in global finance governance had been ongoing since the creation of the G24, but in the 1990s they did not launch any new concerted campaigns to redress this imbalance, although there were some signs that the developing countries might block developed country initiatives (e.g. Mohammed, 1999, p. 34) or strike out on their own, as with the creation of the G15, mentioned above.

Instead, the wealthy countries began to realize that if they did not bring emerging market countries into the policy process, international financial regulation would not work: the policies would not take emerging market conditions sufficiently into account, and emerging market countries would feel no ownership of the rules and would thus be less likely to implement them. This was much more the case than previously, because many rules vital to the functioning of the global securities markets that dominated core–periphery financial relations in the 1990s, such as the rules governing emerging market stock exchanges, were controlled in the emerging markets countries. Even in banking there were a great many more home jurisdictions than had been the case in previous decades.[7] Thus the original central feature of the international regulatory regime, agreement by the G10 on how to regulate the vast majority of internationally active banks that were headquartered in their jurisdictions, was much less effective. One could interpret this new need for active participation of emerging market countries in governance as signifying an increase in their power relative to the wealthy countries, but this increased power was not the outcome of these countries deliberately pursuing it, but rather a consequence of institutional and technological changes in the character of global finance.

The Basel Committee on Banking Supervision took a number of steps to increase the role of emerging market countries in its work. Following its 1988 Accord, it sought to encourage the Accord's adoption at its biennial conference of bank supervisors from around the world; it hosted training visits of emerging market regulators, and it began to establish a network of regional supervisory groups. Some of these regional groups existed prior to their relationship with the Basel Committee, while others were established in response to the Basel Committee's initiatives. By 1998 there were ten of these, covering Latin America and the Caribbean, the Gulf states, Central and Eastern Europe, the Arab countries, East and Southern Africa, Southeast Asia, New Zealand and Australia, Transcaucasia and Central Asia (Porter and Wood, 2002, p. 245). Most of the work of the regional groupings was to comment on initiatives that remained firmly under the control of the Basel Committee and to foster the sharing of information and best practices among regulators in a region, but in the late 1990s there was a more vigorous discussion, of the implications of the reform of the Basel Capital Adequacy Accord for countries outside the Basel Committee's G10 membership in which regional groups played some part.

A significant step in the inclusion of emerging market regulators in the work of the Basel Committee was the creation of an agreed set of Core Principles for Banking Supervision in 1997. These, along with a Compendium of existing standards, were aimed at addressing the types of issues most relevant to emerging markets, in contrast to much of the Basel Committee's work, which had been about complex systems of controlling financial risks that are beyond the need or capacity of emerging market regulators and banks to spend time debating. Moreover, the working group that developed the Core Principles included representatives from seven developing countries, and nine other emerging market countries were consulted extensively (Porter and Wood, 2002).

Despite the increased role of countries outside the G10 in the Basel Committee's work, there are signs that its work remains heavily biased towards the concerns of its wealthy members and the banks headquartered in their jurisdictions. The proposed revision of the Capital Adequacy Accord, as discussed in chapter 4, would allow banks with the capacity to do so to rely on their own risk management systems, and in so doing to reduce the levels of capital they would be required to hold against risky assets. The data collection and analysis requirements for getting regulatory approval to do this are daunting and will likely be limited to a small number of the largest international banks from the G10, giving them a competitive advantage not available to other banks. Costs of compliance have been estimated at 7.5 percent of big banks' technology and operations budgets over four years, but closer to 15 percent over six years for smaller banks in developing markets.[8] The new capital accord also envisions greater reliance on private-sector ratings agencies in assessing risk weights, and this has been criticized as biased, because the big internationally active ratings agencies are USA-based, and may have little familiarity with emerging markets, or may not produce ratings in some markets at all.

The changing role of more formal intergovernmental organizations in the regulation of global finance is also important in understanding the expanding role of emerging markets in global financial governance. In the case of the Bank for International Settlements, by 2003 its membership had been expanded well beyond its traditional industrialized country membership to 55, including Algeria, Argentina, Bosnia and Herzegovina, Brazil, Bulgaria, Chile, China, Croatia, the Czech Republic, Estonia, Hong Kong SAR, Hungary, India, Indonesia, Israel, South Korea, Latvia, Lithuania, the Republic of Macedonia, Malaysia, Mexico, the Philippines, Poland, Romania, Russia, Saudi Arabia, Singapore, Slovakia, Slovenia, South Africa, Thailand, and Turkey. Its first office outside Basel was opened in 1998, in Hong Kong.

In the case of IOSCO the Development Committee was created in 1989 to provide a focus for developing country participation. It was subsequently renamed the Emerging Markets Committee (EMC), and in the 1990s was more closely aligned with the powerful Technical Committee, to facilitate increased input by the former into the work of the latter, and more emerging markets were included in the latter, which was traditionally heavily dominated by the wealthiest member states. In 1999 the EMC met on its own and issued a report on global financial turbulence, the views in which differed from the views of the developed countries in emphasizing the role of investor and systemic factors and in criticizing "one-size-fits-all" solutions (Porter and Wood, 2002, p. 247).

In 1999 the IMF's Interim Committee was renamed the International Monetary and Financial Committee, signaling formally the increased role played by the IMF in financial-sector governance. Despite the criticisms that have been made of the IMF for its lack of consideration of the input and interests of developing and transition countries, it is more representative than the G7, the G10, or Basel Committee. The IMF's partial shift away from its emphasis on macroeconomic and structural adjustment towards an emphasis on poverty reduction, with the Poverty Reduction Strategy Papers (PRSP), a more participatory process involving an increase in NGO and borrowing country input, can be seen as a response to the dissatisfaction of developing countries and NGO critics with the older way of doing things.

The OECD, in working on corporate governance standards, a crucial issue for emerging markets after the global crises of 1997 and 1998, was careful to work through the Global Corporate Governance Forum (<www.gcgf.org/about.htm>), a joint arrangement with the World Bank, and to consult widely in emerging markets, a sharp contrast to the secretive and elitist character of the failed Multilateral Agreement on Investment that it had sponsored in an earlier period.

The most dramatic move to increase the participation of emerging markets in the governance of global finance was the creation of the G20 in 1999, and the G22 process that preceded it, discussed in chapter 3. The G20, with its inclusion of 11 large developing and transition countries along with the G7 countries, Australia, and the EU, was a significant improvement over the traditional exclusion of developing countries from processes dominated by the G7 and the G10. Nevertheless, the G20 is relatively new, and questions remain about its future role. It clearly remains less important than the G7, as evident in the G20 not meeting at the head-of-government level, and in the lack of meaningful developing or transition country representation in the G7-dominated Financial Stability Forum, also created in 1999.

A change in the center of gravity of debates about the future of the international financial system is further evidence, along with the increased inclusion of emerging markets in policymaking processes discussed above, that the top-down governance of global finance is beginning to change. Three examples provide a sense of this change.

First, high-profile conflicts at the World Bank, including the controversial resignation of Ravi Kanbur in 2000 in the midst of his editorship of the flagship *World Development Report*, reportedly over US opposition to his emphasis on empowerment, and the angry public assessment of the role of the IMF, the World Bank, and globalization more generally by former World Bank Chief Economist Joseph Stiglitz, indicate a rift in the formerly monolithic Bretton Woods organizations. A series of high-profile liberal economists, formerly unequivocal supporters of international economic liberalization and globalization, have also harshly criticized aspects of the governance of global finance, including Jeffrey Sachs, the inventor of "shock therapy" for countries moving towards more liberalized markets, George Soros, who made a fortune speculating in global financial markets as head of his hedge fund, and prominent economists Paul Krugman and Jagdish Bhagwati.

Second, the emphasis had shifted by the late 1990s from an aggressive push for liberalized cross-border flows under all circumstances, to wide agreement that "sequencing" was important – that strong prudential regulations should be in place before liberalization is allowed to proceed. Serious consideration at the IMF of the merits of capital controls, and of the creation of mechanisms for "private-sector burden sharing" such as rules creating a standstill on outbound capital flows during crises, is also striking, and a sharp contrast to the beginning of the decade, when such discussion would have been anathema.

Third, the disarray in Mexico in 2003 of the Doha Round of trade talks, at which the industrialized countries had hoped to get agreement on new issues, including investment and financial services rules, signaled the increased clout of developing countries and their unwillingness to be the recipients of policies formulated by the industrialized countries.

Conclusion

The past quarter-century has been remarkable for the degree to which areas of the world that were previously only minimally connected to the global financial system have become much more closely integrated. In the years following World War II, international financial relations for developing countries consisted primarily of grants and loans channeled through the public sector in aid of national development strategies. Some developing countries also relied on the direct foreign investment of multinational corporations, but others sharply restricted the activities of MNCs and instead relied on state-owned enterprises. Large parts of the world, including the Soviet bloc and China, remained completely detached from global finance.

Since then, almost all these countries have experienced dramatic waves of integration with global finance. It is clear, however, that this is much more complex than simply the expansion of market forces. It has required the construction of new institutions and social practices, and when these have failed, the results have been catastrophic. The shift from bank lending to portfolio investment illustrates both the growth of the cross-border institutions that are a precondition for the integration of developing and transition countries into global securities markets, and the great dangers that accompany this integration if these institutions are poorly designed and managed.

As will be discussed further in the concluding chapter of this book, a key factor in the performance of these institutions is the degree to which those affected by them have influence over their development and management. Looking back over the period since the early 1990s, it is clear that developing countries have increased their participation in the governance of global finance, and it is no longer run exclusively by the wealthiest governments and banks. At the same time it is also evident that huge asymmetries of power persist, and some developments have not been positive in their implications for developing country influence, such as the creation of the FSF by the G7 with no developing country representation, or the biases in the new Basel Capital Adequacy Accord discussed above. As in other areas, the question of whether globalization brings greater hardship or is beneficial depends crucially on the capacity, openness, and fairness of the institutions that make it possible.

9

Non-Governmental Organizations and Global Civil Society

One of the most prominent aspects of globalization has been the emergence of *global civil society*, evident, for instance, in the increased involvement of those seeing themselves as part of global civil society in the activities of the United Nations and the international economic institutions such as the IMF and the World Bank. Although the definition of the concept remains contested, as discussed further below, it refers in general to the idea that citizens spontaneously engage in policy-relevant transnational activities. In some definitions the concept includes the activities of business associations, while in others it refers primarily to new social movements concerned about issues such as the environment, human rights, or peace. This chapter considers both business and new social movements in its conceptual discussion, but its primary empirical focus is non-business non-governmental associations. Chapter 7 of this book focused on business associations, and that chapter can be read in conjunction with this one. The chapter will argue that although civil society has played an increasingly important role in global finance, it exhibits certain important limitations that should be recognized.

Like many of our most important social science concepts, *civil society* has both analytical and practical political significance. Scholars can attempt to discern regularities and offer explanations by using the concept of civil society, but efforts to develop the concept further are also part of a larger reworking of the practice of democracy, with practical implications for the governance of global finance.

There are a number of reasons for expecting that global civil society will be especially prominent in global finance. In numerous respects global finance has the types of characteristics that Beck (1992) has linked to an upswing grassroots activism in *Risk Society*. These include the severity, complexity, science-based, socially constructed, and global character of the risks involved, as discussed in chapter 11. We shall see below that global civil society has become more important in global finance in recent years, but it remains much weaker than one might expect, and this reveals some deficiencies in the concept of global civil society.

The chapter begins with a general discussion of the concept of global civil society. It then discusses the history of civil society involvement in global finance, before turning to more contemporary developments.

Global Civil Society as Concept and Practice

As with any important political concept, including democracy, rights, and freedom, *civil society* is what Laclau and Mouffe have called "a floating signifier, a 'wild' antagonism which does not predetermine the form in which it can be articulated to other elements in a social formation" (1985, pp. 170–1). The concept derives its significance – its ability to have meaning – from the conceptual traditions on which it builds, from the hopes people have invested in it, from its performance in scholarly models, and from the degree to which it seems to capture successfully developments in political practices that other concepts cannot. Therefore, to understand the concept, it is useful to look at its past, present, and future.

Throughout its history civil society has involved two qualities that display some tension with one another. The first is an emphasis on *association*, a form of sociality that can be counterposed to the individualism of markets and might seem to have some affinity with the collectivity-enhancing effects of the state. The second is an emphasis on *autonomy*, a sense of spontaneity and independence that can be counterposed to the state and might seem to have some affinity with the individualism and fluidity of markets. While the tension between them reflects to some degree the clashing interests of those who have converged on the concept, it also expresses the distinctive historical role played by civil society. This is the role identified by Habermas (1989) in his analysis of the emergence of the *public sphere* in the nineteenth century, sustained by coffee houses and newspapers, and primarily constituted by the era's business elite. A discursively constituted public emerged at the intersection of state and market, legitimizing both and mutually enabling their respective effectiveness, a development with which the concept of civil society was closely linked.

In more recent times an upswing in enthusiasm for the concept of civil society can be traced, paradoxically, to developments on both sides of the Cold War divide in its last decade. The concept was vigorously promoted by dissidents in Eastern Europe, as it was seen to usefully capture the development of a complex of voluntary associations that were autonomous from the centralized socialist states. It was thought that such autonomy was essential for the exercise of freedom by citizens. The concept was also embraced by critics of capitalism in the West. Here, the associational aspect of civil society was emphasized, rather than the autonomous aspect, and it offered an alternative vision to the anomie, excessive individualism, and decay of community and commitment to a greater good that seemed to be associated with the expansion of market forces in the West.

This second use of the concept seemed to capture the heightened importance of new social movements, but also resonated with broader concerns shared across the political spectrum, such as, for instance, in the relationship between attitudes of civility, of treating others with respect, and civil society. These uses were consistent with the thinking of the originators of the concept, who saw civil society as important in social cohesion.

While the concept of civil society has traditionally been invoked with reference to domestic politics, in recent years it has become widely used as well at the international level. Its dual aspects were evident there as well. On the one hand, the concept was connected with the increased prominence of transnational social movements, many of which were arrayed in opposition to the individualism, greed, and destruction of social obligation and belonging that the global expansion of market forces was bringing. At the same time these social movements generally were also highly critical of individual states, as with the international human rights movement, and of the state-centric character of governance at the global level, as with those movements and groups that saw power politics as connected to a wide variety of abuses, ranging from wars to trade agreements biased in favor of the wealthy states.

Like any political concept with theoretical and practical implications, civil society has subtle strengths and weaknesses relative to alternative overlapping concepts, such as transnational policy networks, citizen diplomacy, ethno and other *scapes*, private authority, and the global polity. All these concepts seek to capture the significance of the increasing density and complexity of global politics, including the erosion of states' monopoly over politics at the international level as non-state actors become increasingly involved. These concepts vary significantly, however, in the significance and value they grant to the role of states, and in the degree to which they see the density of relationships varying across global issue areas, as opposed to being connected to more holistic phenomena such as post-modernity or globalization. Relative to other overlapping concepts, the concept of global civil society tends to stress the value of initiatives that are independent of states, and to imply that such citizen involvement is an inherent feature of globalization, rather than a response to particular types of problems or policy settings.

This chapter will argue that although civil society has made some very important contributions to some aspects of the governance and organization of global finance, especially in altering the policies of the World Bank and the International Monetary Fund, it has remained very weak with regard to other aspects, especially the private-sector financial flows which now account for a much larger share of global finance than does the lending of the multilateral public-sector economic organizations.

While this can partly be attributed to the shorter time that large private-sector international financial flows have been a prominent feature of global finance, it also points to two weaknesses of civil society. First, its capacity to engage with the fast-moving, highly technical issues involved in the regulation and organization of private-sector cross-border flows is limited, especially in comparison to business, making effective intervention very difficult. Second, civil society remains highly dependent on public-sector initiatives, and since public-sector initiatives and institutions in the governance of private-sector flows remain complex and diffuse, it is harder for civil society to play a role here, as compared to other issue areas. This should lead to caution about the limits of the capacity of civil society to contribute to global governance as a whole and with regard to assertions that civil society is a product of epochal or worldwide change, as opposed to distinctive conditions that vary by issue area.

The next section discusses the historical evolution of civil society in global finance as compared to other issue areas. It then assesses more fully the current contributions of civil society to the governance of global finance.

Civil Society and Global Finance:
Historical Evolution

One useful measure of the influence of civil society is the listings in the *Yearbook of International Organizations*. The *Yearbook* is the most comprehensive such listing, and has been used by scholars seeking to analyze the growth of international non-governmental organizations. It has certain deficiencies, including a reliance on self-reporting, an inability to measure influence accurately, and its lack of inclusion of networks without a formal identity. Nevertheless, with more than 40,000 international organizations and constituencies listed in 2003, the *Yearbook*'s coverage is extensive, and one can treat an entry in it as signaling an organization's surpassing of a minimum threshold profile.[1]

Table 1 displays the finance-oriented entries listed in three editions of the *Yearbook*. The columns do not add to the total because the total may include treaties, organizations that should not have been listed under finance, and inactive organizations. In the rows appearing below "Active NGOs," an organization may be listed more than once if it carries out more than one function. There has been a dramatic increase in the number of NGOs involved in global finance, from 14 in 1951–2 to 351 in 2003.

In 1951–2 the *Yearbook* listed 20 organizations that had some orientation towards finance, of which six were intergovernmental organizations (IGOs) such as the IMF, the World Bank, and the Tripartite Committee for the Restitution of [Nazi] Monetary Gold, and 14 were non-governmental organizations (NGOs). Most of the NGOs

Table 1   Finance entries in the *Yearbook of International Organizations*

	1951–2	1980	2003
Finance-oriented entries, total	20	295	560
Intergovernmental	6	127	161
Active NGOs	14	129	351
Business	3	62	126
Civil society organization with social mission	2	10	104
Professional or employee groups	5	18	56
Foundations/charities	0	8	65
Agro or micro-credit	1	3	26
Educational and research	3	47	85
Regional	1	58	131
National with international focus	0	20	52

were professional or research associations that were more concerned with cross-national sharing of information than with influencing international finance, and in some cases finance was only one of their interests. Examples include the Econometric Society, the International Fiscal Association, and the International Congress of Actuaries. Three were credit associations: the International Thrift Institute, the International Credit Insurance Association, and the Confédération internationale du credit agricole. Two were primarily advocacy groups: the International Interchange Committee, which promoted "a concerted lowering of customs and monetary barriers," and the International Union for Land Value Taxation and Free Trade, which aimed to raise taxes on land to reduce poverty and other taxes. The Chamber of Commerce was a multi-purpose organization, only partially focusing on financial issues.

In the two later periods there are large increases in each category. The largest NGO category is business-related, which increased from 62 in 1980 to 126 in 2003. In 1980, 65 NGOs were professional or employee groups (for example, the Association of International Accountants), or educational (such as the International Banking Research Institute), a number which had increased to 141 in 2003. Eight were foundations or charities, a number that had increased to 65 in 2003. Some of these were listed as financial only because they disbursed money across borders. Three were agro or micro-credit organizations, a number that had increased to 26 in 2003. Some of the organizations listed were not global, but rather were regional in either origin or focus, or were national organizations with an international focus.

This chapter's focus is on citizen's groups that seek to influence global finance rather than international business associations, which were the focus of chapter 7. Using *civil society organization with a social mission* (CSO) as a label to refer to this category, the number of active financial CSOs listed in the *Yearbook* increased from 10 in 1980 to 104 in 2003. However, this is a very broad category, which includes multi-purpose foundations and charities such as the Catholic Organization for Joint Financing of Development Programmes, and micro-financing organizations such as Women's World Banking or PlaNet Finance. Only about eight listings are for non-business NGOs that seek primarily to influence the governance of global finance. These eight include, for instance, ATTAC (Association for the Taxation of Financial Transactions for the Aid of Citizens), the Bretton Woods Project, New Rules for Global Finance, and Women's Eyes on the World Bank. We now look briefly at each of these types of organizations in turn.

The material impact of multi-purpose foundations and charities on international finance is significant: in 1995 the International Council of Voluntary Associations estimated that NGOs spent $9–10 billion annually on development assistance. While a great many of these development-financing NGOs are entirely independent of states, the sector as a whole also enjoyed a substantial increase in importance over time as states began to rely more heavily on NGOs for the implementation of their own aid policies. However, many of these NGOs have only a minimal influence on global governance.

Micro-financing has been a distinctive contribution made by civil society organizations to global finance and was already well under way in the mid-1990s. As noted in chapter 10, micro-financing has often been targeted at women, and one of the most extensive micro-financing networks is provided by New York-based Women's World Banking (WWB). Micro-financing was originally developed primarily by non-governmental organizations that were interested in it as a means of promoting economic development or gender equality.

Micro-financing is unusual in combining non-commercial ethics and forms of organization with more business-oriented ones. As it grew in popularity, the World Bank and large international commercial banks began to get more heavily involved, even if the sector as a whole remained very small relative to other forms of development assistance or private-sector financial flows, and questions remained about its commercial viability. Micro-financing was also one of the first instances of global civil society engaging with the practical regulatory issues involved with private-sector financial flows. For instance, an officer of one micro-financing institution, BancoSol, has criticized the mismatch between the international regime for bank regulation being developed at Basel and the needs of the micro-financing sector (Krutzfeldt, 1996, pp. 3–4).

The first concerted effort of NGOs to influence the governance of global finance emerged in connection with the great number and variety of NGOs devoted to advocacy regarding Third World debt issues that became prominent in the 1980s and 1990s. Many of these were brought together in the NGO–World Bank Working Group, established in 1981. The International Council of Voluntary Agencies provided the secretariat for this group initially, but this function passed to the Asociación Latinoamericana de Organizaciones de Promoción (ALOP) in Costa Rica in the early 1990s. The "50 Years is Enough" campaign, targeting the Bretton Woods institutions, brought together a variety of NGOs, including the Bank Information Center, the Center of Concern, the Development Group for Alternative Policies, and others. Other NGOs involved in Third World debt issues included the European Network on Debt and Development (EURODAD), the Freedom from Debt Coalition based in the Philippines, the Forum on Debt and Development, an independent policy research center based in the Netherlands, Oxfam, Bretton Woods Project, the Jubilee campaign, and the Brussels-based Committee for the Cancellation of Third World Debt. Other NGOs who had been involved in environmental or trade issues, such as Friends of the Earth, began to pay more attention to the governance of global finance when the negotiation of investment treaties along with other aspects of cross-border capital mobility and structural adjustment policies seemed to threaten to undermine the capacity of governments to engage in environmental regulation or to pursue national industrial and employment goals.

These NGO efforts had some significant successes in contributing to the establishment of the Heavily Indebted Poor Countries (HIPC) debt relief initiative run by the World Bank, discussed in chapter 4, and the IMF's Poverty Reduction Strategy Papers, which added reduction of poverty as a priority to the previous heavy emphasis on macro-economic variables, and which required borrowing governments to consult with local NGOs.

Another way in which civil society began to get involved with the regulation of cross-border financial flows was through the advocacy of a tax on international financial transactions, often called a Tobin tax after Nobel laureate James Tobin who first suggested the idea in 1972. Tobin argued that a very small tax, perhaps a quarter percent, would have little effect on long-range transactions but would be an effective brake on speculative flows, since the cumulative effects of moving in and out of currencies daily, for instance, and paying the tax each time, would soon make such activities unattractive. For some global civil society organizations this was attractive, not just because it restrained cross-border financial flows and their destructive effects, but also because even a small tax promised to raise enormous revenues, given the massive size of cross-border financial flows. If the tax was collected by an international organization such as the United Nations, it would be a big step forward in strengthening the autonomy of the institutions of global governance. It could also generate vast new levels of funding to address global social problems such as poverty.

Discussion of the Tobin tax first garnered significant international attention at the World Summit for Social Development in 1995. In addition to those civil society actors promoting the idea at that conference, there were some initial expressions of interest from the Swedish, Australian, Canadian, and French governments. A further indication of support was the enthusiasm of the UN Development Program (UNDP), which sponsored an edited volume *The Tobin Tax*, published by Oxford University Press (ul Haq, Kaul, and Grunberg, 1996) in which prominent economists, including Tobin, discussed the idea relatively favorably and began to put serious thought into issues that might arise in its implementation.

Hopes grew that the Tobin tax might be put on the agenda of the G7 at its 1995 summit in Halifax by its Canadian government hosts. While the summit, held in the wake of the Mexican peso crisis that had ignited in 1994, was indeed preoccupied with how to stabilize global finance, the Canadian government dropped its initial consideration of the Tobin tax after it was panned by officials in its finance ministry. Nevertheless, the Tobin tax was given a further boost by the efforts of the Halifax Initiative, a civil society group, at that summit – an effort that continued after the summit.

Following the Halifax summit the lead on the Tobin tax was taken by a Paris-based NGO, ATTAC, created in 1998, an "international movement for democratic control of financial markets and their institutions" (<www.attac.org>). Since then, ATTAC, which is set up as a decentralized network, has developed affiliated individuals and groups in 38 countries. ATTAC and other groups have begun to address the technical questions that remain about its feasibility and design.

One such group is the New Rules for Global Finance coalition, which began in 1998 in response to the East Asian financial crisis. It "is a coalition of development, human rights, labor, environmental, and religious organizations and scholars dedicated to the reform of the global financial architecture" (<www.new-rules.org>). In addition to other activities, it organized a conference on the Tobin tax and published a book *Debating the Tobin Tax* (New Rules for Global Finance, 2004), based on that conference. The efforts of CSOs like these to engage the technical questions about the Tobin tax's feasibility and implementation are significant in indicating the broadening of the range of financial governance issues of concern to civil society beyond debt relief.

Despite some notable victories in the campaign for the Tobin tax, such as the Canadian Parliament's endorsement of the idea of looking further into it in 1999, the idea was dealt a deadly blow when Republicans in the USA began to angrily oppose it, portraying it as an outrageous tax grab by the United Nations that violated the sovereign constitutional exclusive authority of the US government on tax matters. After the Republicans threatened to cut off UN funding through congressional legislation should the tax even be *discussed* at the UN, the topic was dropped by the UNDP like a hot potato. This US opposition also guaranteed that it would not be taken up by other key intergovernmental bodies such as the G7, the IMF, or the World Bank.

Another important sign of development in civil society's relationship to global finance is a series of books that have been published on this topic in recent years. There are a vast number of books on global finance, but until relatively recently they have had little to say about civil society. Because books take substantial effort to pull together, and because their publication represents a distinctive degree of concreteness and approval, they can be a useful indicator of the development of a much broader and more eclectic body of shared understandings produced in written and other forms. Books can be a record of the development of civil society and global finance, both in reporting on that development and in themselves being an expression of that development by bringing civil society participants together as contributors, or by presenting new analysis by civil society actors. Three books are especially noteworthy in this regard, and each will be examined each in turn.

The first book to have thoroughly examined civil society and global finance is *Contesting Global Governance*, written jointly by four scholars (O'Brien, Goetz, Scholte, and Williams, 2000) and published by Cambridge University Press. The focus in this book is the relationship of global social movements to the IMF, the World Bank, and the WTO, with the first two being most relevant to global finance. The book recorded significant but uneven progress that had been made in the ability of global social movements to influence the governance of global finance. The IMF was much slower than the World Bank to establish mechanisms to engage in dialogue with global social movements, and many of the initiatives seen as positive by IMF and World Bank officials are seen as rhetorical and inadequate by civil society actors. The book made an important contribution in identifying and explaining variation in the influence of civil society actors on the governance of global finance across issue areas (gender, environment, and labor) and organizations. It provided a great deal of detailed analysis of the significance of institutions, practices, and cognitive frameworks internal to the World Bank and the IMF, and to the global social movements. In focusing on the World Bank and the IMF, the book reflected the focus of civil society at the time on cross-border flows managed by the public sector rather than the governance of private-sector flows.

A second book that marks an important advance in the relationship between civil society and global finance is *Global Finance: New*

Thinking on Regulating Speculative Markets, edited by Walden Bello, Nicola Bullard, and Kamal Malhotra, and published in 2000 by Zed Books. All three editors were senior figures in a civil society organization, Focus on the Global South, and contributors included others active with civil society, including Susan George, Director of l'Observatoire de le Mondialisation, Bruno Jetin of ATTAC, Martin Khor, Director of the Third World Network, and Jessica Woodroffe, Head of Campaigns at the World Development Movement. The editors note that the book was "the result of a ground-breaking conference held in Bangkok in March 1999 which brought together 340 activists and scholars from the North and the South under the banner 'Economic Sovereignty in a Globalizing World: Creating People-Centred Economics for the 21st Century'. The views, ideas, analyses and proposals in this book are different from those coming out of the IMF and BIS simply because their starting point is different" (p. xii). The book is significant because it is oriented towards providing concrete analytical and policy propositions for the regulation of private-sector financial flows, including the Tobin tax, capital controls, the creation of a world financial authority, a new international investment agreement with standards of corporate conduct, and international bankruptcy provisions to allow countries in crisis to hold off creditors.

A third book is *Civil Society and Global Finance*, edited by Jan Aart Scholte and Albrecht Schnabel, published by Routledge in 2002. The book differs from *Contesting Global Governance* in making the relationship between civil society and global finance its main focus, in the breadth of financial policy issues that are addressed, and in its inclusion of actors with practical involvement in building relations between civil society and finance as authors of the majority of chapters. The book differs from *Global Finance: New Thinking on Regulating Speculative Capital Markets*, which focused on putting forward civil society perspectives, in its inclusion of contributions from officials of intergovernmental organizations, such as a Foreword by Andrew Crockett, General Manager of the Bank for International Settlements and Chair of the Financial Stability Forum, as well as officials from the IMF, the World Bank, and the UN, along with contributions from civil society organizations, such as the Uganda Debt Network, Greenpeace, and Friends of the Earth. A number of the public-sector officials had previously spent extensive time working in civil society. Thus the organization of the book signals a significant step forward in the degree to which global civil society has become a participant and interlocutor in the policy process associated with the governance of global finance as a whole, rather than simply a critic of IMF and the World Bank policies – a step of which not all civil society actors would approve.

The content of the book provides further confirmation of this. Although the book acknowledges the many civil society actors who would prefer to dismantle official institutions and policy processes rather than become involved in them, the overall tone is one that stresses constructive engagement rather than complete rejection. For instance, in his analytical chapter Scholte comments: "in sum, civil society has considerable positive potential to improve the governance of global finance" (p. 26), although he cautions against the danger of co-optation where "the critical element becomes diluted and eventually lost altogether" (p. 28). A number of contributors call for civil society to get more involved in issues connected with cross-border private-sector flows, not just by working to reform public-sector institutions, but also by putting direct pressure on financial firms. Issues of legitimacy of civil society are also prominent, including the need for mechanisms to ensure greater internal accountability of civil society organizations, to clarify who is or should be represented, and an acknowledgement of the ongoing North–South gap in civil society capacity. The book's consideration of all these issues could be taken as pointing in the direction of a more formal and extensive incorporation of global civil society in the arrangements for governing global finance, even if this involves maintaining the critical distance from the official institutions to which Scholte refers.

The demise of the Washington consensus, which was discussed in chapter 8, has improved the prospects for civil society making a meaningful contribution to the governance of global finance. The Washington consensus, with its heavy emphasis on IMF conditionality, macro-economic stabilization, and cutbacks in social spending, strengthened the relationship between international and national public-sector authorities, against which were arrayed most civil society actors. The successes of civil society in sensitizing the Bretton Woods institutions, especially the World Bank, to social, environmental, and gender issues, and the evident shortcomings of the Washington consensus in the wake of the East Asian crisis, including its neglect of the need for a social safety net, set the stage for an upswing in collaboration between the public-sector institutions and civil society. The IMF's Poverty Reduction Strategy Papers, with their explicit expectation that governments will consult civil society, and the UN Financing for Development process, which brought the IMF and the World Bank together with the more civil society-friendly UN for the first time, and involved an unprecedented effort to foster genuine dialogue among civil society and these public-sector institutions, are important signs of the change that is occurring, even if some civil society actors remain critical of the pace of change.

Conclusion: The Limits and Potential of Global Civil Society

The experience of civil society and global finance highlights civil society's strengths and weaknesses as a concept and a political practice, both in this issue area and with respect to global governance more generally. On the one hand, civil society has grown substantially in its capacity to put forward alternative perspectives to those found in official financial institutions and to have these perspectives heard, and in the range of global financial issues that it is able to comment upon. On the other hand, most non-governmental organizations concerned with finance are not directly interested in governance issues but rather in their charitable, professional, or business work. The relatively small number of civil society organizations that seek to influence the governance of global finance have only relatively recently begun to comment on the governance of private-sector cross-border financial flows, even though these flows have become as large or larger in volume and effect than flows managed by the public sector.

This weakness is symptomatic of a larger weakness: the dependence of civil society on the initiatives of states. The civil society concept lends itself to the idea that civil society is an autonomous self-organizing force that operates in between and relatively independently of market and state. While there are some examples of this type of independence, such as micro-financing initiatives started without World Bank assistance, or aid projects that have been carried out without public-sector support, the most important developments in civil society have been in response to highly visible initiatives of states or intergovernmental organizations. Thus civil society's involvement in global finance was focused initially on the IMF's and World Bank's handling of the 1980s debt crisis, or came about as a result of a lateral shift from trade or environmental issues, where civil society was strongly mobilized in response to important initiatives of states, such as the UN's evolving environmental policies from the 1972 Stockholm Conference, through the 1992 Rio conference and the negotiations of the Montreal and Kyoto Protocols, or the creation of the World Trade Organization with its strong dispute-settlement provisions. Similarly, and more recently, the UN Financing for Development process provided an important focal point for CSO mobilization (Herman, 2002, pp. 172–5).

While this dependence on state initiatives does not mean that civil society does not make an important contribution in influencing these initiatives, it does mean that civil society is at a disadvantage in issue areas where governance is more nebulous and complex, and where business actors are strongly organized. This is the case for issues concerning the international regulation of private-sector financial flows. For these types of issues, other concepts, such as Cox's (2000, p. 27) *nébuleuse*, or the idea of global public policy networks, may be better suited to capturing analytically the challenges and potential associated with influencing global governance, since these concepts highlight more effectively the relatively closed and obscure circuits of policymaking that tie powerful private-sector and public-sector actors together.

Where civil society has been most successful at the global level, it has combined highly detailed analysis of feasible policy options with insistent highlighting of the big-picture questions that official and other prevailing perspectives neglect. For instance, the environmental movement includes the remarkably thorough reporting of the *Earth Negotiations Bulletin*, on which many states rely, as well as the profound critique of modernity of deep ecologists. The arms control movement similarly combines the detailed monitoring of treaty developments carried out by *Nuclear Non-Proliferation News* with the profound philosophical and spiritual questioning of militarism that motivates many peace activists. The human rights movement combines the practical expertise of Amnesty International with a powerful tradition of reflection on the ethical meaning of rights.

While the weakness of this type of integration of practical policy detail and systemic critique in the area of global finance can be partly attributed to the shorter length of time that serious global financial problems have been evident, it also reflects the greater difficulty of linking these in an issue area where state initiatives are subtle and the private sector can easily monopolize all opportunities for non-state influence.

These weaknesses of civil society do not mean that it is a mistake to have any hope that it will be able to have a meaningful impact on the evolution of the governance of global finance. On the contrary, civil society has a crucial role to play. At the same time, it is important to recognize the challenges it faces and to acknowledge the differences across issue areas, rather than seeing global civil society as a general feature of globalization or late modernity. It will only be by engaging with the complex new policy networks and governance arrangements that have been constructed that it will be possible for civil society to extend its influence beyond IMF structural adjustment and other state-centric issues that dominated past agendas to begin to influence the ways in which the risks of private-sector financial markets are managed and distributed.

Part IV

Democracy and Politics in the Governance of Global Finance

10

Gender and the Globalization of Finance

Gender can be defined as the expectations associated with being male or female. Despite being one of the most pervasive and important differentiations among people, gender has traditionally not received much attention in analysis of international and financial affairs, a neglect associated with the predominance of men among those involved at the elite levels in the practice and analysis of world politics and finance. The experiences of men were taken to be those of humans generally, and the experiences of women, as well as the significance of the differences and relations between men and women, and between images of masculinity and femininity, have been obscured. This neglect was exacerbated by the tendency to focus on the decisions of powerful actors for whom international and financial affairs were seen as an external environment to be manipulated or as involving a structurally driven set of constraints to which it was necessary to conform, rather than a set of institutions and social practices, as has been emphasized in this book. In this chapter we shall see that gender is very relevant to the unfolding practices associated with the globalization of finance.

A distinctive characteristic of gender is the way in which it operates simultaneously and interdependently at the most micro, personal level, such as the way in which a man and a woman organize their relationship to their child and to one another, and at the most macro global level, such as the cumulative effect on the violence of world politics of a centuries-long division of labor between men and women in fighting wars. Social traditions and relations of power have built on, exaggerated, and used as an arbitrary justification the biological characteristics of women that are related to their unique capacity to bear children, so that gender's effects extend in vast patterns across time and space in ways that are only very remotely and indirectly related to actual biological differences.[1] Gender can operate simultaneously at the economic level, as in the changing participation of women in the labor market, at the social level, as in patterns of exclusion of women from particular influential social networks, at the political level, as in the changing conception of the role the state should play in complementing or substituting for the types of care traditionally provided by women, and at the cultural level, as in variations between men and women in attitudes towards risk taking or variations in images associated with masculinity and femininity.

Both globalization and finance are also characterized by a rapidly growing simultaneity and interdependence between levels and spaces of social practice; so to identify the relevance of gender to the globalization of finance, we need to trace out its effects in these levels and spaces (Marchand, 1996, p. 587; Van Staveren, 2001, p. 10). Globalization brings together the local and the personal with vast extended global social practices. Thus, part of gender's significance for the globalization of finance is due to the way in which changes in the relationship of men and women at the micro, personal level are connected in a more immediate way with global changes than may have been the case in the past.

The expanded role of financial markets that is such a prominent feature of late modernity is highly ambiguous in its relationship to gender. On the one hand, as the quintessential competitive, anonymous, individualized, self-interested type of market interaction, it can be seen as consistent with masculinized behavior and attitudes and as hostile to the type of non-market caring relationships such as child rearing that tend to be more closely associated with women. The expansion of financial markets, then, can be seen as building on and reinforcing long-term historical patterns of gender inequality and patriarchy. On the other hand, the expansion of finance has involved new employment opportunities for women, in comparison to previous periods, when heavy industry dominated the economy or when the financial industry only employed men. As well, even though the privatization of pensions and other social benefits provided by welfare states has serious negative consequences for women having to take up the burden of providing care when it becomes unaffordable, on the other hand, when financial products such as health or life insurance displace a traditional reliance on women's care in the family, one can say that the expanded role of finance in late modernity has weakened the traditional relationships associated with gender inequalities.

The rest of the chapter divides the ways in which gender is relevant to the globalization of finance into three related sections: one concerned primarily with gendered occupational patterns in global finance, one with the impact of gendered attitudes and images on global finance, and one on the gendered aspects of the relationship between the developing world and the global financial system.

Occupational Patterns in Global Finance

Studies of employment patterns in the financial industry attest to the growing role played by women in it, even if this participation continues to be marked by traditional gendered inequality. At the same time, the upper echelons in global finance, both in private-sector and public-sector institutions, remain heavily dominated by men.

In the United States, in 1964, 47 percent of those employed in financial activities were women, a number that increased at a constant rate, until it levelled off at 61 percent for all years from 1989 to 2002.[2] Considerable differences persisted in the types of jobs that women do within the industry, however. For instance, in 2002 women made up 87 percent of bank tellers, 59 percent of accountants and auditors, but only 29 percent of those involved in securities and financial services sales. Women had only a 19 percent share in financial management in 1970, but this had increased to 50 percent by 2002.[3]

At the more senior levels of US financial decision making, improvements in the representation of women have been minimal. At the Federal Reserve, which has primary responsibility for monetary policy and financial regulation, of the 82 governors appointed between 1913 and 2002, the first 56 were men, with the first woman, Nancy Teeters, appointed in 1978, and the next, Martha Seger, in 1984. The remaining women were appointed after 1990, constituting four of the 12 appointments in that time period.[4] At the Securities and Exchange Commission, the key securities market regulator, of the 85 commissioners appointed between 1934 and 2003, six have been women, with the first, Roberta Karmel, appointed in 1977. Two of the 16 commissioners appointed since 1990 have been women.[5] The American Bankers Association, the largest bank association in the USA, is an important player in decision making in finance and can serve as a gauge of the situation in the private sector. Of the 24

ABA board members in 2002–3, three were women. Of the 49 senior executives holding the position of ABA's State Membership Chairs, only three were women, although all three of the ABA's Regional Membership Managers were women.[6] For securities markets, the leading association, the Securities Industry Association had three of 31 members of the Board of Directors who were women, but none amongst its six officers.[7]

The situation in Europe is similar. An extensive survey sponsored by the European Commission and the European Expert Network, "Women in Decision-Making in Finance" (Quack and Hancké, 1997), noted that in 1995 women constituted 47 percent of employees in European banks, but 8.2 percent of higher bank management (up from 5.9 percent five years earlier), 18 percent of middle management, and 27 percent of lower management. Women constituted 4.9 percent of boards of directors, and 13.5 percent of heads of departments. With regard to banking associations, women accounted for one of 12 presidents, one of 114 board members, zero of 39 executive committee positions or directorships, and five of 77 heads of departments. Women held five of 15 board positions for the London Stock Exchange, one of 17 positions for the Bourse de Paris, one of 43 positions for the European Savings Bank Association, one of 40 for the European Association of Co-operative Banks, and three of 17 for the Fédération Européene des Fonds et Sociétés d'investissement.

The above study found that on the public-sector side in Europe, in national finance ministries, women made up one of 17 finance ministers and nine of 139 heads of department, while their share of total staff ranged from 42 percent to 55 percent. For national central banks, women constituted two of 15 governors, two of 16 deputy governors, and 12 of 157 heads of department, while their share of staff positions overall ranged from 25 percent to 61 percent. Women accounted for two of eight top positions in national-level European bank supervisory institutions. At the European level, women's share of board positions were one of 42 for the public-sector European Investment Bank and 16 of 163 Executive Directors of the European Bank for Reconstruction and Development.

In Canada the share of women in finance, insurance, and real estate occupations increased from 51 percent in 1971 to 62 percent in 1991. By comparison, women accounted for 30 percent of those in manufacturing occupations in 1991, up from 24 percent, and for 43 percent of those in occupations in public administration, up from 26 percent. Looking in more detail at the distribution of employment within the financial industry, however, the persistence of gendered patterns is evident. For instance, in 1991 women accounted for 76 percent of employees in deposit-accepting intermediary industries (banks), 60 percent of insurance employees, but only 50 percent of investment intermediary industries, and 42 percent of other financial intermediary industries. These last two include firms involved in stock markets. Women constituted 40 percent of those in professional occupations in business and finance, 77 percent of finance and insurance administrative positions, and 99 percent of secretaries in business, finance, and administrative occupations. Women's weekly earnings in finance, insurance, and real estate in 1990 were 58 percent of men's.[8]

Statistics on the proportion of women in finance in Japan are less available, but suggest that the situation is similar or worse to that described above. One of nine members of the Policy Board of the Bank of Japan is a woman.[9] None of the 19 directors of the Japanese Bankers Association is a woman.[10] In 2002, 19 of 95 Japanese professional staff members in the Asian Development Bank were women.[11] The first woman general manager at a Japanese bank was appointed in the early 1990s, and in the corporate sector more generally only 0.3 percent of department heads and 1.3 percent of section chiefs at Japan's top 300 corporations are women.[12]

Forty-eight countries provide statistics to the International Labour Organization, covering 363 million women workers, and these statistics can be used to provide a broader overview than the above country-specific statistics. As of the late 1990s, the average proportion of women in the employment in the financial industries of these countries was 52 percent, as compared to their share of total employment of 42 percent. There was high variation across countries, ranging from a share of women in finance greater than 65 percent for eight countries in transition,[13] plus Finland, to less than 25 percent for Egypt and the United Arab Emirates. Altogether 3.5 percent of the 363 million women workers were employed in finance. The share of women in employment in finance had increased by 0.5 percent over the mid-1990s.[14]

The international institutions concerned with global finance also display deficiencies with regard to the representation of women at the senior levels. A study by the Women's Environment and Development Organization (n.d.) found that women accounted for 2.2 percent of the 175 members of the IMF Board of Governors, and zero percent of the 24-member IMF Board of Directors. The World Bank was marginally better, with women accounting for 5.5 percent of their 171 governors, and 8.3 percent of their 22-person Board of Directors. With regard to the regional development banks, the figures for the

Board of Governors were 7.1 percent for the European Investment Bank, 8.6 percent for the Asian Development Bank, 5.3 percent for the African Development Bank, and 13.6 percent for the Inter-American Development Bank.[15] At the Bank for International Settlements, in 2003, there were no women among the 17 board members or 12 senior managers in 2003, although there was one among the 12 alternates to the Board,[16] and one, Danièle Nouy, held the important position of Secretary-General of the Basel Committee on Banking Supervision. At the International Organization of Securities Commissions, of the 177 people listed as members in all membership categories, 21 are women.[17]

Qualitative analysis of the changing structure of employment in finance provides a useful complement to the statistical analysis above. On the public-sector side, finance ministries, central banks, and financial regulators have gained great power relative to more social ministries as the globalization of finance has proceeded, and combined with the narrow focus of these institutions on macroeconomic performance, this has led to a downgrading of the parts of the public sector that otherwise might be more sensitive to gender issues. Women's organizations have been much less able to influence the public-sector agencies concerned with finance than other agencies, in part because of the resistance of high-level financial officials, and in part because of the difficulty of developing the technical expertise needed to engage in the necessary debates (Sen, 2000; Palmer, 1995).

On the private-sector side, the overall picture is one in which the lower and middle levels of the financial industries have been dramatically feminized in most industrialized countries over the past century, but where senior levels at which key decisions are made and some segments, such as the more aggressively competitive world of securities trading, remain heavily dominated by men. Feminization at the lower and middle levels may be attributed in part to changes that characterize post-World War II patterns of employment in these economies in general, and in part to distinctive characteristics of the financial industries. General patterns include the increased labor force participation of women and the rapid expansion of service industries in which formerly high-prestige jobs held by men are differentiated into a large number of routinized factory-like white-collar jobs held mostly by women, controlled by those holding a smaller number of managerial and professional positions, most of whom are men.

Crompton, in her detailed studies of the transformation of work in banks in Britain and France, provides numerous examples of heavy discrimination in the three decades after World War II, where women were channeled into lower-level positions while men were rapidly promoted (Crompton, 1989; see also McDowell and Court, 1994). She also provides examples of change, where women began to successfully push for more training and management responsibilities. In many countries they have been assisted in this by equal opportunity or anti-discrimination initiatives of governments (Crompton and Le Feuvre, 2000, p. 341; Quack and Hanké, 1997, pp. 19–22). However, the effectiveness of these government initiatives has often been limited by their emphasis on public-sector employees, or by a failure to take implementation seriously. One study in the mid-1970s noted that the US Equal Employment Opportunity Commission had a backlog of over 100,000 unprocessed cases in the banking industry, and even faced charges of discrimination against its own female employees in its Atlanta office (Simcich, 1977, p. 9).

The problem is in part due to the persistence of discriminatory attitudes among individuals in the banking industry, and in part more indirect or structural, including the exclusion of women from influential informal networks that can be important in building careers, the small proportion of women in the economics, MBA, or public policy programs that can be a prerequisite for appointment to senior positions, and a lack of flexibility in expectations regarding career paths or daily schedules that can be damaging for those women who often continue to have primary responsibility for care of children. For instance, one study of a UK bank that had strong formal anti-discrimination policies and commitments, but with women constituting only 2 percent of senior managers and 5 percent of applicants to senior posts, found negative informal perceptions of women's capabilities, lack of informal networking opportunities, and other structural problems to be a significant problem (Liff and Ward, 2001; see also Parker, Pascall, and Evetts, 1998, and McGuire, 2002).

A horrifying account of discriminatory attitudes on Wall Street was given when Pamela Martens, who started as a stockbroker trainee at Shearson/American Express in the mid-1980s, initiated legal action in 1995 against her employer, Smith Barney, a leading Wall Street firm. According to Martens and other women at the firm, Smith Barney's Garden City branch was rife with extreme sexual harassment, including groping of women employees in its frat-style "boom-boom room," threats of rape, calling women employees whores and using unprintable language in slurring them, and systematically refusing opportunities for advancement to women. At the time only eight of the firm's 390 branch managers were women.[18] After finally protesting, Martens was fired, despite an exemplary record, and she and a co-worker then filed a class-action suit against Smith Barney, which more than 2,000 women across the country eventually joined. The case was complicated by the employees having signed an agreement to bring employment disputes to a confidential arbitration procedure run by the industry. Originally designed to avoid disclosures to clients, the arbitration procedure became subject to intense criticism for allowing the industry to suppress problems of discrimination. The class action was settled, but Martens refused to accept the settlement, pointing out some serious concerns with the process, including the fact that plaintiffs' lawyers were awarded more than $12 million in fees from Smith Barney when they agreed to settle, before the plaintiffs had received any money. In the end Smith Barney agreed to spend $15 million over four years putting in place a process to encourage workplace diversity, and paid damages to plaintiffs, even if they avoided having to disclose further evidence of discrimination. This case inspired a number of other similar legal actions against major Wall Street firms.[19]

One outcome of the Smith Barney settlement was its financing of an extensive independent survey of the experiences of women on Wall Street, run by Catalyst, a research group working to advance women in business. The Catalyst report (2001) found that while the age and experience profiles were similar for women and men in senior positions in the securities industry, 75 percent of women had spouses or partners who worked full time, as compared to 20 percent of men, even though 94 percent of men had spouses or partners. As well, only 58 percent of women had children, as compared to 88 percent of men. In other words, most men had wives at home to take care of children, while most women had to forgo having children or to juggle care for children with a spouse who also had a full-time job outside the home. As one senior woman noted, "I cannot imagine ever having children and doing this business" (p. 22). About three-quarters of women and men were satisfied with their employers and their current positions, but women were less satisfied than men with their networking opportunities and compensation. Three-quarters of women reported that they needed to develop a style that male managers and partners were comfortable with if they were to succeed, and 61 percent saw stereotyping and preconceptions of women's roles and abilities as an obstacle to advancement. Thirty-two percent of women reported experiencing sexual harassment. There is some change. As one man noted, "There's an awareness now that . . . you can't get away with the locker room mentality" (p. 52). However, many of the more subtle forms of discrimination continue, and overall change is slow, with only 18 percent of women reporting that opportunities for advancement to senior leadership had increased over the previous five years (p. 42). Catalyst's findings in a report on the Canadian investment industry were similar.[20]

Recruitment of women employees has also been stimulated by the changing nature of the financial services industry. The industry, concerned as it is with high-value intangible products, has always relied on trust, but the older gentlemanly ways of fostering trust, such as shared memberships in exclusive male clubs, have become less adequate as finance has become more freewheeling and less an activity restricted to a small wealthy elite. In the London markets a key instance of this was the intrusion of aggressive US banks in the 1970s with a more performance-oriented and professional approach to sustaining trust. This emphasis on achieved over ascribed qualities has helped erode gender discrimination (McDowell and Court, 1994, p. 1407). Indeed, having women in senior management was found by Welbourne (1999) to be correlated with superior financial performance of a company when its stock is issued on stock markets.

In some financial activities, as in other service occupations such as fast foods, the intense modulation of facial expression, tone of voice, and body language that is used by sales and customer service representatives to gain the trust of customers is an (often dehumanizing) activity that women are seen as better at than men (Leidner, 1993; Folgerø and Fjeldstad, 1995; on harassment in financial services sales, see Collinson and Collinson, 1996). As women have become more responsible for their own personal financial decisions or those of their family, many financial services firms have seen the hiring of women as important in marketing their services to these women clients.[21] Many financial services sales are moving out of old financial districts, into department store or supermarket chains or onto the internet, where the share of women investors is higher than in other venues (Haegele, 2000; Harrison, 2001, p. 159).

Much of the expansion of women in financial services employment is driven by the huge increase in back-office clerical work that is done mostly by women (Sassen, 1991). Globalization has made it possible to move some of this back-office work offshore, to lower-wage English-speaking locations such as Ireland or India.

The Impact of Gendered Attitudes and Images on Global Finance

While the gendered character of employment in the regulatory and private-sector financial services organizations has serious implications for those working in the industry, its significance extends much further. The organizations discussed in the preceding paragraphs are ones that play key roles in the globalization of finance, and since the financial system allocates resources in ways that have important consequences for the well-being of individuals and collectivities, it is important that it not have biases that systematically and arbitrarily favor some peoples' preferences and needs and neglect those of others. The types of gendered employment patterns discussed above are associated with gendered attitudes and images that can be significant for the organization of global finance as a whole.

Both theory and evidence suggest that a financial system that is dominated by men is likely to engage in higher levels of individualistic risk taking at the expense of systemic and individual stability than would be the case in a system in which men and women played equally influential roles.[22] Part of this is due to the traditionally differing structural relationship of women and men to the family. Women, who traditionally have had primary responsibility for the well-being of children, are likely to place a higher value on security than risk taking relative to men who do not (Floro and Dymski, 2000). Some of this may be a simple rational calculation, but it can also involve more profound enduring inclinations that are related to the differences in the value placed on care for others relative to striking out on one's own that are linked to the differential life experiences of the two genders (Flax, 1990). Numerous empirical studies have confirmed the greater preference for risk of men relative to women.[23] These attitudes can be reinforced in high-pressure male-dominated environments such as trading floors. As one woman financial executive put it, "trading is a hugely stressful, macho type job where, you know, putting the big bet on the line is what is rewarded."[24]

The attitudes and behavior with regard to risk that are prevalent in areas of global finance where men predominate are reinforced and reproduced by recurrent images drawn from cultural themes that have been emblematic of a type of masculinity associated with danger, heroism, combat, and aggression. In the most extensive study of these images to date, Mayhall (2002) examined the three most prominent trade journals in global finance – *The Banker, Euromoney*, and *Institutional Investor* – along with other relevant financial journals such as *Fortune* and *The Economist*, and found them infused with recurrent metaphoric uses of such imagery, including gunslingers, samurais, knights, high-stakes poker players, Superman and other superheroes, and football players.

One long-standing theme in the culture of high finance emphasizes the dispassionate rational control of contingency, a trait often associated with masculinity, while contingency has often been conceived as possessing feminine characteristics (de Goede, 2000). Yet, this dualism can obscure the role of emotion in male-dominated financial settings, which, as Pixley (2002, p. 49) notes, can include a killer instinct and fearless aggression – and the emotional male bonding that functions to sustain trust. Taken together, these gendered characteristics of financial markets can lead to suppression of concerns with the effects of excessive risk taking on people's well-being.

The skewing of the risk taking/stability balance in finance can have negative consequences at both micro and macro levels. At the micro level, particular individuals may lose savings as a consequence of excessive risk taking. An empirical study of 35,000 households by Barber and Odean (2001) notes that overconfident investors tend to trade excessively, and that men trade 45 percent more than women, reducing their net returns significantly relative to women. In countries in which men have higher educational levels than women, they may be better positioned to cope with the economic volatility that comes with financial liberalization (Sen, 2000, p. 1383), and thus they may expose the family units that they control to a higher than optimal level of risk. At the macro level, this skewing can have negative consequences for the role played by the financial system and institutions in our globalizing late-modern world (Van Staveren, 2002). Capital flows may be liberalized prematurely, before adequate regulatory arrangements are in place, as is now widely agreed was the case with the global financial crises of the 1990s. There may be a bias towards channeling resources towards higher-return and riskier financial markets that could otherwise be channeled through lower-return stable public-sector arrangements, as with the privatization of pensions that has been a major policy initiative in most jurisdictions over the past decade. There may be a favoring of financial performance indicators that systematically undervalue the unpaid labour of women, as with the tendency to evaluate government performance with excessively heavy reference to GNP growth, low taxes, or more generally the perceptions of governments held by financial market actors (Bakker, 2001). Social services, such as early childhood education or health care, may be systematically undervalued because the men who assess the role of these services in society are not as aware of their importance as women would be, and assume incorrectly that these functions can be costlessly taken on by women carrying out their traditional roles. These biases can result in pressures to cutback excessively the social spending of the welfare state, pressures that come from both private-sector actors in global finance and international financial institutions such as the IMF.

Gender and Developing Countries
in Global Finance

The experience of developing countries with the global financial system differs significantly from the experience of developed countries, and this is evident in issues related to gender as well. Because finance plays a key role in development, the management of internal and external financial relations has been a key priority for developing countries. Unfortunately, it has not always been clear how best to mobilize finance for development, and the political weakness of citizens in the developing countries has often put them at a disadvantage relative to other more powerful actors as the global financial system has evolved. This is even more the case for poor women, especially in the many developing countries in which women's rights are severely restricted on traditional or religious grounds. Thus, while developing countries have seen some important benefits from their involvement in the global financial system, they have also been exposed to recurrent severe consequences from deficiencies in that system, especially the debt crisis that began in the early 1980s and the global financial crises of the 1990s, discussed in more detail elsewhere in this book. As discussed further below, these negative consequences have been experienced most acutely by women.

Even without crises, the experience of the developing countries with the global financial system would have been heavily shaped by gender-related factors. There are many factors that explain North–South financial flows. They include the market-oriented emphasis on the tendency of capital to move from the industrialized countries, where it is relatively abundant, to developing countries, where it is scarce and therefore able to foster greater productivity increases and earn higher returns, and the more critical approach that makes a similar point, while casting it instead as the shift in the opportunities for exploitative profits in the two locations. We can add a further gender-oriented explanation by extending the point made in the previous section about the excessive preference for risk over stability that is related to the dominance of the global financial system by men: premature involvement of developing countries in highly risky international financial markets may have led to sub-optimal outcomes, especially when the often neglected impacts of this involvement on the unpaid work of women are considered. Enloe (1990), in a book chapter entitled "Blue Jeans and Bankers," has highlighted the disjuncture between the role played by the male-dominated centres of the global financial system in shaping the export-oriented development strategies of the newly industrializing countries and the reliance of these countries on export-processing zones in which up to 80 percent of workers are women. It is not surprising that development strategies can fail to reflect the best interests of the women that are relied upon to implement these strategies.

As well, these North–South financial flows are stimulated by differences in the demographics of the two regions, which in turn are closely related to the role of women. In the immediate post-World War II period both industrialized countries and developing countries were experiencing high birth rates, the former because of the "baby boom" that followed the war. This demographic profile oriented the financial system towards the needs of young families, including the creation of credit for financing of social infrastructure and the expansion of employment opportunities. However, in the last quarter of the twentieth century, the age profile of the developed countries had altered dramatically, as the baby boomers aged and birth rates dropped. The focus of the financial system in developed countries shifted from the needs of young families to the worries of financing the elderly, including guaranteeing high returns on the assets that the aging baby boomers had accumulated in their mutual funds, returns that could be increased by supplying the continuing high need for credit in the developing world (Dobson and Hufbauer, 2001, pp. 20–8). In short, North–South financial flows can be explained in part by the differential roles of women in the two regions: in the South, high birth rates continue to be more common, and these can be attributed to the lack of alternatives for women, the income generated for the family by children, and to the reliance upon children for the care of the elderly, while in the North the financial system has substituted for the old-age-related functions previously carried out by families, a change closely related to the changing role of women. The heavy emphasis on concerns of creditors relative to debtors in the global financial system can be explained in part by the ability of those experiencing this changed age profile in the North to impose their preferences on those in the South.

In the period before the debt crisis of the 1980s, gender bias was also evident in the mechanisms by which international and domestic financial resources were distributed within developing countries. The expansion of the role of money and finance in developing countries, which is often seen as a positive indicator of development, can often have negative consequences for the type of subsistence family-oriented farming in which women have played a key role. Earlier on, in colonial times, requirements that families pay taxes in cash forced them to reorient their farming towards world markets in order to obtain this cash, and colonial authorities strongly favored men over women in their interactions regarding these tax and trading matters, thereby shifting authority relations in the household in men's favor.

This type of gender bias continued in the post-World War II period, where the emphasis was on large-scale foreign infusions of capital into heavy industry and globally oriented infrastructure. These investments, mostly managed by governments, produced occupations in which men predominated, and often the rate of return on this investment was far lower than would have been the case had the money been invested in the types of activities in which women specialized, such as early childhood health care and education, or access to clean water and cooking fuel. Women have a tendency to spend a much greater proportion of the income they earn on children than do men, and this can have positive effects on the long-range prospects for development.[25] More educated women have fewer children, and this helps increase savings and contributes to sustainability (World Bank, 2002, p. 6). Feminist scholars have inspired a large literature on these problems, and in response most official lending agencies have sought to incorporate consideration of these gender issues in their programs. For instance, the World Bank notes that it "has made progress in integrating gender issues into country work and lending." It lent $3.4 billion for girls' education between 1995 and 2000, included gender-related considerations in more of its lending, created a Gender and Development Board in 1997, initiated a plan for Country Gender Assessments for all active borrowers, and issued lengthy reports on gender, although it has also been consistently criticized for moving too slowly by advocates of gender equality.[26]

In addition, many developing country governments sought to make cheap finance available for industrialization by setting ceilings on interest rates. This had the unintended consequence of biasing the financial system against the smaller-scale economic activities in which women played key roles, since banks could not charge the higher interest rates needed to cover the greater costs of lending to these more dispersed projects, and therefore simply lent to the same large projects that international lenders were targeting (Floro and Dymski, 2000, p. 1270; Baden, 1996). The interest rate ceilings also made it difficult for poor women to accumulate savings, since even if a bank branch opened in their community, the interest rates would be low. Wealthy citizens, by contrast, would often place their financial assets in international markets to get around the interest ceilings.

The debt crisis of the 1980s, as discussed in chapter 4, involved the imposition of strict IMF structural adjustment policies (SAPs) on indebted developing countries. Ostensibly these were accepted voluntarily by the sovereign developing states, but in practice these states had little choice, since they were dependent on IMF approval to manage their heavy debt, which to a large degree they were not responsible for incurring, and which in any case could not be wished away now that it was there. Given their lack of representation in financial decision making, women in developing countries had even less influence on the SAPs than did their governments.

The SAPs have been severely criticized for their negative effects on women (Floro, 1995; Seguino, 1997; Sen, 2000, p. 1382). One set of criticisms revolves around the cutbacks in social spending that they required. This social spending, which was often characterized as wasteful, was especially important to women, since it addressed the needs for which women bore greatest responsibility. Women's already unequal burden would increase further as they substituted their own unpaid labor in an effort to substitute for the lost services, in some cases taking female children out of school to work to supplement lost income. Many of the social services, such as health care systems, had also been an important source of employment and upward mobility for women. The hardships would drive women in large numbers into dangerous and dehumanizing work in areas that were growing, with government assent or active encouragement, because they involved the type of access to foreign currency that the SAPs required.[27] This work included assembly work in export-processing zones in which women's low pay or poor working conditions were justified with reference to sexist stereotypes such as their use of earnings for frivolous luxury spending, or their naturally nimble fingers' capacity for dehumanizing assembly work, or other abuses, such as firms forcing women workers to take birth control pills so that the firms can avoid addressing the implications of pregnancies. In some countries such as South Korea and Mexico, women's share of employment, after initially rising, began to drop as some industries developed and became higher-skilled (Mehra and Gammage, 1999, pp. 540–1). Many women have been employed in domestic work in foreign countries, far from their children, and vulnerable to abuse by employers, or engaged in prostitution and sex tourism. Other women were employed in very small businesses that were not able to compete or engage in partnerships with foreign multinationals to the same degree as medium-sized businesses owned by and primarily employing men (Sen, 2000, p. 1383). The SAPs seemed to be a quintessential example of a plan devised by male-dominated financial elites, the successful implementation of which depended on a reprehensible increase in the exploitation of women (Elson, 2001).[28]

Similar criticisms were made in response to the effects of the East Asian financial crisis of 1997–8. Catastrophic drops in income in the affected countries often led to greater increased hardship for women than for men, because women's lower seniority led them to be fired first, because they sought to protect their children's well-being by increasing their unpaid labor or reducing their own consumption, or because men used their control over households to shift the greater part of the burden of adjustment to women (Aslanbeigui and Summerfield, 2000; Young, 2002; Francisco and Sen, 2000; Lim, 2000; Singh and Zammit, 2000; White and Sharma, 1999; Zhiqin, 2002).

The persistence of these types of problems is evident in the shortcomings of the UN's Financing for Development (FfD) initiative (Floro, 2001), which culminated in a conference in Monterrey in 2002. The UN Secretary-General's Report on FfD, for instance, failed to consider the gender implications of its analysis (Waghray, 2001). Despite some scattered references to gender in the Monterrey consensus that was agreed by governments at the conference, including a call to "mainstream the gender perspective into development policies at all levels and in all sectors" (paragraph 64), and the innovativeness of bringing the IMF and the World Bank together with the more gender and socially sensitive UN organizations, there was disappointment that the process did not go beyond the Washington consensus in as significant a way as had been hoped (Durano, 2002, p. 69).[29] A similar criticism has been made of the New Partnership for Africa's Development (NEPAD), a major effort by developed and African countries in 2001 to address Africa's development problems (Randriamaro, 2001).

There are some positive developments that offset to some degree the bleak picture painted so far. These revolve mainly around the degree to which financial markets provide opportunities for women to escape from oppressive relations in their community or family (Marchand, 1996, p. 581; Ruiz, 2000; Sparr, 1994, pp. 29–30). For instance, despite the sexism and exploitation in the export-processing zones, for many women they offered more independence and higher wages than would have been the case in the communities from which they came, and may have provided them with a source of income that was more reliable than some of the male-dominated domestically oriented industries, even if in some countries many women are expected to hand their earnings over to male family members (Elson, 1999, p. 615). Liberal economic theory suggests that competitive markets will reduce discrimination against women, as discriminatory firms will be outperformed by firms that make optimal use of all the skills of available employees, including underpaid women whose wages consequently rise in response to this demand. There is a modest amount of evidence supporting this view in financial and other industries (World Bank, 2001, p. 197; but see also Razavi, 2001, p. 18). At the managerial and executive levels, there is some evidence that multinational corporations can contribute to enhancing the role of women when they hire more women than more traditional host economies, such as Japan (Adler, 1993).

Some research has found that export-oriented growth that is stimulated by financial liberalization reduces inequality between women and men, although these findings are challenged by other research (Benería, Floro, Grown and MacDonald, 2000, p. xii). In some cases reduced inequality can occur when industries in which men predominate, such as construction or heavy industry, experience a severe loss of jobs. Or economic hardship may lead families to pull boys out of school, bringing their educational participation closer to the low level of girls. Cases such as these are hardly the optimal way to address gender inequalities, because the absolute condition of women has not improved. In other cases, however, women have gained in both absolute and relative terms, as when the emphasis on exports that has come with SAPs has expanded employment in industries in which women predominate (World Bank, 2001, ch. 5).

One type of financial initiative to improve women's conditions that has attracted a great deal of attention is micro-financing (United Nations Expert Group on Women and Finance, 1995; Mehra, Drost-Maasry, and Rahman, 1995). Often the lending is managed or assisted by non-governmental organizations working closely with informal networks of women, and trust that a loan will be repaid is often based on the force of community expectations rather than traditional collateral, although it can also be based on the greater vulnerability of women to pressures to repay (Van Staveren, 2001, p. 13). Both interest rates and repayment rates are typically much higher than for more conventional loans. The high interest rate reflects the cost of administering this type of decentralized lending, the high rate of return of the investments the borrowers make, and the fact that the only alternative source of financing is often even higher interest rates from informal money-lenders. While many poor men have benefited from micro-financing, its primary focus has been women. Micro-financing attracted much attention at the Beijing Fourth World Conference on Women,[30] and has been eagerly promoted by the worldwide International Coalition on Women and Credit, for which the New York-based Women's World Banking provides the Secretariat (see <www.swwb.org>). Micro-financing is attractive to supporters of markets as well, since it involves a commercial relationship rather than a charitable one, and the World Bank has been very active in assisting micro-financing initiatives.[31]

Despite the enthusiasm for it, micro-financing has certain deficiencies (United Nations Expert Group on Women and Finance, 1995; Baden, 1996; Berger, 1989). Some of these relate to the ongoing types of discrimination faced by women, especially if they want to use micro-financing as a stepping stone to get to more conventional financing. For instance, in some countries women do not have the right to have title to property or to control the revenues from their enterprises. Their responsibility for their family can make it difficult to separate out business and family accounting, or to avoid drawing from business funds for food in times of hardship. Despite assistance from NGOs, the time and skills involved in written loan documentation can be daunting for many poor women. Often the borrowers' enterprises are in activities that, while familiar, also bring very low returns. More generally, despite the millions of women who have been helped by micro-financing, the size of the micro-financing sector is dwarfed by other types of financial activities, and even with the best efforts of its advocates, it is unlikely to ever be able to really compete with the vastly larger number of more profitable financial instruments.

Conclusion

There are numerous ways in which the evolution of the global financial system is profoundly linked to gender. These connections can be obscured by approaches that treat the global financial system as involving powerful states and atomistic markets, and that do not consider the way in which social practices link micro-level activities, such as the macho culture of a trading floor, and macro-level activities, such as excessive systemic risk leading to recurrent destructive global financial crises.

Gender is relevant in both the way in which human actors reproduce the global financial system through their daily practices, and in the way in which that system affects people. The domination of finan-

cial decision making by men and the exclusion of women are changing very slowly, and in the meantime the system that is reproduced
daily, in addition to being biased towards excessive risk taking, fails
to consider adequately the effects of new financial market innovations and public policies on women. These are generally experienced
by women, who carry the primary responsibility in the care economy,
as a diminishment of opportunity and increased economic hardship,
only partially offset by the positive effects for those women who
experience new opportunities as they are drawn in high proportions
into an expanding financial services industry, or who benefit from
new financial arrangements that did not exist in a less globalized era.

The globalization of finance has both negative and positive implications with regard to gender, and, as is the case with the other
aspects of financial globalization studied in this book, which of these
two contrary tendencies predominates depends on the rules and nor-
mative expectations, formal and informal, that link the micro and
macro levels. While difficult to measure, the *Martens* v. *Smith Barney*
case and ones like it resulted in positive alterations in the practices
of firms on Wall Street, and over time this is likely to have significant
impacts on the way in which Wall Street helps shape global finance.
Similarly, the effects of the practices of the IMF and the World Bank,
which have a vastly greater span of influence than a few court cases,
are also highly dependent on the way in which the rules shaping these
practices are formulated.

11

Risk Politics and Financial Crises

It is obvious that risk is an important feature of global finance. Everyone is aware that if you choose to speculate in international financial markets you are engaging in a risky activity and can easily lose your money. After the global financial crises of the 1990s, with their catastrophic effects on Mexican and East Asian economies, it is also clear that the global financial system creates risks even for those who do not choose to be involved in it. A look at the history of international insurance will reveal that insurers have been managing risks for hundreds of years, and a casual survey of contemporary global finance will reveal that a great deal of effort is devoted to the development and commercialization of risk management systems.

Although it is easy to see that risk and global finance are closely connected, the social and political significance of the concept of risk is not as self-evident. "Risk" differs from other words such as "hazard," "peril," or "danger" in the degree to which it is associated with the decision to act on the basis of a calculation of the probability of a future occurrence (Ewald, 1991, p. 200). Such a calculation can help in managing risks, as with insurance. Thus the concept of risk involves a relationship between the use of knowledge to bring about control, on the one hand, and the persistence of the unexpected and contingent, on the other. This dialectical relationship is a key feature of finance, not just in insurance, but in innumerable other respects, including saving for one's old age or the state's mobilization of finance to enhance its security.

The relationship is also one of the key paradoxical features of our contemporary world more generally. Never has there been an age when knowledge production and a lack of certainty have simultaneously seemed so central to every facet of life, or where actions are decided with reference to future consequences rather than past traditions. This parallel between finance and life more generally is not coincidental: finance has always played a central role in the structuring of social life. Thus the concept of *risk* can be an important entry point for understanding the connection of the globalization of finance to other large-scale social and political changes that we are living through.

There are many theoretical approaches that are useful in analyzing risk: Ulrich Beck's (1992) concept of *risk society*, the link that Giddens (1990, pp. 124–37; 1991, pp. 109–43) makes between risk management and *colonization of the future*, and the insights of poststructuralism into the relationship between knowledge, control, and contingency, including work on accounting (Hopwood and Miller, 1994), insurance (Ewald, 1991), and "scientific finance" (de Goede, 2001). The chapter begins by discussing these concepts in more detail, highlighting their relevance for understanding contemporary social phenomena in general. It then discusses their relevance for global finance.

Risk as Social Practice

Beck (1992, 1999) argues that in our contemporary world political conflict is increasingly centered on the distribution of risks rather than the distribution of wealth. Today risks are an unintended, manufactured by-product of our complex scientific and economic systems, a sharp contrast to earlier periods, in which the negative effects of natural phenomena posed a greater danger to humanity. Moreover, incalculable socially constructed dangers are increasingly displacing risks, which are calculable. For Beck, then, the growth of expert knowledge tends to be associated with uncertainty and increased risk and danger. This is captured as well in Beck's concept of reflexivity, in which the construction of more elaborate expert systems creates negative feedback.

Giddens (1990, 1991), by contrast, sees proliferating expert systems as providing greater choice and potential for citizens to construct their own life-narratives – to gain control of their own destiny. Giddens provides the example of insurance, which, he argues, allows us to control or *colonize* the future. Where previously we might be helpless victims of catastrophic loss, insurance allows us to anticipate and offset the probability of such a loss. This is in contrast to Beck (1999, p. 31), who sees the significance of insurance in its limits – those dangers that are incalculable and therefore uninsurable. For Giddens reflexivity involves the ability of individuals to learn creatively from past practices. Thus, overall, Giddens is optimistic about our capacity to use more complex systems of knowledge to control risks and to pursue our goals successfully.

A useful complement to Beck and Giddens is provided by post-structuralist approaches, which treat bodies of organized knowledge as discourses that structure social interactions and constitute relations of power. For instance, de Goede (2001) has pointed to the important role played by scientific risk models in creating and legitimizing derivatives markets. These models altered earlier views of derivatives as morally problematic forms of gambling, and also provided the rules that defined the value of them. Accounting similarly constitutes relations of control (Hopwood and Miller, 1994).

All three of these approaches treat risk as involving the structuring of decisions and of contingent dangers by systems of knowledge. Risk is therefore not simply a property of an environment external to social action that risk analysis reveals. The shaping of human conduct by sets of knowledge-derived rules is what has been referred to as "social practices" in chapter 2. Formal and informal risk management, therefore, whether it involves lay actors using rules of thumb to decide whether to save or spend, or highly trained professionals equipped with complex mathematical rules, is creatively drawing on social rules, and the aggregate social effect of the choices such actors make can also be traced to these rules.

The Long Historical Evolution of Risk and Finance

The control of uncertainty has always been an important aspect of finance, and a look back at the evolution of risk in finance helps in better understanding the social implications of the globalization of finance. The history of money and finance can be seen as involving increasingly complex mechanisms for managing risks, with each new innovation creating new risks that supersede the older types of risk they were designed to control: "protecting against one category of risk exposes to another" (Douglas, 1992, p. 14). These complex mechanisms are primarily *social*, even though they have often been misrecognized as involving mainly the search for security through the accumulation of material resources.

The most basic and oldest constituent element of financial systems is money. Money typically is defined as having three functions, and each of these is linked to the reduction of uncertainty and therefore to the management of risk. Money is a store of value, and holding money instead of goods that might deteriorate, such as perishable foods, helps offset risk. Money is a unit of account, providing a common benchmark for ascertaining the value of things. Money is a means of payment, allowing vastly greater control over the timing and range of choice in transactions than barter. As Luhmann (1993, p. 176) has put it, "Money operates without a memory . . . The risk is not passed along with money as it is when goods are transferred." Or as Simmel (1978, pp. 476–7) has noted, money ties people together, and permits "the *conquest* of distance"; but in removing the personalized aspects of economic relationships, it "places an invisible functional distance between people that is an inner protection and neutralization against the overcrowded proximity and friction of our cultural life."

The evolution of money has involved increasingly complex and social mechanisms for managing risk. A common early form of money was a precious metal such as gold or silver that had an intrinsic value connected to its material properties, such as its malleability and beauty. While this value offset the risk that money would not be accepted, it brought other risks, such as theft and adulteration. Over time, more portable and clearly defined paper money, backed up by the reputations and organizational capacity of banks and states, replaced precious metals.

The evolution of the international monetary system over the past two centuries can also be seen as a series of increasingly elaborate social arrangements for the management of risk. Under nineteenth-century British hegemony the gold standard created a system of rules through which states fixed the value of their currencies to gold, thereby reducing the risks from currency fluctuations, but bringing new risks to citizens who were required to adjust their living standards to preserve the value of their currency. By the mid-twentieth century these risks had become politically unacceptable, and after World War II, under US hegemony, a more elaborate system was constructed, with states agreeing to peg their currencies to the dollar, which in turn was fixed in value at $35 per ounce of gold, while the International Monetary Fund was created to authorize periodic adjustments and to provide short-term financing when countries experienced unexpected problems in their balance of payments. This new Bretton Woods system was devised in part to address uncertainties with regard to the supply of gold, and to shield countries from the risks associated with international trade and currency volatility (Ruggie, 1982).

However the Bretton Woods system brought its own unmanageable risks, involving the Eurocurrency markets, as discussed in chapters 2 and 3, along with the increased risks associated with the fragility of the US commitment to exchange gold for dollars at $35 per ounce. Initially, many analysts saw the breakdown of the Bretton Woods system in the early 1970s and its replacement by a system of floating rates as providing a solution to the risks associated with the pegged currencies of the Bretton Woods system, since, for instance, governments could allow their currency to float up or down instead of having to defend it and stabilize it. However, the shift to floating rates can also be seen as a massive privatization of risk, with states repudiating their responsibility for managing monetary and financial risks associated with the international economy. Ultimately, complex forms of private-sector financing, including foreign exchange derivatives, were developed to address the risk management needs that states were no longer handling, but these in turn have brought new risks.

The financing of the state through taxes or borrowing also involved the construction of a social capacity for managing risks. In the early modern period a key reason for states to raise finances was for the conduct of war – for military security. As the state added social welfare to war making as one of its primary functions, the role of finance in the transformation of risks also became apparent. In the nineteenth century, life and disability insurance emerged as a way of protecting citizens from the new risks connected with the Industrial Revolution. The division of labor between the public and private sectors in this was contested (Defert, 1991), and ultimately both would continue to develop, with the state focusing more on broader social insurance and private firms focusing on more specific risks. As Defert (1991) points out, the emergence of private disability insurance involved the construction of new forms of liability law, replacing individual responsibility for misfortune of either the worker or the firm with a generalized commitment to compensate based on statistical measurement of patterns of risk, patterns inherent in the population as a whole and not traceable to individual actors. Both public-sector and private-sector insurance, therefore, involved a socialization of risk (Ewald, 1991, p. 203).

The risk management capacities of financial practices were also very evident in the organization of production in the Industrial Revolution. For instance, a developed personalized system called *factorage* provided financing to cotton plantations, managing their risks over the seasons and years, a system in turn linked to the British banks in London. As transatlantic cotton markets became more developed, and with the establishment of the transatlantic telegraph cable, cotton futures markets replaced the personalized factorage system as a mechanism for managing risks (Porter, 2002b, p. 34). The emergence of limited liability companies and the use of stock markets and investment banks for the financing of industrial firms was also a distinctive feature of the British Industrial Revolution. These financial arrangements were important internationally: "Under the shelter of the liberal imperial authority at Whitehall, but never overshadowed by it, the City of London exercised the major control over the world's capital markets and through these markets over the great process of the production and distribution of wealth" (Ridgeway, 1938, pp. 13–14).

The more recent growth in the application of financial technologies to public- and private-sector management can also be seen as a social mechanism for the management of risk. Generally these were developed as a corrective to the risks associated with inflexible bureaucracy in a world in flux. In large firms, financial strategies of control replaced more personalized management styles, and replaced more intuitive decisions about the internal allocation of resources with quantitative modeling and performance assessment. Similarly, in public administration financial indicators, incentives, and constraints replaced more political programs and plans, and auditing increasingly replaced personalized supervision (Power, 1994; Fligstein, 1990). Growing social inequality, loss of social cohesion, and corporate governance scandals are indications of the new risks that come with these risk management techniques, which emphasized financial performance at the expense of other social concerns.

The above examples of the historical role of the financial system in managing risk show that financial transformations were closely associated with large-scale political, economic, and social transformations. Although there are some developments that owe some of their distinctive features to particular eras, such as the international gold standard's link to British hegemony, there is a clear, long historical trend towards an increased reliance on complex social arrangements for managing risk. Each of these large-scale social innovations was accompanied by new risks, and many, such as the Bretton Woods system, broke down, bringing new waves of system-threatening risk. From this perspective it is not surprising that the financial system has always been characterized by frightening risks, since, like any such massively complex and tightly coupled technical system, it is subject to what Perrow (1984) has called *normal accidents*, in which an unexpected interaction within the system can lead to catastrophic collapse. In the case of finance this can be especially destructive, since its function is to aggregate, absorb, and manage risk from the broader social system of which it is an integral part, and financial system breakdowns lead to the spilling back of risks into the institutions from which the financial system had previously drawn them.

It is clear as well that the increasingly sophisticated character of the financial system's capacity to manage risk is closely associated with globalization. Finance has always played a central role in efforts to construct social institutions to protect citizens or entrepreneurs from international political and economic hazards. The way it has done so has tracked the patterns of sovereignty and cross-border integration that tell the story of globalization more generally.

Control and Disruptions in Financial Risk Management

Finance and risk management more generally are characterized by an increasing dialectical tension between more intense and sophisticated systems of control, on the one hand, and more unmanageable and frightening disruptions, on the other. As noted in the previous section, this dialectic is in part due to the way in which each solution to a risk problem brings new risks, which in turn is in part due to the complexity and tight coupling of the complex social arrangements for managing risk that have evolved over time. This section highlights two other factors contributing to this dialectic: the ambiguous implications of evolution of modes of information for control, and the clashing interests that are in play over this control.

Finance itself is communications-intensive, and knowledge-intensive, and thus it is not surprising that its evolution should correspond to evolutionary patterns in communications technologies. Poster (1990) has identified the following three stages in what he calls the *mode of information*: (1) face-to-face, orally mediated exchanges; (2) written exchanges mediated by print; and (3) electronically mediated exchange.

The transition from the first to second stages is closely associated with the shift from barter to the popular use of standardized coins and paper money, a shift that paralleled the transition from orally mediated religious rituals in churches to the nationalist ideologies that came with newspapers, books, and other print media, and helped consolidate the state. Helleiner (2003) has pointed to the role of mechanically reproduced national currencies, imprinted with national symbols, in the consolidation of state control of its territory and its citizens' loyalty, a process akin to the role of printing in creating uniform national languages and identities (Anderson, 1991), and the role of printing of timetables and technical manuals in the standardization of time (Kern, 1983).

The transition from the second to third stages involves both a disruption and an enhancement of control. Baudrillard (1993) has distinguished two stages in this last electronic mode identified by Poster. The first electronic stage is simulation, in which models create a *hyper-reality* in which the purity of the simulation can seem more real than a non-existent reality that it purports to simulate. Simulations differ from mechanical printed reproductions, which are copies of an original that they can be said to represent. By contrast, a simulation generated by a model has no original that it is copying. Baudrillard's second electronic stage is a "fractal" stage in which "each value or fragment of value shines for a moment in the heavens of simulation, then disappears into the void along a crooked path that only rarely happens to intersect with other paths." Baudrillard is pointing here to the evolution of systems of meaning, in which the link of meaning or value to either an underlying material reality or a coherent unifying model is increasingly displaced by viral processes in which meaning or value is generated by the rapid flow and decentralized interactions of fragmented codes. These developments in communications and information technologies have contributed to the volatility and disruptiveness of such features of global finance as derivatives, the dependence of financial values on mediated perceptions rather than real fundamentals, and the transgressing of territorial and functional boundaries.

On the other hand, developments in communications technologies have also brought about enhanced capacities to exercise control. The emergence of finance itself created a distinct sector, which in turn involves the splitting of simple financial products into more and more specialized derivatives, targeting finer and finer classes of risk, and the creation of increasingly differentiated regulatory instruments, such as the increasing variety in the types of risk models applied to different classes of firms. This process can be seen as the most recent phase of a long historical period of functional differentiation, a constitutive principle of social cohesion in complex societies (Luhmann, 1982). Similarly, Foucault's notion of *governmentality*, the tendency of contemporary societies to rely on the discursive control of the frameworks within which self-regulation can be brought about, rather than the direct control of behavior, fits with the way in which financial technologies can strengthen decentralized control mechanisms.

Accounting and auditing, which have become increasingly important in our contemporary world, highlight these ambiguous developments. On the one hand, they provide precise and effective mechanisms for monitoring and controlling performance. However, this control is mediated, and perhaps confounded, by the experts who are responsible for translating assessments of performance into standardized numerical and textual indicators. The language of accounting and accountability is increasingly displacing the language of democracy and representation, reflecting both the perceived failures of democracy and the perhaps excessive elevation of technical expertise relative to political deliberation. As Power (1994) has pointed out, a great paradox of accounting and auditing is that the processes by which the assessment occurs are confidential and non-transparent. The accounting scandals of the early twenty-first century highlight the potential for collusion between the assessors and the assessed. Thus, ironically, accountability and unaccountability are linked.

Similarly, the prominence of risk discourses in late modernity also involves heightened expectations with regard to officials. As Douglas (1992, pp. 15–16) notes, our current risk-focused "blaming system" is "almost ready to treat every death as chargeable to someone's account, every accident as caused by someone's criminal negligence, every sickness a threatened prosecution. Whose fault? Is the first question." Risk implies choice, and includes the decision not to act. Thus authorities can no longer excuse their conduct with reference to tradition or natural factors beyond their control. Demands on governments and firms to modify risky policies can be seen as the outcome of these heightened expectations. As Luhmann (1993, p. 138) notes, "The fact that risk has become a new focus for protest is to be explained by the contingency arrangement that this concept names. The temporal contingencies in relation to decision and loss (both need not be!) provoke . . . social contingencies. They permit varying observer stances without offering a redeeming unity."

On the other hand, Beck (1999) highlights the negative consequences associated with the use of technical expertise as a source of risk management in his analysis of *unawareness* and *organized irresponsibility*. He (Beck, 1999, p. 119) states: "the 'medium' of reflexive modernization is not knowledge, but – more or less reflexive – unawareness." He (Beck, 1999, pp. 126–30) identifies a number of types of unawareness. These include both willful creation or acceptance of absences or distortions in knowledge and the types of unawareness that are more connected to those aspects of the knowledge-producing process that are beyond the control of expert or lay actors. Expertise can be implicated in all these forms of unawareness. At a more structural level, unawareness is associated with organized irresponsibility: the failure to acknowledge or act upon risks. The opacity of the financial system to lay actors and the failure to manage systemic risks adequately are paradigmatic examples.

Risk is distinctive as well in the degree to which it exercises control over action with reference to expectations about the future rather than the past. The contemporary prominence of risk can be seen as another instance of the post-traditional character of our times that is evident in all social institutions. Risk does not involve a reduction of rules, but rather a rule-governed substitution of a probabilistic esti-mation of future contingencies in place of guides to action derived from a shared understanding of how things have always been done. The past can enter into risk analysis in providing the data set that helps generate the probabilities of future contingencies. Moreover, statistical concepts such as the normal distribution can normalize pre-vailing conduct while casting innovative or oppositional conduct as unacceptably risky. Risks have long been used to consolidate social cohesion, as when dissidents are portrayed as foreign-inspired threats to the social order (Douglas, 1992). Nevertheless, in contrast to traditional norms and formal law, risk analysis is far more change-oriented in providing guidelines for maximizing future benefits relative to costs and in legitimizing choice under uncertainty. As Luhmann (1993, p. 59) notes, unlike a norm, "a risk cannot be violated."

These points about risk and control highlight the degree to which the prominence of finance in contemporary social phenomena, including globalization, is due to the role played by finance in man-aging risk and, in turn, the central role played by risk in constituting a social order in a knowledge-intensive world experiencing rapid change. Financial and other risk practices both accelerate change and seek to guide it. These practices do not simply help in weighing costs and benefits of alternatives presented by an environment beyond our capacity to change. On the contrary, they generate new risks, Beck's areas of *unawareness* and *organized irresponsibility*, and Perrow's (1984) *normal accidents*, with no guarantee that the capacity to manage risk will keep pace as new risks are unleashed.

Risk Politics and Global Finance

The control and the negative consequences that can be associ-ated with financial and other risk practices draw our attention to the politics of risk. "Politics" here refers to contestation over the authoritative allocation of resources. Drawing on the work of Beck (1992, 1999), Giddens (1990, 1991), and others, we can identify five main political aspects of contemporary risk practices.[1]

A first political aspect of risk is the impact of social inequality on the experience of risk: "the poor risk more" (Douglas, 1985, p. 6). For instance, Marske (1991) found a correlation between the frequency of crashes of planes carrying college basketball teams and the standing of the team: teams with fewer resources relied upon more poorly maintained and regulated airlines. In a study of military casualties, Leigh and Berney (1991, p. 130) found that "hostile casualties tended to be disproportionately concentrated among those draftees and reluctant volunteers with relatively low civilian income potentials." The risks associated with AIDS and other diseases are similarly greater for those without the resources to learn about, avoid, and treat them. For global finance too, those with resources can anticipate, offset, and take advantage of risks in a way that those without cannot. Sometimes this relationship between social inequality and risk can operate unnoticed, a neglect reinforced by the lack of capacity of those most adversely affected to recognize and act on the problem. However, anger at this type of injustice can also fuel political conflict.

A second political aspect of risk stems from its indeterminacy. Scientific and technical approaches often aspire to avoid politics by adjudicating disputes with reference to empirical evidence and empirically validated laws. The uncertainties associated with risk render this problematic. Political deliberation and contestation may be the only viable ways of making choices where the probability of a risk's occurrence or the magnitude and character of its effects are unclear, or where preferences vary regarding acceptable levels of risk. As Beck (1999, pp. 58–9) argues, in risk society science is politicized as it is drawn into conflicts about distribution of risks, undermining its own legitimacy as competing scientific claims clash. These clashing rationalities disrupt the coherence of the prevailing social and political order. This is evident in global finance in the shortcomings of the economic models used by proponents of liberalization to legitimize it. Despite their elegance, such models can fail to capture unexpected disturbances, or to match the lived experience of those for whom the costs of financial liberalization outweigh the benefits.

A third political aspect of risk is the new distributional conflicts it introduces between the experts it empowers and everyone else. These conflicts may revolve around the appropriation by experts of decisions that others feel those experts do not have the right to make. Or they may revolve around the economic resources that flow to experts, either in exchange for their scarce knowledge or because experts have abused their position and have arbitrarily expropriated resources at the expense of others, as with insider trading.

Financial and other risk practices may generate political conflict when the emergence of these practices themselves is seen as a problem. Political conflict can arise when risk practices are seen as creating new risks, or as displacing other less change-oriented ways of doing things to which people are attached. Often insurance has been criticized for creating a problem of *moral hazard*, where people are more careless because they expect to be compensated if things go wrong. Financial globalization has been criticized for bringing about excessively volatile change that undermines the institutions that have been built up over the years to protect citizens, such as the welfare state or the norm of full-time permanent employment.

Financial and risk practices may become the vehicle for political conflicts that primarily originate elsewhere. These practices are so linked to decision making, and their practitioners and discourses are so highly respected, that they may be used as a vehicle for achieving certain goals that might otherwise have been pursued by alternative decision-making techniques, such as democratic deliberation. For instance, neoliberal governments have often been accused of using financial constraints, such as external debt, as an excuse to pursue an underlying desire to reduce the power of the state, or to turn public property over to favored groups through privatization. Similarly, neoliberals often accuse labor unions and traditional national industries of criticizing financial liberalization when their real concern is protecting their own interests.

A related way in which political conflict can be associated with financial and other risk practices is in the degree to which they create individual responsibility for one's problems, transforming earlier patterns of mutual obligation into a cold statistical socialization of risks. As Beck notes, sub-system rationalities and experts "dump their contradictions and conflicts at the feet of the individual" (1992, p. 137). For some this brings an exhilarating sense of freedom, while for others it can bring a terrible burden of dealing with hardships alone, without the help of others.

Conclusion

Aside from the political conflict that is directly linked to financial and other risk practices, the issues discussed in this chapter raise serious questions with regard to the implications of these practices for how politics is conducted. Beck has noted that environmental and other risks can cut across social classes, policy fields, and other social categories that previously would have created boundaries that would have helped manage risk. As a result of these changes, political practices are transformed, with legislatures declining in importance relative to the active direct engagement of citizens in political practices, often in defense of a decentralized and multi-level system of rights rather than voting for one's favorite political party. Despite this proliferation of new types of political engagement, troubling questions remain about the implications for democracy of the concentrations of private-sector and technical authority that come with financial and other risk practices. This is a topic to which chapter 12 returns.

12

Democracy and Legitimacy in the Governance of Global Finance

This book started by arguing that global finance is a topic that should not just be left to experts, and the preceding chapters have aimed to draw lessons that are of interest not only to such experts. This concluding chapter brings together the threads from previous chapters, and seeks to highlight the types of issues that have relevance for our understanding of our contemporary world more generally, as well as for problems specific to global finance, and thereby to contribute to the type of discussion about the place of global finance in our contemporary world that should be an important part of democratic deliberation and contestation today.

This challenges a common tendency to think of global finance as too complicated for the average citizen to understand. Those involved in policymaking in global finance are often eager to keep politics at a distance and to solve problems through careful technical work rather than public debate. Previous chapters have provided many reasons to question this separation of politics and technical questions, especially the arbitrariness of many risk allocations and the probability that such allocations will be explained more by the power at the disposal of the actors that shape these allocations rather than by technical models or standards. These types of concerns were evident, for instance, in chapter 4, in the suggestion that the new Basel Capital Accord may unfairly favor large sophisticated banks, and in the examples in other chapters of the way in which the costs of financial crises have been borne to a large degree by citizens of the affected countries and only minimally by financial market actors, even though these actors' search for high returns was a major factor in bringing the crises about. The structural problems associated with gender inequalities in finance discussed in chapter 10 can likewise be addressed only by political creativity, not technical analysis. The upswing in interest in global finance on the part of a highly politicized global civil society discussed in chapter 9 is a further indication of the limits of an approach that seeks to restrict discussion to technical matters.

While it is a mistake to try to restrict discussion of global financial issues to experts, it is certainly important not to ignore technical issues. It is important for those concerned about the negative effects of global finance to take these technical issues more fully into account if practical solutions to current and future problems are to be advocated in addition to highlighting past injustices. Shaping the direction of the private-sector financial markets that presently constitute the largest part of global finance will require more new technical knowledge than would be the case if the lending of the IMF, the World Bank, and other public-sector bodies were still as central to global finance as it was in the past. It is best not to ignore or dismiss technical detail, or to insist that this detail be left to experts, but rather to try to understand the political and ethical implications of this technical complexity. Technical issues involve much more than just a set of incremental adjustments to a system that is often portrayed by its supporters as self-evidently and necessarily the best one possible.

Democracy is relevant to global finance not just because the issues at stake are sufficiently important and political that they should involve wider deliberation and accountability than is possible when it is shaped solely by technical decisions made by experts. Democracy is also important because the stability of global finance requires much more active and widespread engagement than was the case in previous times when decisions were made through informal old boys' networks in the City of London, or when the G10 member states could regulate global finance by relying on their control over international banks which were overwhelmingly headquartered in their jurisdictions. As discussed in chapters 5 and 8, the globalization of securities markets and the incorporation of emerging markets into global finance have brought increased recognition of the importance of agreed international standards, peer review, and the fuller inclusion of developing and transition countries in decision-making processes, in place of the more exclusive, secretive G10-centric process of the past. An additional sign of this recognition amongst policymakers is an upswing in the use of the concept of *legitimacy*, along with other similar words such as "accountability," "ownership," and good governance.[1]

A key theme of this book – namely, the importance of recognizing the role of international social institutions and practices, as opposed to portraying global finance as involving a tension between fluid anonymous markets and centralized, hierarchical competitive states – is relevant to the theme of democracy and global finance for a number of reasons. Recognizing the role of social institutions and practices highlights much more accurately the way in which both financial transactions and global public policy are carried out, and this helps draw out the issues that should be discussed, as well as expanding the range of feasible policies. An extreme case of the negative consequences of an elitist approach that ignored the role of social institutions is the disastrous reform and exposure to globalization of Russian finance, discussed in chapter 8. Similarly, the common and dangerous assumption that global finance cannot be regulated is usually based on a serious underestimation of the emergence of a complex set of governance networks, an emerging *regime* for global financial regulation, as discussed in chapter 3. Such an assumption prematurely rules out policy options that should be explored in debates about global finance.

The rest of the chapter develops these points more fully, looking first at the lessons about social practices to be drawn from other chapters, then at the problem of democracy and legitimacy in global finance, and finally at lessons to be drawn about the future of global finance.

Global Finance and Social Institutions and Practices

Chapter 2 presented an emphasis on institutions and practices in understanding global finance as an alternative to prevailing market-oriented, state-centric, and critical approaches. It argued that social institutions and practices constitute a form of formal or informal rule-governed behaviors that can be more decentralized than states, but more organized than fluid anonymous markets. It suggested that these institutions and practices play an important part in the structuring and regulation of global finance.

The evolution of the regime for global financial regulation discussed in chapter 3 provides support for this emphasis on institutions and practices. Over the past quarter-century there has been a set of progressively more complex and capable institutions constructed at the global level to help regulate private-sector financial flows. These generally took the form of expert committees whose technically focused work gradually grew into more formalized and linked collaborative arrangements, both at the individual committee level, as with the Basel Committee's progression from its early agreements to today's far more complex ongoing revisions of the Basel Capital Accord, and in the ties between groupings, as with the way in which the Financial Stability Forum, created in 1999, drew together in its membership representatives from the main bodies concerned with global financial regulation.

This history challenges both the idea that the fluidity and anonymity of global financial markets make them impossible to regulate and the alternative frequent assumption that powerful competitive states, and perhaps formal intergovernmental organizations such as the IMF, are the only relevant actors for understanding the regulation of global finance. Instead, the emerging regime for international financial regulation relies a great deal on the shared understandings among regulators engaged in decentralized rule making. While some of these rules draw on the enforcement capacities of states, all enhance their authority by being seen as a guide to future best practices and by summing up past best practices: a reflexive process in which regulators and other standards-setters are constantly examining and adjusting the practices in which they and the regulated firms are engaged.

The account of international bank regulation in chapter 4 provides further evidence of the role of social institutions and practices. The bank regulations developed by the Basel Committee have involved an ever-increasing reliance by regulators on the internal organization of banks and on financial market practices, most evident in the revised Basel Accord's emphasis on the banks' risk management systems. This is increasingly the regulation of self-regulatory processes, instead of direct control or surveillance of the activity that regulators actually want to control. This integration of regulatory practices and financial market practices is very different from the common perception of global finance as consisting primarily of a struggle between two distinct forms of social organization, fluid markets and hierarchical states.

The account of international securities markets in chapter 5 showed that these markets are highly dependent upon complex institutions and social practices. This is evident in the lag between the emergence of international banking and that of international securities markets, because of the latter's greater dependence on complex institutions; in the great difficulty that exchanges have had in developing viable cross-border linkages, in the importance of the organization of exchanges for the functioning of global securities markets, in the role of informal practices in the Eurobond market, and in the way that large new markets can grow out of the creative financial practices of financial firms. Similarly, as discussed in chapter 6, the importance of the organizational character of the multinational firm for explaining foreign direct investment, the role of a sequence of bilateral and other investment treaties in establishing new practices with regard to the treatment of MNCs, and the differences in the volatility of direct foreign investment relative to portfolio flows all point to the density and significance of the social institutions involved in global financial markets.

The discussion in chapters 7 and 9 of two types of non-governmental organization, business associations and civil society organizations, provided further examples of the importance of social institutions and practices. Chapter 7 showed that there are a great many forms of business organization and rule making that are important in global finance, ranging from informal business practices through formal standard-setting bodies. It also argued that the many types of interactions between public-sector and private-sector institutions were more important than the rule-making and enforcement capacity of organized business alone. Thus there is a dense and varied range of private-sector business institutions and practices that organize global finance. The development of civil society organizations in global finance also reflects the importance of social institutions. Contrary to the tendency to see global civil society as an expression of globalization or late modernity in general, the case of global finance shows that civil society's role varies greatly across issue areas, tends to respond to the organized initiatives of states rather than spontaneously emerging everywhere, and tends to build on existing related practices, such as environmentalism or the anti-free trade movement, rather than starting afresh when a new issue area emerges.

The importance of social institutions and practices in the relationship of the developing countries to the global financial system, discussed in chapter 8, was evident in the differences between the debt crisis of the early 1980s, centered on bank lending, and the global crises of the 1990s, in which securities markets played a key role. While both these periods involved crises in global finance, the differences in the practices and organization of the cross-border flows were important. The crisis of bank lending in the 1980s was managed by commercial banks working closely with their Institute of International Finance, the IMF, and the US government, and developing countries had little role to play in shaping the response that emerged, and instead simply had to adjust to the policies developed by more powerful actors. The focus was on getting developing country governments to adjust their macro-economic policies. In contrast, the crises of the 1990s involved much more dispersed financial flows, and accordingly, the solutions proposed asked the developing country governments to reform their domestic financial regulation and corporate governance. This more complex and decentralized project required more active participation by developing countries in coming up with solutions to the problems and, through both the G20 and more *ad hoc* arrangements, steps were taken to bring about this participation.

Chapters 10 and 11 highlight the role of two specific types of practices important in global finance: gendered practices and risk practices. Neither of these can be understood with reference to centralized states or fluid market forces alone. The effects of gender permeate the system as a whole, from the most micro-level discriminatory practices in particular financial firms, through a systemic propensity to encourage excessively risky behavior and to undervalue non-monetary contributions to human well-being. Risk practices also operate in decentralized fashion, through the application of rules and models in ways that shape the conduct of individual investors and firms as well as the evolution of the system as a whole.

Overall, then, the globalization of finance has involved much more than the overwhelming of states by anonymous fluid financial markets. It has been carried out by a vast expansion of institutions and practices that have provided sets of rules and stabilized expectations, drawing vast networks of public- and private-sector actors into patterns of shared understandings and collaborative activities. Many of the features of globalization and post- or late modernity that have been highlighted by social theorists are evident in this: the emphasis on self-regulation and the entanglement of power and knowledge of Foucault, the reflexivity and the ways in which actors reproduce rules by using them highlighted by Giddens's concept of structuration, and the way in which risk disrupts centralized forms of political power and scientific discourse, as discussed by Beck. Both problems and solutions in global finance increasingly involve an engagement in these vast networks rather than a dismantling or strengthening of the state's capacity to control the entry or exit of financial flows at the border.

Democracy and Legitimacy

There has been a great deal of debate about the relationship between globalization and democracy. On the one hand, many fear that globalization will undermine democracy, by shifting decision making to international institutions that are more remote from citizens, by undermining the state, the traditional locus of democratic decision making, or by enhancing the power of MNCs or markets at the expense of citizens. On the other hand, many have seen globalization as enhancing democracy, by bringing new forms of *cosmopolitan* democracy at the global level, by providing new opportunities for citizen initiatives through global civil society, or by creating new types of pressures from markets or international institutions to hold poorly run states accountable to perform in ways that support democracy.

As noted in chapter 2, these types of debates have been evident in global finance, just as they are in discussions about globalization more generally. Some have seen the constraints imposed on states by global financial markets or international financial institutions as making the leaders of those states more accountable to standards of performance that are associated with democracy. For instance, the transparency increasingly demanded by global investors or by the IMF can help citizens better control their own governments. On the other hand, financial policies or financial market pressures developed at the global level can themselves lack transparency, relying heavily on elitist, exclusive decision-making processes that the average citizen has little chance of influencing, or even understanding.

Global finance differs from some other global issue areas because the democratic deficit created by a shift of decision making to a more remote global policy process has been exacerbated by the exclusivity of the highly technical language and concepts with which policy discussions are carried out and by the disproportionate influence of business associations and dominant international firms relative to global civil society or national citizenries. Thus the benefits for democracy of globalization for this issue area as compared to others, like human rights, are much smaller, and are outweighed to a greater degree by the negative effects of globalization. The prominent roles of technical and private-sector authority in global finance not only exclude those who are not technical experts or business actors, but also narrow the range of issues that can be considered, taking off the agenda large-scale questions about the relationship of the globalization of finance to social inequality, or about the distribution of risks that exceed the capacity of markets to handle.

Many of these larger issues involve questions about our tolerance of risk, or about the ethics of risk distribution, that cannot be resolved by technical risk models or by claiming that these risks are a private matter to be worked out by those involved. Large issues of this kind are best addressed through democratic public deliberation. Such deliberation requires participants to justify their claims with reference not to self-interest, but to shared social and ethical norms, a process that is similar, but much broader than, the technical deliberation that characterizes most current policymaking in global finance.

Traditionally, democratic deliberation has relied upon constitutions, legislatures, voting, and other democratic practices that have been built into national states, and finding functional equivalents to these at the global level is difficult. Even at the domestic level, the relevance of traditional formal democratic procedures has been challenged by the complexity of technical systems (Schmidt and Werle, 1998), leading to fears that these procedures will be subverted by scientists, bureaucrats, and other experts, by the disproportionate influence of business actors, and by voter apathy, a sign that citizens do not find traditional formal procedures to be sufficiently meaningful to deserve their attention. As noted above, at the global level all these problems are more severe, and in place of the stable foundation of the nation-state for domestic democratic procedures, a system has evolved of competitive states zealously guarding their own sovereignty, regarding collaborative arrangements with other states with suspicion.

Some democratic theorists, most notably David Held, have sketched out fairly elaborate institutional arrangements that could support cosmopolitan democracy at the global level. While some aspects of these offer some support for their feasibility, such as the growth of cosmopolitan law – global law that references citizens directly instead of states – in general such elaborate plans have tended to fail, and instead more decentralized collaborative arrangements among states, such as the *international regimes* discussed in chapter 3, have seemed to offer more promise of success, at least in the foreseeable future. Regimes are more flexible, less costly, and pose less of a threat to sovereign states.

It is useful to develop some criteria that can be used in assessing the quality of deliberative democracy in the complex emerging polity that characterizes contemporary global governance. Coleman and Porter (2000), drawing on the work of others, have proposed six such criteria: (1) transparency, (2) openness to direct participation, (3) quality of discourse (substantive debate versus empty rhetoric), (4) representation, (5) effectiveness (citizens' interests can be addressed if institutions lack the capacity to carry out the policies they choose), and (6) fairness (the adequacy of rules about rule making). These types of generic criteria can be applied to a very wide variety of policy processes, ranging from traditional national formal democratic processes to complex trans-border technical networks involving both public- and private-sector actors.

Chapter 7 on business associations, chapter 8 on developing and transition countries, chapter 9 on NGOs, and chapter 10 on gender all provide lessons about the degree to which global finance exhibits characteristics matching the above generic measures of democracy. In each case progress has been made, but much more is needed.

In the case of business associations, interest in their capacity to hold public-sector officials accountable to their members must be balanced against the danger that they will "capture" policy processes at the expense of the broader public. Chapter 7 showed that there has been a substantial increase in the capacity of private-sector associations in global finance, and that their members are better represented in global policy processes than would have been the case had this increase in capacity not occurred. However, chapter 7 also showed that, much like the civil society organizations discussed in chapter 9, business associations remain weaker at the global level than is often assumed. There are no significant cases of private-sector rule making and enforcement at the global level that do not rely to some degree on public-sector institutions. Just as interesting as the private-sector role in self-regulation is the relationship between public- and private-sector rules and institutions. While in some cases it has raised fears of "capture," this relationship can also provide public-sector actors and institutions with a form of leverage over private-sector actors, extending the reach and effectiveness of public-sector rules, and offering some hope that private-sector practices can more effectively be made compatible with the wider global public interest.

Chapters 8, 9, and 10 showed substantial progress in the incorporation of developing countries, civil society, and women in global finance. For instance, developing and transition countries have been drawn more fully into consultations at the Basel Committee on Banking Supervision, and the creation of the G20 in 1999 was a step forward in providing a mechanism for them to participate at a high level in policy deliberations about the direction to be taken in the governance of global finance. The Bretton Woods institutions have consulted civil society more carefully and have altered their policies in significant ways. Civil society has slowly begun to develop the capacity to engage those who have dominated global policy processes in debates about the governance of private-sector finance. In the case of micro-financing, civil society organizations have directly involved themselves in private-sector finance, seeking especially to benefit poor women in developing countries. Women have been drawn into global financial firms in ever increasing numbers, and gender-based analyses are engaging with the traditional public-sector actors and economic analysis in significant new ways.

Despite this progress, there are still serious deficiencies in the degree of democracy in global finance experienced by developing and transition countries, civil society, and women. The Basel consultations have mainly involved existing leading actors in international banking, and thus it is not surprising that the proposed revisions of the Basel Capital Accord are being criticized for favoring firms headquartered in the most developed markets. The G20 remains much weaker than the industrialized countries' G7 – for instance, in not meeting at the heads-of-government level. Despite progress, civil society enjoys only a weak presence in the new areas of governance of global private-sector financial flows. Women remain severely under-represented in the upper echelons of global finance, and the problematic distribution and quantity of risk to which the gendered character of finance has contributed continues.

Addressing the democratic deficit in global finance will require initiative from a variety of actors. Public-sector actors need to expand the range of conceptual approaches and actors they consult in considering their role in global finance, opening up excessively exclusive policy networks and discourses. Highly technical approaches have been attractive to these public-sector actors, because they appear to offer pragmatic effective solutions while avoiding the wasteful rhetoric and conflict that often characterizes more politicized international negotiations. However, this has come at the price of lack of ability to mobilize political support for useful measures that are currently kept off the agenda because they seem too costly or are too heavily opposed by influential financial firms. For instance, the idea of "private-sector burden sharing," which proposes to create legal mechanisms so that investors do not impose costs of crises that they should bear on others, is consistent with the economic logic used by international regulators and would offer a way of stabilizing the financial system without relying on costly public-sector bail-outs – but so far the political will has not been mobilized to bring this idea to fruition.

Private-sector actors need to take more responsibility for the global financial architecture than they do at present, but in a way that links their favored policies to principles that have more generalized validity than ones that are to the benefit of a small number of leading firms that typically dominate industry associations. A positive example is the concern of the World Federation of Exchanges to strengthen standards to foster confidence in the markets in general, despite the tendency of unregulated exchanges to free-ride on the regulatory and institution-building efforts of the WFE and its members. With some notable exceptions, such as the WFE and the International Accounting Standards Board, the contribution of private-sector actors to the governance of global finance is surprisingly weak. If the private sector does not take a more active role in broad-ranging debates about the future of the global financial system, then it will find either that solutions it might not have chosen will be imposed on it or trust in the benefits of global financial markets will evaporate. The active engagement of the chemical and forestry industries with sustainability and other environmental issues is an example of how other risk-intensive industries have begun to do this.

Civil society actors also need to engage in more meaningful dialogue with the approaches, issues, and actors that currently dominate the policy process in global financial governance. This does not mean blunting their criticisms, but rather sharpening them by homing in on the practical mechanisms and subtle but dangerous and exploitative abuses that are at the leading edge of the developing infrastructure for financial policy and market transactions, and that can determine the future direction of this development. Civil society is not strong enough on its own to successfully oppose public-sector and private-sector actors. Even if street protests have been important in allowing civil society to gain the attention of policymakers and the general public, mobilizing effective broad political support requires showing that a favored policy – such as a restriction on capital mobility – can be framed in ways that make sense beyond the immediate supporters and members of a particular civil society organization.

All the above initiatives point to the need for further increases, at the global level, of the type of deliberation that is at the heart of democracy.

The Future of Global Finance

The globalization of finance is emblematic of globalization more generally, and thus drawing implications for its future development from its development to this point has relevance beyond the concerns of those most directly involved in it. At the same time, the experience of globalization in other issue areas can provide lessons and signposts for the future development of global finance.

Like globalization more generally, the globalization of finance has been both hugely beneficial and hugely costly. These costs and benefits have been distributed very unevenly, which accounts for much of the conflict and debate associated with this issue area. The heavy focus of liberal economic theory on the aggregated balance sheet in seeking to add up the costs and benefits of global finance is problematic. Even if that balance sheet could be shown to be positive, this would fail to address the greater hardship experienced by a poor person thrown out of their $1,000 a year job as a consequence of uncontrolled financial risk, as compared to the bond-trader who makes an extra $1,000 from a skillful speculation on a price change, for whom that $1,000 accounts for a small fraction of a six-figure annual income. This distributional problem is political and ethical rather than economic. Moreover, as noted especially in chapter 10 with regard to gender, not only is the distribution of risk problematic, but the total amount of risk associated with global finance, as with globalization more generally, is higher than optimal.

Turning back the clock and eliminating globalization, both in finance and more generally, is neither feasible nor desirable, not because it is driven by forces beyond human control, but because it is likely that more people, and especially people with money and influence, will favor trying to harness global finance rather than killing it. As Harmes (2001, p. 103) has noted, a "mass investment culture" has expanded along with global finance, as for instance in the increase in the proportion of US households with a share in the stock market from 3 percent before the 1929 crash to over 50 percent in the late 1990s.

The globalization of finance brings three main potential overlapping benefits if its negative effects can be controlled better: its ability to transfer resources, its organizational properties, and its ability to reallocate risk. It is worth looking briefly at each in turn.

The potential benefit of global finance is its capacity to allow those in need of financial resources to borrow these resources from those who have more than they wish to use at present. If they are wisely used, these borrowed resources can be used to meet needs, such as for physical or social infrastructure or the creation of new industries, that can generate more than enough growth to return the financial resource along with the interest or other fee that those providing it have charged. At the global level, the aging of the population in the wealthy industrialized countries, and this population's need to save, along with the younger population in the developing countries, with their great need for development of infrastructure and industry, means that the potential for mutually beneficial cross-border financial flows will remain high in the foreseeable future (Dobson and Hufbauer, 2001).

This beneficial aspect of global finance should not be exaggerated: it is often outweighed by global finance's negative effects. Moreover, this type of financial transaction does nothing to address the ethical obligation of those with abundant financial resources to help those in need, especially if the abundance and need are connected through some past exploitative relationship or structural deficiency in the global economy. Too often the types of mutually beneficial financial transactions that the globalization of finance is supposed to bring about are treated as a substitute for this ethical obligation, an easy and self-interested way for those with wealth to avoid caring about those without. This negative consequence of the globalization of finance should be taken seriously, but it does not necessarily cancel out the positive potential of cross-border financial transfers described in the previous paragraph.

The second potential benefit of the globalization of finance is organizational. Finance has always involved ways of shaping and stabilizing mutual expectations, and this often involves a type of ongoing mutually beneficial collaboration that is at the heart of social cohesion. Finance has also always involved control, which can be beneficial, as when one increases one's control of the future through insurance, or which can involve negative effects, as when powerful actors abuse their financial control and engage in fraudulent or exploitative activities.

Control mechanisms in finance are enormously varied, including accountancy, financial planning, budgeting, contracts, price signals, the exercise and transfer of ownership rights associated with capital, and the attachment of conditions to lending. In fast-moving, complex global economies, the organizational capacities of finance can be important and beneficial in helping to organize resources and people. However, as in all forms of organization and control, there is no guarantee that the organizational features of global finance will bring good things. Whether they do depends crucially upon the accompanying levels of accountability, openness, equality, and other conditions that we associate with democracy.

The third potential benefit of global finance is its capacity to reallocate risk in useful ways. As discussed in chapter 10, the arbitrary distribution and excessive growth of risks is a prominent and problematic feature of our contemporary world, to which global finance has contributed greatly. At the same time, the potential contribution of global finance to better controlling risks should not be overlooked. Insurance, with its socialization of risk, is an obvious example; but even derivatives, which have been associated with some of the most destructive aspects of global finance, if properly regulated, can usefully shift risks, from those who don't want them to those who do, for a price. While gender-based and other critiques of excessive and harmful levels of systemic risk in global finance are very important and should be acted upon, not all the increased risk taking in our globalized late-modern world is problematic – some of it comes with the restless change that brings benefits as well as costs.

What can be done to assure that the many negative effects of global finance do not outweigh its benefits? While measurement problems make it impossible to know conclusively whether overall poverty and inequality have been decreasing or increasing with globalization (IMF, 2002), there is widespread agreement that China's experience weighs heavily on the positive side of the balance sheet, and that experience is a story of careful, controlled integration with global finance. There is also widespread agreement that behind the aggregate figures there are large numbers of people whose lives have become more precarious and impoverished. This has occurred at the same time as others have been able to take advantage of their connections to global finance to vastly increase their wealth. Poverty, inequality, and arbitrary and unequal exposure to harmful risks are likely to continue to be severe problems if mechanisms are not developed to strengthen the institutions that both make and manage the rules associated with global finance and facilitate democratic deliberation about the political issues relevant to global finance that were identified above.

This book has highlighted the importance of complex social institutions and practices in the governance of finance, and this chapter has emphasized the importance in general of democracy; but there are many specific initiatives that would be useful. Critics of global finance, in making proposals for change, have focused especially on the Tobin tax and capital controls, and while these are ideas worth pursuing, there are many other measures that deserve consideration as well. For instance:

- Proposals for "bailing in" the private sector in times of crisis through the use of "standstills" on outward financial flows would shift the costs more fairly to the private sector by creating legal and political mechanisms for preventing a catastrophic race for the exit.

- The Basel Capital Adequacy standards helped in imposing more of the costs of excessively risky behavior on holders of bank capital, and its deficiencies, such as the lax treatment of short-term lending which was a major contributor to the East Asian crisis of 1997–8, should be corrected.
- The increased international sensitivity to the importance of the sequencing and pace of financial globalization should be further developed, and the reckless, self-interested badgering of government by financial firms seeking to open financial markets should be subjected to critical scrutiny.
- The formal mechanisms for reconciling prudential regulation and trade liberalization, such as the vague "prudential carve-out" in the NAFTA and WTO agreements, should be strengthened, a task that is currently being left largely to the Working Party on Domestic Regulation at the WTO, which only public-sector and business actors follow.
- The destructive effects of hedge funds can be reined in, either by regulating them directly or by regulating the banks on whose loans they depend.

These types of change require an engagement with, and a strengthening of, the emerging regime for financial regulation, as well as an imaginative and careful use of the social institutions and practices that constitute global finance.

While such practical initiatives are very important, just as important is an insistence that finance be kept in its place in our conceptions of our globalized world. A defining property of globalization is our shared awareness of the world and our connection to it. Globalization both creates and is created by this awareness, and each of our parts in reproducing this shared awareness helps shape globalization's future. During the 1980s and early 1990s financial globalization seemed mysterious, explosive, exhilarating, and frightening, and came to play a massive, extravagant role in our collective imaginations, as well as our practical experience. Vast areas of life were subordinated to financial technologies, evaluative assessments, and risks. The challenge of globalization has always been to untangle its benefits from its costs, to offset its aggressive momentum with a careful preservation of the values it threatens to destroy. Finance has its place, but the human experience cannot be reduced to numbers. Awe of global finance has been replaced by a healthy caution and skepticism in the wake of our awareness of the persistent dangers of global financial crises. Our challenge now is to build on what we have learned, to do what we can to make sure finance plays the part we want it to play in the globalized world we are building, rather than periodically leaving vast swathes of destruction or a less dramatic but equally troubling incremental flattening of our imaginations, where non-financial values fade amidst the froth of financial turbulence and the harsh linearity of financial technologies of control.

Notes

Chapter 1   Introduction: Why Study Global Finance?

1   For a definitive assessment of globalization, with some excellent measures of financial globalization, see Held et al., 1999.
2   For a more extensive discussion, see Held et al., 1999, pp. 216–20; Herring and Litan, 1995, ch. 2.

Chapter 2   Debates and Controversies in the Conceptualization of Global Finance

1   Consolidated cross-border claims in all currencies and local claims in non-local currencies. Data from <www.bis.org>.

Chapter 3   The Emerging Regime for Regulating Global Finance

1   An exception is some forms of insurance, such as that managed by Lloyds. Lloyds is discussed in chapter 7.
2   For information on the G7/G8 see <www.g8.utoronto.ca>, especially the work by John Kirton.
3   G20 members include the G7 plus Argentina, Australia, Brazil, China, India, Indonesia, Mexico, Russia, Saudi Arabia, South Africa, Korea, Turkey, and the European Union.

Chapter 4 International Banking

1 Data and information on the HIPC initiative is available at <www.worldbank.org>. For a critical view, see Shah, 2001.

Chapter 5 The Governance of Global Securities and Derivatives Markets

1 Unless otherwise noted, data in this paragraph and the next are from <www.bis.org>. World output is gross domestic product, current prices, from <www.imf.org>.
2 The first figure is notional amounts outstanding of OTC (Over the Counter) foreign exchange derivatives net of inter-dealer double counting by instrument, counter-party, and currency at the end of June 2003. The second figure is the outstanding value of all types of futures and options, over the counter and on organized exchanges, from June 2003. Data in this paragraph are from <www.bis.org>.
3 World Federation of Exchanges (WFE) data based on its member exchanges.

Chapter 6 Foreign Direct Investment

1 Unless otherwise stated, data are from the United Nations Conference on Trade and Development (2003).
2 "Pressure eased on NAFTA governments over investor protection," *Financial Times* (London), August 2, 2001, p. 7; "Canada seeks narrowing of NAFTA lawsuit terms," *National Post*, October 22, 2002, p. FP10.

Chapter 7 Business Institutions and Private-Sector Norms

1 This label was coined in Cutler, Haufler, and Porter, 1999, and the eight categories discussed here draw on that work as well.
2 Much of the discussion of private-sector associations in this section appears also in Porter, 2002a, and has been submitted for publication in a chapter of a book on public policy and financial services by McGill–Queen's Press scheduled to appear in Fall, 2004.
3 See <financialservices.house.gov/banking/3399coth.htm>.
4 See, for example, <www.publicampaign.org/publications/studies/goldenleashes/hollings.htm>.

Chapter 8   Developing and Transition Countries

1   Data in this paragraph are from Armijo, 1999, p. 6.
2   See, for instance, Armijo, 1999; Blustein, 2001; Dobson and Hufbauer, 2001; Eichengreen, 1999; Glick, Moreno, and Spiegel, 2001; Goldstein, 1998; Haggard, 2000; Lukauskas and Rivera-Batiz, 2001; Pempel, 1999; Soros, 1998; Underhill and Zhang, 2003.
3   For useful analysis of the Russian financial problems, see Benn, 2001, and the books he reviews: Johnson, 2000; Stiglitz, 1999, and Westin, 2001.
4   This chapter's discussion of China draws on an unpublished research report prepared for the author by Lan Zhang (2002) on China's financial integration, which in turn drew on the English- and Chinese-language literatures. Interviews with regulators in Hong Kong were also helpful. In addition to the references in the text, the following are useful sources that have also been drawn upon: press releases of the People's Bank of China at <www.pbc.gov.cn>; *People's Daily Online* at <english.peopledaily.com.cn>; BIS, 1999; Chen, Dietrich, and Fang, 2000; Feeney, 1994; Lampton, 2001; Norton, 1998; OECD, 2002; Shi, n.d.
5   This paragraph is based on Zhang, 2002.
6   The Centro de Estudios Monetarios Latinoamericanos (CEMLA) is a research, information-sharing, and training institute set up by Latin American central bankers in 1952. However, it was not involved in regulatory matters until 1982, when it began to provide the secretariat for a regional group of bank supervisors which would become the Association of Banking Supervisory Authorities of Latin America and the Caribbean in 1991 (<www.cemla.org>).
7   An example of this dispersion of banking is that the worldwide operations of banks headquartered in the USA accounted for 8.7 percent of the external positions of all BIS reporting banks in 1983, but only 1.5 percent in 1998. Its share increased sharply after the 1997–8 crisis, however, to over 4 percent in 2001, before dropping to 2.9 percent in 2003 (calculated from BIS data available at <www.bis.org>).
8   "Asia Faces a Stark Choice," *Far Eastern Economic Review*, September 25, 2003.

Chapter 9   Non-Governmental Organizations and Global Civil Society

1   For a more extensive discussion of the use of the *Yearbook of International Organizations* as a data source, see Boli and Thomas, 1999, pp. 20–2. In this chapter the 2003 data are based on both the printed

Yearbook and the electronic listing available at <www.uia.org>. This is supplemented by information on organizations available on the internet, where it was not possible to categorize the organization based on the information provided by the *Yearbook* alone.

Chapter 10   Gender and the Globalization of Finance

1   There is debate about the merits of the gender/sex distinction that revolves around a concern not to obscure biological variation that is not captured by a male/female dichotomy, and a concern not to obscure the degree to which biological differences and our understanding of them are socially constructed. See the essays in Ferree, Lorber, and Hess, 1999.

2   Calculated from US Bureau of Labor Statistics, Series Ids CEU5500000001 and CEU5500000002, at <www.bls.gov>.

3   US Bureau of Labor Statistics, "Employed persons by detailed occupation, sex, race and Hispanic origin," at <www.bls.gov/cps>. 1970 figure from Wirth, 2001, p. 42.

4   Based on list at <www.federalreserve.gov/bios/1199member.pdf>.

5   Based on list at SEC Commissioners, <http://www.sec.gov/about/concise.shtml#history>.

6   "ABA Elects New Board for 2002–2003," ABA news release, at <www.aba.com>.

7   Listing at <www.sia.com>.

8   All data in this paragraph are from Statistics Canada, as compiled by Gunderson, 1998, pp. 96, 141, 165, 168, 169.

9   <www.boj.or.jp/en/about/about_f.htm>.

10   <www.zenginkyo.or.jp/en/abstract/ board/abstract0300.html>.

11   <www.adb.org/Documents/Fact_Sheets/JPN.asp>.

12   "Japan: Bank of Merit", *Asiaweek.com*, July 13, 2001.

13   Romania, Georgia, Croatia, Slovakia, Poland, Russia, Hungary, and the Czech Republic.

14   These are the author's calculations, based on data in the *Yearbook of Labour Statistics*, 61st edn, (Geneva: International Labour Organization, 2002), Table 2B: Total employment by economic activity. Only those countries reporting ISIC 3 data for the mid- and late 1990s were included, in order to make comparison possible. Data for the year closest to 1995 and 2000 were selected, except for countries reporting from 1997 to 2001 only, in which case the end points of this reporting period were used.

15   Women's Environment and Development Organization, n.d.

16   <www.bis.org/about/index.htm>.

17   <www.iosco.org>.

18   On the Marten's–Smith Barney case, see "Lowering the Boom: Brokers'

6-year Fight vs. Office Sex Abuse," *New York Post*, November 17, 2002, p. 17; "Whistle-Blower's Grim Tale: Naughty Boys on Wall Street," *Financial Observer*, December 2, 2002, p. 11; "Smith Barney's Woman Problem," *Business Week*, June 3, 1996; "Speaking Truth to Citi's Power: Interviews with Citi's Critics," *Multinational Monitor*, 23 (4), April 2002; and the court decisions such as *Martens et al. v. Smith Barney*, decided June 28, 1998, or *Martens v. Smith Barney*, decided May 15, 2000, both United States District Court for the Southern District of New York, available through LexisNexis.

19 See, for instance, <www.womenonwall.com>, which comments on suits against Morgan Stanley and Merrill Lynch.

20 For a report on Catalyst's *Women in Canadian Investment Dealers* study, see "Challenges for Women in Finance," *Canadian HR Reporter*, July 16, 2001, Proquest version. A survey by the Financial Women's Association confirmed the Catalyst findings, including with regard to the slow pace of change. See Mollison, 2002. For an account of the situation in London see McDowell and Court, 1994. The US Securities Industry Association created a Diversity Committee in 1996 and initiated industry-wide diversity surveys, in 1999 and 2001, produced by Catalyst, which showed some improvement over time. See "Survey Shows Increased Securities Industry Commitment to Diversity," SIA press release, November 8, 2001, at <www.sia.com>.

21 For instance, Barclay's bank (2001) produced a report entitled "Women in Business – The Barriers Start to Fall," which noted that women entrepreneurs were responsible for a third of all business start-ups, an increase of 22 percent from four years previous.

22 This is not intended to suggest that all men or all women exhibit attitudes and behaviors associated with prevailing images of masculinity and femininity respectively.

23 For a summary of the studies, see Barber and Odean, 2001, p. 285.

24 Quoted in McDowell and Court, 1994, p. 1412.

25 See Women's Environment and Development Organization, 2001.

26 See World Bank, 2002, pp. xii, 32, 59. By 2000, eight countries had completed Country Gender Assessments. For a thorough and and more critical assessment, see O'Brien, Goetz, Scholte, and Williams, 2000, ch. 2.

27 Empirical evidence on the relationship between SAPs and the feminization and worsening income distribution in the economies subject to them is reported in Çağatay and Özler, 1995. They identify a U-shaped pattern in which women's participation first declines then increases as countries develop economically.

28 For a useful analysis of the gendered character of neoclassical economics and SAPs, see Sparr, 1994, p. 16, who notes: "Policy-makers have assumed that women's unpaid domestic work is infinitely flexible and free – regardless of how resources are allocated. Obviously this is not true."

29   The paragraph draws on the collection of essays in "Financing for Development: Women Challenging Globalization," at <www.wedo.org>.

30   The 1995 Platform for Action that came out of the conference called for "scaling-up of institutions dedicated to promoting women's entrepreneurship, including, as appropriate, non-traditional and mutual credit schemes, as well as innovative linkages with financial institutions" (paragraph 166a), and "expand[ing] women's access to financial markets by identifying and encouraging financial supervisory and regulatory reforms that support financial institutions' direct and indirect efforts to better meet the credit and other financial needs of the micro, small and medium-scale enterprises of women" (paragraph 167c), at <www.un.org/womenwatch/daw/beijing/platform/economy.htm>. Women's World Banking led three UN Expert Groups on micro-financing in preparation for the conference, and brought together 100 financial leaders at a Global Policy Forum in April 1995. See <www.swwb.org/English/pdf/wwb%20Global.pdf>.

31   Accurately assessing the impact of micro-financing is difficult. For a quantitative study that finds it to have a positive effect on women's empowerment, see Amin, Becker, and Bayes, 1998. However, it is possible that it was women's empowerment that led them to engage more in micro-financing.

Chapter 11   Risk Politics and Financial Crises

1   On risk and politics, see also Douglas, 1992; Luhmann, 1993; Nelkin, 1992; Winner, 1977.

Chapter 12   Democracy and Legitimacy in the Governance of Global Finance

1   For instance, the Chair of the Basel Committee commented: "In developing the Core Principles, the Committee sought to craft a document that would have the legitimacy, quality, and flexibility to meet the needs of bank supervisors around the world" (McDonough, 1999). See also comments by Martin (1999), who would become Chair of the G20.

References

Abu-Lughod, Janet L. (1989) *Before European Hegemony: The World System A.D. 1250–1350* (New York: Oxford University Press).

Adler, Nancy J. (1993) "Competitive Frontiers: Women Managers in the Triad," *International Studies of Management and Organization*, 23 (2), Summer, pp. 3–23.

Aggarwal, Reena (2002) "Demutualization and Corporate Governance of Stock Exchanges," *Journal of Applied Corporate Finance*, 15 (1), Spring, pp. 105–13.

Altvater, Elmar, and Birgit Mahnkopf (1997) "The World Market Unbound," *Review of International Political Economy*, 4 (3), Autumn, pp. 448–71.

Amin, Ruhul, Stan Becker, and Abdul Bayes (1998) "NGO-Promoted Microcredit Programs and Women's Empowerment in Rural Bangladesh: Quantitative and Qualitative Evidence," *Journal of Developing Areas*, 32 (2), Winter, pp. 221–36.

Anderson, Benedict (1991) *Imagined Communities: Reflections on the Origin and Spread of Nationalism*, rev. edn (London: Verso).

Andrews, David M. (1989) "Capital Mobility and State Autonomy: Toward a Structural Theory of International Monetary Relations," *International Studies Quarterly*, 83, pp. 193–218.

Armijo, Leslie Elliott, ed. (1999) *Financial Globalization and Democracy in Emerging Markets* (Basingstoke: Macmillan).

Arrighi, Giovanni (1994) *The Long Twentieth Century* (London: Verso).

Aslanbeigui, Nahid, and Gale Summerfield (2000) "The Asian Crisis, Gender and the International Financial Architecture," *Feminist Economics*, 6 (3), November, pp. 81–103.

Baden, Sally (1996) "Gender Issues in Financial Liberalization and Financial Sector Reform," topic paper prepared for Directorate General for

Development (DGVIII) of the European Commission, Bridge Report Number 39, at <www.ids.ac.uk/bridge/reports/re39c.pdf>.

Bakker, Isabelle (2001) "Who Built the Pyramids? Engendering the New International Economic and Financial Architecture," paper prepared for Feminist Political Economy and the Law: Revitalizing the Debate, Conference, March 24, Osgoode Hall Law School.

Bank for International Settlements (1996) *Settlement Risk in Foreign Exchange Transactions*, report prepared by the Committee on Payment and Settlement Systems (Basel: BIS, March).

Bank for International Settlements (1999) *Strengthening the Banking System in China: Issues and Experience* (Basel: BIS).

Bansia, Parveen (2002) "Suffering Under the Weight," *Banker*, 151 (190), December 2, pp. 16–20, available at <www.thebanker.com>.

Barber, Brad M., and Terrance Odean (2001) "Boys will be Boys: Gender, Overconfidence and Common Stock Investment," *Quarterly Journal of Economics*, 1, February, pp. 261–92.

Barclay's Bank (2001) "Women in Business – The Barriers Start to Fall", report at <www.smallbusiness.barclays.co.uk>.

Basel Committee on Banking Supervision (1996) "Amendment to the Capital Accord to Incorporate Market Risks," January, at <www.bis.org>.

Baudrillard, Jean (1993) *The Transparency of Evil: Essays on Extreme Phenomena*, trans. James Benedict (London and New York: Verso).

Bautier, Robert-Henri (1971) *The Economic Development of Medieval Europe* (London: Thames and Hudson).

Beck, Ulrich (1992) *Risk Society: Towards a New Modernity* (London: Sage).

Beck, Ulrich (1999) *World Risk Society* (Cambridge: Polity).

Bello, Walden, Nicola Bullard, and Kamal Malhotra, eds (2000) *Global Finance: New Thinking on Regulating Speculative Markets* (London: Zed Books).

Benería, Lourdes, Maria Floro, Caren Grown, and Martha MacDonald (2000), "Introduction: Globalization and Gender", *Feminist Economics*, 6 (3), November, pp. vii–xviii.

Benn, David Wedgwood (2001) "Review Article: Warm Words and Harsh Advice: A Critique of the West's Role in Russian Reforms," *International Affairs*, 77 (4), pp. 947–55.

Berger, Marguerite (1989) "Giving Women Credit: The Strengths and Limitations of Credit as a Tool for Alleviating Poverty," *World Development*, 17 (7), pp. 1017–32.

Bhagwati, Jagdish (1998) "The Capital Myth," *Foreign Affairs*, 77 (3), May/June, pp. 7–12.

Blustein, Paul (2001) *The Chastening: Inside the Crisis that Rocked the Global Financial System and Humbled the IMF* (New York: Public Affairs).

Boli, John, and George M. Thomas, eds (1999) *Constructing World Culture: International Non-Governmental Organizations since 1875* (Stanford, CA: Stanford University Press).

Braudel, Fernand (1984) *Civilization and Capitalism: Fifteenth to Eighteenth Centuries*, iii: *Perspectives of the World* (New York: Harper and Row).

Buckley, Ross P. (2000) "The Role and Potential of Self-Regulatory Organizations: The Emerging Markets Traders Association from 1990 to 2000," *Stanford Journal of Law, Business and Finance*, 6 (1), Fall, pp. 135–51.

Burchell, Graham, Colin Gordon, and Peter Miller, eds (1991) *The Foucault Effect: Studies in Governmentality* (Chicago: University of Chicago Press).

Çağatay, Nilüfer, and Şule Özler (1995) "Feminization of the Labor Force: The Effects of Long-Term Development and Structural Adjustment," *World Development*, 23 (11), pp. 1883–95.

Catalyst (2001), *Women in Financial Services: The Word on the Street* (New York: Catalyst).

Cerny, Philip G. (2000) "Political Globalization and the Competition State," in Richard Stubbs and Geoffrey R. D. Underhill, eds, *Political Economy and the Changing Global Order*, 2nd edn (Toronto: Oxford University Press), pp. 300–9.

Chancellor, Edward (1999) *Devil Take the Hindmost: A History of Financial Speculation* (New York: Farrar, Straus, Giroux).

Chen, Baizhu, J. Kimball Dietrich, and Yi Fang, eds (2000) *Financial Market Reform in China: Progress, Problems and Prospects* (Boulder, CO: Westview Press).

Cline, W. R. (1995) *International Debt Reexamined* (Washington: Institute for International Economics).

Coleman, William D., and Tony Porter (2000) "International Institutions, Globalisation and Democracy: Assessing the Challenges," *Global Society*, 14 (3), July, pp. 377–98.

Collins, Alexis L. (2002) "Regulation of Alternative Trading Systems: Evolving Regulatory Models and Prospects for Increased Regulatory Coordination and Convergence," *Law and Policy in International Business*, 33, pp. 481–505.

Collinson, Margaret, and David Collinson (1996) " 'It's Only Dick: The Sexual Harassment of Women Managers in Insurance Sales," *Work, Employment and Society*, 10 (1), pp. 29–56.

Cox, Robert W. (2000) "Political Economy and the World Order: Problems of Power and Knowledge at the Turn of the Millennium," in Richard Stubbs and Geoffrey R. D. Underhill, eds, *Political Economy and the Changing Global Order*, 2nd edn (Toronto: Oxford University Press), pp. 25–37.

Crompton, Rosemary, and Nicky Le Feuvre (2001) "Gender, Family and Employment in Comparative Perspective: The Realities and Representations of Equal Opportunities in Britain and France," *Journal of European Social Policy*, 10 (4), pp. 334–48.

Crompton, Rosemary (1989) "Women in Banking: Continuity and Change since the Second World War," *Work, Employment and Society*, 3 (2), pp. 141–56.

Culpeper, Roy (1997) *Titans or Behemoths: The Multilateral Development Banks*, V (Ottawa: North–South Institute; Boulder, CO: Lynne Rienner).

Cutler, A. Claire, Virginia Haufler, and Tony Porter, eds (1999) *Private Authority and International Affairs* (Albany, NY: SUNY Press).

DaCosta, Maria Manuela Neveda, and Jennifer Ping Ngoh Foo (2002) "China's Financial System: Two Decades of Gradual Reforms," *Managerial Finance*, 28 (10), pp. 3–18.

Dávila, Francisco Suárez (1999) "The Developing Countries and the International Financial System: 25 Years of Hope, Frustration, and Some Modest Achievements," in Eduardo Mayobre, ed., *G-24: The Developing Countries in the International Financial System* (Boulder, CO: Lynne Rienner), pp. 3–26.

Defert, Daniel (1991) " 'Popular life' and Insurance Technology," in Graham Burchell, Colin Gordon, and Peter Miller, eds, *The Foucault Effect: Studies in Governmentality* (Chicago: University of Chicago Press), pp. 211–33.

De Goede, Marieke (2000) "Mastering 'Lady Credit': Discourses of Financial Crisis in Historical Perspective," *International Feminist Journal of Politics*, 2 (1), pp. 58–81.

De Goede, Marieke (2001) "Discourses of Scientific Finance and the Failure of Long-Term Capital Management," *New Political Economy*, 6 (2), pp. 149–70.

Dell, Sidney (1990) *The United Nations and International Business* (Durham, NC: Duke University Press/UNITAR).

DeLuca, Dallas (1994) "Trade-Related Investment Measures: US Efforts to Shape a Pro-Business Legal System," *Journal of International Affairs*, 48 (1), Summer, pp. 251–77.

Dobson, Wendy, and Gary Clyde Hufbauer, assisted by Hyun Koo Cho (2001) *World Capital Markets: Challenge to the G-10* (Washington: Institute of International Economics).

Douglas, Mary (1985) *Risk Acceptability according to the Social Sciences* (New York: Russell Sage Foundation).

Douglas, Mary (1992) *Risk and Blame: Essays in Cultural Theory* (London and New York: Routledge).

Dunning, John H. (1988) *Explaining International Production* (London: Unwin Hyman).

Durano, Marina Fe B. (2002), "The Monterrey Consensus: Consolidate Globalisation at the Expense of Women," *Social Watch*, p. 68, at <www.socialwatch.org/en/informeImpreso/pdfs/themonterrey2002_eng.pdf>.

Eichengreen, Barry (1999) *Toward a New International Financial Architecture: A Practical Post-Asia Agenda* (Washington: Institute for International Economics).

Eichengreen, Barry, James Tobin, and Charles Wyplosz (1995) "Two Cases for Sand in the Wheels of International Finance," *Economic Journal*, 105 (428), pp. 162–72.

Elson, Diane (1999) "Labor Markets as Gendered Institutions: Equality, Efficiency and Empowerment Issues," *World Development*, 27 (3), pp. 611–27.

Elson, Diane (2001) "International Financial Architecture: A View from the Kitchen," paper presented to the International Studies Association Annual Conference, Chicago, February.

Enloe, Cynthia H. (1990) *Bananas, Beaches and Bases: Making Feminist Sense of International Politics* (Berkeley: University of California Press).

Ewald, François (1991) "Insurance and Risk," in Graham Burchell, Colin Gordon, and Peter Miller, eds, *The Foucault Effect: Studies in Governmentality* (Chicago: University of Chicago Press), pp. 197–210.

Feeney, William R. (1994) "China and the Multilateral Economic Institutions," in Samuel S. Kim, ed., *China and the World: Chinese Foreign Relations in the Post-Cold War Era* (Boulder, CO: Westview Press), pp. 226–51.

Fennema, Meindert, and Kees van der Pijl (1987) "International Bank Capital and the New Liberalism," in Mark S. Mizruchi and Michael Schwartz, eds, *Intercorporate Relations* (New York: Cambridge University Press), pp. 298–317.

Ferree, Myra Marx, Judith Lorber, and Beth B. Hess (1999) *Revisioning Gender* (Thousand Oaks, CA: Sage Publications).

Financial Stability Forum (2000) Report of the Working Group on Highly Leveraged Institutions, 5 April, at <www.fsforum.org>.

Flax, Jane (1990) *Thinking Fragments: Psychoanalysis, Feminism and Postmodernism in the Contemporary West* (Berkeley: University of California Press).

Fligstein, Neil (1990) *The Transformation of Corporate Control* (Cambridge, MA: Harvard University Press).

Floro, Maria Sagrario (1995), "Economic Restructuring, Gender, and the Allocation of Time," *World Development*, 23 (11), pp. 1913–29.

Floro, Maria Sagrario (2001) "Gender Dimensions of the Financing for Development Agenda," Working Paper prepared for the United Nations Development Fund for Women in preparation for the 2002 UN Conference on Financing for Development.

Floro, Maria Sagrario, and Gary Dymski (2000) "Financial Crisis, Gender and Power: An Analytical Framework," *World Development*, 28 (7), pp. 1269–83.

Folgerø, Ignebjørg, and Ingrid H. Fjeldstad (1995) "On Duty – Off Guard: Cultural Norms and Sexual Harassment in Service Organizations," *Organization Studies*, 16 (2), pp. 299–313.

Francisco, Josefa (Gigi), and Gita Sen (2000) "The Asian Crisis: Globalization and Patriarchy in Symbiosis," February, at <www.socialwatch. org/2000/eng/thematicreports/theasiancrisis_eng.htm>.

Froud, Julie, Sukhdev Johal, and Karel Williams (2002) "Financialisation and the Coupon Pool", *Capital and Class*, 78, Autumn, pp. 119–39.

Germain, Randall (1997) *The International Organization of Credit: States and Global Finance in the World-Economy* (Cambridge: Cambridge University Press).

Giddens, Anthony (1990) *The Consequences of Modernity* (Cambridge: Polity).

Giddens, Anthony (1991) *Modernity and Self-Identity: Self and Society in the Late Modern Age* (Cambridge: Polity).

Gill, Stephen (1990) *American Hegemony and the Trilateral Commission* (Cambridge: Cambridge University Press).

Gill, Stephen (2003) *Power and Resistance in the New World Order* (Basingstoke: Palgrave).

Gill, Stephen, and David Law (1989) "Global Hegemony and the Structural Power of Capital," *International Studies Quarterly*, 33, pp. 475–99.

Glick, Reuven, Ramon Moreno, and Mark M. Spiegel, eds (2001) *Financial Crises in Emerging Markets* (Cambridge: Cambridge University Press).

Goldstein, Morris (1998) *The Asian Financial Crisis: Causes, Cures and Systemic Implications* (Washington: Institute for International Economics).

Goodfriend, Marvin (1998) "Eurodollars," in Timothy Q. Cook and Robert K. Laroche, eds, *Instruments of the Money Market*, Federal Reserve Bank of Richmond, available at <www.rich.frb.org/pubs/instruments>.

Gowan, Peter (1999) *The Global Gamble: Washington's Faustian Bid for World Dominance* (London: Verso), with a version also at <www.gre.ac.uk/~fa03/iwgvt/files/9-gowan.rtf>, to which page numbers in the text refer.

Gunderson, Morley (1998), *Women and the Canadian Labour Market: Transitions towards the Future* (Ottawa: Statistics Canada).

Habermas, Jürgen (1989) *The Structural Transformation of the Public Sphere* (Cambridge, MA: MIT Press).

Haegele, Katie (2000) "Women Investors," *Target Marketing*, 23 (10), October, pp. 226–31.

Haggard, Stephan (2000) *The Political Economy of the East Asian Financial Crisis* (Washington: Institute for International Economics).

Haley, Mary Ann (1999) "Emerging Market Makers: The Power of Institutional Investors," in Leslie Elliott Armijo, ed., *Financial Globalization and Democracy in Emerging Markets* (Basingstoke: Macmillan), pp. 74–90.

Harmes, Adam (2001) "Mass Investment Culture," *New Left Review*, 9, May/June, pp. 103–24.

Harmes, Adam (2002) "The Trouble with Hedge Funds," *Review of Policy Research*, 19 (1), Spring, pp. 156–76.

Harrison, Debbie (2001) "The Changing Role of Women in Finance," *Women: A Cultural Review*, 12 (2), pp. 158–63.

Harvey, David (1989) *The Condition of Postmodernity: An Enquiry into the Origins of Cultural Change* (Cambridge, MA: Blackwell).

Hasenclever, Andreas, Peter Mayer, and Volker Rittberger (1997) *Theories of International Regimes* (Cambridge: Cambridge University Press).

Haufler, Virginia (1997) *Dangerous Commerce: Insurance and the Management of International Risk* (Ithaca, NY: Cornell University Press).

Held, David, Anthony McGrew, David Goldblatt, and Jonathan Perraton (1999) *Global Transformations: Politics, Economics and Culture* (Cambridge: Polity).

Helleiner, Eric (1994) *States and the Reemergence of Global Finance: From Bretton Woods to the 1990s* (Ithaca, NY: Cornell University Press).

Helleiner, Eric (2003) *The Making of National Money: Territorial Currencies in Historical Perspective* (Ithaca, NY: Cornell University Press).

Herman, Barry (2002) "Civil Society and the Financing for Development Initiative at the United Nations," in Jan Aart Scholte and Albrecht Schnabel, eds, *Civil Society and Global Finance* (London: Routledge), pp. 162–78.

Herring, Richard J., and Robert E. Litan (1995) *Financial Regulation in the Global Economy* (Washington: Brookings Institution).

Hexner, Ervin (1946) *International Cartels* (London: Pitman).

Holz, Carsten A. (2002) "Long Live China's State-Owned Enterprises: Deflating the Myth of Poor Financial Performance," *Journal of Asian Economics*, 13, pp. 493–529.

Hopwood, Anthony G., and Peter Miller, eds (1994) *Accounting as Social and Institutional Practice* (Cambridge: Cambridge University Press).

Hymer, Stephen (1975) "The Multinational Corporation and the Law of Uneven Development," in Hugo Radice, ed., *International Firms and Modern Imperialism* (Harmondsworth: Penguin), pp. 37–62.

Inter-American Development Bank (1997) *A Strategy for Poverty Reduction*, (Washington: IADB, March, D.C.) available at <www.iadb.org>.

International Labour Organization (2002) *Yearbook of Labour Statistics* 61st edition (Geneva: International Labour Organization).

International Monetary Fund (2002) "Is Global Inequality Rising?," transcript of an IMF Economic Forum, IMF, Washington, October 8, at <www.imf.org/external/np/tr/2002/tr021008.htm>.

Jacobson, Harold K., and Michael Okensburg (1990) *China's Participation in the IMF, the World Bank, and GATT: Toward a Global Economic Order* (Ann Arbor: University of Michigan Press).

Johnson, Juliet (2000) *A Fistful of Rubles: The Rise and Fall of the Russian Banking System* (Ithaca, NY, and London: Cornell University Press).

Jones, Geoffrey, and Harm G. Schröter (1993) "Continental European Multinationals, 1850–1992," in Geoffrey Jones and Harm G. Schröter, eds, *The Rise of Multinationals in Continental Europe* (Aldershot: Edward Elgar), pp. 3–27.

Kaplan, Arthur M. (2002) "Anti-Trust as a Public–Private Partnership: A Case Study of the NASDAQ Litigation," *Case Western Law Review*, 52 (1), pp. 111–32.

Kapstein, Ethan B. (1994) *Governing the Global Economy: International Finance and the State* (Cambridge, MA, and London: Harvard University Press).

Karmel, Roberta S. (2002) "Turning Seats into Shares: Causes and Implications of Demutualization of Stock and Future Exchanges," *Hastings Law Journal*, 53, pp. 367–430.

Keohane, Robert O. (1988) "International Institutions: Two Approaches," *International Studies Quarterly*, 32, December, pp. 379–96.

Kern, Stephen (1983) *The Culture of Time and Space, 1880–1918* (Cambridge, MA: Harvard University Press).

Kerr, Ian M. (1984) *A History of the Eurobond Market: The First 21 Years* (London: Euromoney Publications).

Kindleberger, Charles P. (1989) *Manias, Panics and Crashes: A History of Financial Crises* (New York: Basic Books).

Kotz, David (2003) "Neoliberalism and the U.S. Economic Expansion of the '90s", *Monthly Review*, 54 (11), April, electronic version from <findarticles.com>.

Krutzfeldt, Hermann (1996) "The Experience of BancoSol," in Craig F. Churchill, ed., *An Introduction to Key Issues in Microfinance: Supervision and Regulation, Financing Sources, Expansion of Microfinance Institutions* (Washington: Microfinance Network, February).

Laclau, Ernesto, and Chantal Mouffe (1985) *Hegemony and Socialist Strategy: Towards a Radical Democratic Politics*, trans. Winston Moore and Paul Cammack (London: Verso).

Lague, David (2002) "China/Banking: On the Road to Ruin," *Far Eastern Economic Review*, November 14, pp. 32–5.

Lampton, David M., ed. (2001) *The Making of Chinese Foreign and Security Policy in the Era of Reform, 1978–2000* (Stanford, CA: Stanford University Press).

Langley, Paul (2002) *World Financial Orders: An Historical International Political Economy* (London: Routledge).

Lardy, Nicholas (2002) *Integrating China into the Global Economy* (Washington: Brookings Institution).

Leidner, Robin (1993) *Fast Food, Fast Talk: Service Work and the Routinization of Everyday Life* (Berkeley: University of California Press).

Leigh, Duane E., and Robert E. Berney (1991) "The Distribution of Hostile Casualties on Draft-Eligible Males with Differing Socio-Economic

Characteristics," in Charles E. Marske, ed., *Communities of Fate: Readings in the Social Organization of Risk* (Lanham, MD: University Press of America), pp. 123–32.

Lenin, Vladimir Illyich (1917) "Imperialism, the Highest Stage of Capitalism," repr. in *Selected Works*, part I (New York: International Publishers, 1943).

Levitt, Kari (1970) *Silent Surrender* (Toronto: Macmillan).

Lex Fori (n.d.) "La Meilleure Pratique dans le recours à des norms juridiques 'douces' et son application au consommateurs au sein de l'Union européen", study produced at the request of the European Commission DG SANCO.

Liff, Sonia, and Kate Ward (2001), "Distorted Views through the Glass Ceiling: The Construction of Women's Understandings of Promotion and Senior Management Positions," *Gender, Work and Organization*, 8 (1), January, pp. 19–36.

Lim, J. (2000) "The Effects of the East Asian Crisis on the Employment of Men and Women: The Philippine Case", *World Development*, 28 (7), pp. 1285–1306.

Lin, Z. Jun (2000) "Asian Financial Crisis and Accounting Reforms in China," *Managerial Finance*, 26 (5), pp. 63–79.

Lothian, James R. (2002) "The Internationalization of Money and Finance and the Globalization of Financial Markets," *Journal of International Money and Finance*, 21, pp. 699–724.

Luhmann, Niklas (1982) *The Differentiation of Society*, trans. Stephen Holmes and Charles Larmore (New York: Columbia University Press).

Luhmann, Niklas (1993) *Risk: A Sociological Theory* (New York: Aldine de Gruyter).

Lukauskas, Arvid John, and Francisco L. Rivera-Batiz, eds (2001) *The Political Economy of the East Asian Crisis and its Aftermath* (Cheltenham: Edward Elgar).

Macey, Jonathan R. (2003) "Regulatory Globalization as a Response to Regulatory Competition," *Emory Law Journal*, 52, pp. 1353–79.

Marchand, Marianne H. (1996) "Reconceptualizing 'Gender and Development' in an Era of 'Globalisation'," *Millennium: Journal of International Studies*, 25 (3), pp. 577–603.

Marske, Charles E. (1991) "The Political-Economics of Risk in College Athletic Travel," in Charles E. Marske, ed., *Communities of Fate: Readings in the Social Organization of Risk* (Lanham, MD: University Press of America), pp. 97–121.

Martin, Paul (1999) "The International Financial Architecture: The Rule of Law," Remarks before the Conference of the Canadian Institute for Advanced Legal Studies, Cambridge, UK, July 12.

Marx, Karl (1844) "Economic and Philosophic Manuscripts," in David McLellan, ed., *Karl Marx: Selected Writings* (Oxford: Oxford University Press), pp. 75–112.

Mayhall, Stacey (2002) "Riding the Bull/Wrestling the Bear: Sex and Identity in the Discourses of Global Finance" (doctoral dissertation, York University).

McDonough, William J. (1999) "Global Financial Reform: A Regulator's Perspective," Remarks by President William J. McDonough before the Foreign Policy Association, November 17, at <www.ny.frb.org/newsevents/speeches/1999/mcd991117.html>.

McDowell, L., and G. Court (1994) "Gender Divisions of Labour in the Post-Fordist Economy: The Maintenance of Occupational Sex Segregation in the Financial Services Sector," *Environment and Planning A*, 26, pp. 1397–1418.

McGuire, Gail M. (2002) "Gender, Race and the Shadow Structure: A Study of Informal Networks and Inequality in a Work Organization," *Gender and Society*, 16 (3), June, pp. 303–22.

McKenzie, Richard B., and Dwight R. Lee (1991) *Quicksilver Capital: How the Rapid Movement of Wealth has Changed the World* (New York: The Free Press).

McWilliams, Wayne C., and Harry Piotowski (1993) *The World since 1945: A History of International Relations* (Boulder, CO: Lynne Rienner).

Mehra, Rekha, and Sarah Gammage (1999) "Trends, Countertrends, and Gaps in Women's Employment," *World Development*, 27 (3), pp. 533–50.

Mehra, Rekha, Annelies Drost-Maasry, and Ruba Rahman (1995) *Credit for Women: Why is it So Important?* (Santo Domingo: International Center for Research on Women/UN International Research and Training Institute for the Advancement of Women).

Mohammed, Aziz Ali (1999) "The Future of the Group of 24," in Eduardo Mayobre, ed., *G-24: The Developing Countries in the International Financial System* (Boulder, CO: Lynne Rienner), pp. 27–41.

Molano, Walter T. (1996) "From Bad Debts to Healthy Securities? The Theory and Financial Techniques of the Brady Plan," at <www.bradynet.com/n025.html>.

Mollison, Caitlin (2002) "Financial Women Really Paid Less? Data are Scarce," *American Banker*, May 21, p. 12.

Moran, Michael (1984) *The Politics of Banking: The Strange Case of Competition and Credit Control* (London: Macmillan).

Mytelka, Lynn Krieger, ed. (1991) *Strategic Partnerships: States, Firms and International Competition* (London: Pinter).

Neal, Larry (1990) *The Rise of Financial Capitalism: International Capital Markets in the Age of Reason* (Cambridge: Cambridge University Press).

Nelkin, Dorothy, ed. (1992) *Controversy: Politics of Technical Decisions*, 3rd edn (Newbury Park, CA: Sage Publications).

New Rules for Global Finance (2004) *Debating the Tobin Tax* (Washington, DC: New Rules for Global Finance), available at <www.new-rules.org/debatingtobintax.htm>.

Norton, Joseph J. (1998) "Towards an International Financial Centre for Greater China: Hong Kong and Infrastructural Reform," *Hong Kong Law Journal*, 28, pp. 209–29.

Oatley, Thomas, and Robert Nabors (1998) "Redistributive Cooperation: Market Failure, Wealth Transfers, and the Basle Accord," *International Organization*, 52 (1), pp. 35–54.

O'Brien, Robert, Anne-Marie Goetz, Jan Aart Scholte, and Marc Williams (2000) *Contesting Global Governance: Multilateral Economic Institutions and Global Social Movements* (Cambridge: Cambridge University Press).

Organization for Economic Cooperation and Development (2002) *China in the World Economy: The Domestic Policy Challenges* (Paris: OECD).

Palmer, Ingrid (1995) "Public Finance from a Gender Perspective," *World Development*, 23 (11), pp. 1981–6.

Parker, Susan, Gillian Pascall, and Julia Evetts (1998) "Jobs for the Girls? Change and Continuity for Women in High Street Banks," *Women in Management Review*, 13 (4), pp. 156–61.

Pascual, Ma. Teresa D. (1995) "China, the IMF and the World Bank," in Ma. Teresa D. Pascual, ed., *China's Economy and Asia* (Quezon City: Philippine–China Development Resource Center), pp. 55–69.

Pauly, Louis W. (1997) *Who Elected the Bankers? Surveillance and Control in the World Economy* (Ithaca, NY: Cornell University Press).

Pempel, T. J. (1999) *The Politics of the Asian Economic Crisis* (Ithaca, NY: Cornell University Press).

Perrow, Charles (1984) *Normal Accidents: Living with High-Risk Systems* (New York: Basic Books).

Pistor, Katharina (2002) "The Standardization of Law and its Effect on Developing Economies," G-24 Discussion Paper Series, no. 4, June (New York and Geneva: United Nations), available at <www.g24.org/res-prog.htm>.

Pixley, Jocelyn (2002) "Finance Organizations, Decisions and Emotions," *British Journal of Sociology*, 53 (1), pp. 41–65.

Porter, Tony (1993) *States, Markets, and Regimes in Global Finance* (Basingstoke: Macmillan and New York: St Martin's).

Porter, Tony (1995) "Innovation in Global Finance: The Impact on Hegemony and Growth since 1000 A.D.," *Review: A Journal of the Fernand Braudel Center for the Study of Economics, Historical Systems, and Civilizations*, 18 (3), Summer, pp. 387–429.

Porter, Tony (1996) "Capital Mobility and Currency Markets: Can They be Tamed?," *International Journal*, 51 (4), Autumn, pp. 669–89.

Porter, Tony (1999) "Hegemony and the Private Governance of International Industries," in A. Claire Cutler, Virginia Haufler, and Tony Porter, eds, *Private Authority and International Affairs* (Albany, NY: SUNY Press), pp. 257–82.

Porter, Tony (2002a) "Private Sector Associations and Governance in Global Finance," report prepared for the National Research Program in Financial Services and Public Policy, Schulich School of Business, York University, Toronto, Canada.

Porter, Tony (2002b), *Technology, Governance and Political Conflict in International Industries* (London: Routledge).

Porter, Tony (2003) "Technical Collaboration and Political Conflict in the Emerging Regime for International Financial Regulation," *Review of International Political Economy*, 10 (3), August, pp. 520–51.

Porter, Tony, and Duncan Wood (2002) "Reform without Representation? The International and Transnational Dialogue on the Global Financial Architecture," in Leslie Elliott Armijo, ed., *Debating the Global Financial Architecture* (Albany, NY: SUNY Press), pp. 236–56.

Postan, Michael M. (1973) *Medieval Trade and Finance* (Cambridge: Cambridge University Press).

Poster, Mark (1990) *The Mode of Information: Poststructuralism and Social Context* (Chicago: University of Chicago Press).

Power, Michael (1994) "The Audit Society," in Anthony G. Hopwood and Peter Miller, eds, *Accounting as Social and Institutional Practice* (Cambridge: Cambridge University Press), pp. 299–316.

Quack, Sigrid, and Bob Hancké (1997) "Women in Decision-Making in Finance," report prepared in cooperation with the European Network "Women in Decision-Making" for the European Commission.

Randriamaro, Zo (2001), "The NEPAD, Gender and Poverty Trap," in "Financing for Development: Women Challenging Globalization", Women's Environment and Development Organization, at <www.wedo.org>.

Razavi, Shahra (2001) "Globalization, Employment, and Women's Empowerment," United Nations Division for the Advancement of Women, Expert Group Meeting on "Empowerment of Women Throughout the Life Cycle as a Transformative Strategy for Poverty Eradication," Discussion Paper, November 26–9, New Delhi, available at <www.un.org/womenwatch/daw/csw/empower/documents/Razawi-BP.pdf>.

Reinicke, Wolfgang, and Francis Deng (2000) *Critical Choices: The United Nations, Networks, and the Future of Global Governance* (Ottawa: International Development Research Centre).

Ridgeway, George L. (1938) *Merchants of Peace* (New York: Columbia University Press).

Ruggie, John Gerard (1982) "International Regimes, Transactions and Change: Embedded Liberalism in the Postwar Economic Order," in Stephen Krasner, ed., *International Regimes* (Ithaca, NY, and London: Cornell University Press), pp. 195–231.

Rugman, Alan (1981) *Inside the Multinationals: The Economics of Internal Markets* (New York: Columbia University Press).

Ruiz, Sonia (2000) "Engendering International Trade: Gender Equality in a Global World," European Women's Lobby on the Gender Aspects of International Trade and Globalization in General, November, at <women.socioeco-org/documents/43pdf_rui2.pdf>.

Sassen, Saskia (1991) *The Global City: New York, London, Tokyo* (Princeton: Princeton University Press).

Sassen, Saskia (1995) "When the State Encounters a New Space-Economy: The Case of Information Industries," *American University Journal of International Law and Politics*, 10 (2), Winter, pp. 769–89.

Schmidt, Susanne K., and Raymund Werle (1998) *Coordinating Technology: Studies in the International Standardization of Telecommunications* (Cambridge, MA: MIT Press).

Scholte, Jan Aart, and Albrecht Schnabel, eds (2002) *Civil Society and Global Finance* (London: Routledge).

Schuijer, Jan (2002) "OECD Members' Experience with Capital Account Liberalization and its Relevance to Other Countries," Presentation at the Global Forum on International Investment, Shanghai, December 5–6, available at <www.oecd.org>.

Seguino, Stephanie (1997) "Export-Led Growth and the Persistence of Gender Inequality in the Newly Industrializing Countries," in Janet M. Rives and Mahmood Yousefi, eds, *Economic Dimensions of Gender Inequality: A Global Perspective* (Westport, CT, and London: Praeger), pp. 11–34.

Sell, Susan K. (1999) "Multinational Corporations as Agents of Change: The Globalization of Intellectual Property Rights," in A. Claire Cutler, Virginia Haufler and Tony Porter, eds, *Private Authority and International Affairs* (Albany, NY: SUNY Press), pp. 169–98.

Sell, Susan K. (2000) "Big Business and the New Trade Agreements: The Future of the WTO?," in Richard Stubbs and Geoffrey R. D. Underhill, eds, *Political Economy and the Changing Global Order*, 2nd edn (Toronto: Oxford University Press), pp. 174–83.

Sen, Gita (2000) "Gender Mainstreaming in Finance Ministries," *World Development*, 28 (7), pp. 1379–90.

Servan-Schreiber, Jean Jacques (1967) *Le Défi americain* (Paris: Denoël).

Shah, Anup (2001) "The Heavily In-Debt Poor Countries Initiative is Not Working," at <www.globalissues.org>.

Shi, Jianhuai (n.d.) "Financial Innovations in China, 1990–2000," China Center for Economic Research, Peking University, Beijing, unpublished paper.

Simcich, Tina (1977) *Shortchanged: Women and Minorities in Banking*, Council on Economic Priorities, updated and edited by Wendy C. Schwartz (New York: Praeger).

Simmel, Georg (1978) *The Philosophy of Money*, trans. by Tom Bottomore and David Frisby (London: Routledge and Kegan Paul).

Sinclair, Timothy J. (1994) "Passing Judgement: Credit Rating Processes as Regulatory Mechanisms of Governance in the Emerging World Order," *Review of International Political Economy*, 1 (1), Spring, pp. 133–59.

Singh, Ajit, and Ann Zammit (2000) "International Capital Flows: Identifying the Gender Dimension," *World Development*, 28 (7), pp. 1249–68.

Smythe, Elizabeth (1998) "The Multilateral Agreement on Investment: A Charter of Rights for Global Investors or Just Another Agreement?," in Fen Osler Hampson and Maureen Molot, eds, *Canada among Nations 1998: Leadership and Dialogue* (Toronto: Oxford University Press), pp. 239–66.

Soederberg, Susanne (2004) "Unravelling Washington's Judgement Calls: The Cases of the Malaysian and Chilean Capital Controls," *Antipode*, 36 (1), January, pp. 43–65.

Soros, George (1998) *The Crisis of Global Capitalism* (New York: Public Affairs).

Sparr, Pamela (1994) "Feminist Critiques of Structural Adjustment," in Pamela Sparr, ed., *Mortgaging Women's Lives: Feminist Critiques of Structural Adjustment* (London: Zed), pp. 13–39.

Stiglitz, Joseph E. (1999) "Whither Reform? Ten Years of the Transition," Annual World Bank Conference on Development Economics, Keynote Address, Washington, DC, April 28–30.

Stout, Lynn A. (1999) "Why the Law Hates Speculators: Regulation and Private Ordering in the Market for OTC Derivatives," *Duke Law Journal*, 48, pp. 701–86.

Strange, Susan (1986) *Casino Capitalism* (Oxford: Basil Blackwell).

Suter, Christian (1992) *Debt Cycles in the World Economy: Foreign Loans, Financial Crises, and Debt Settlements, 1820–1990* (Boulder, CO: Westview Press).

Thrift, Nigel (1994) "A Phantom State? The De-traditionalization of Money, the International Financial System, and International Financial Centres," *Political Geography*, 13 (4), July, pp. 299–327.

ul Haq, Mahbub, Inge Kaul and Isabelle Grunberg, eds (1996) *The Tobin Tax: Coping with Financial Volatility* (Oxford: Oxford University Press).

Underhill, Geoffrey R. D. and Xiaoke Zhang, eds (2003) *International Financial Governance under Stress: Global Structures versus National Imperatives* (Cambridge: Cambridge University Press).

United Nations Conference on Trade and Development (2003) *World Investment Report* (New York: UN).

United Nations Expert Group on Women and Finance (1995) "Transforming Financial Systems," Women's World Banking, at <www.swwb.org/english/pdf/expert%20group.pdf>.

US Banker (2002) "Basel II Mandates a Nest Egg for Banks," July, p. 48.

US President's Working Group on Financial Markets (1999), "Hedge Funds, Leverage, and the Lessons of Long-Term Capital Management," Report, April, available at <www.treas.gov/press/releases/report3097.htm>.

Van Staveren, Irene (2001) "Gender Biases in Finance," *Gender and Development*, 9 (1), March, pp. 9–17.

Van Staveren, Irene (2002), "Global Finance and Gender," in Jan Aart Scholte and Albrecht Schnabel, eds, *Civil Society and Global Finance* (London: Routledge), pp. 228–46.

Vernon, Raymond (1971) *Sovereignty at Bay: The Multinational Spread of U.S. Enterprises* (New York: Basic Books).

Women's Edge (2002) "The Asian Financial Crisis: Hearing Women's Voices," at <www.womensedge.org/trade/asiancrisis.htm>.

Women's Environment and Development Organization (2001) "Issue I: Mobilizing Domestic Financial Resources for Development," Financing for Development Briefing, Gender Policy Briefing Kit, at <www.wedo.org/ffd/kitmain1.htm>.

Women's Environment and Development Organization (n.d.) "The Numbers Speak for Themselves," Fact Sheet #1, at <www.wedo.org>.

Waghray, Rajyashri (2001) "Is the FfD Investing in Women," Women's Environment and Development Organization, at <www.wedo.org/ffd/investing.htm>.

Winner, Langdon (1977) *Autonomous Technology: Technics-out-of-Control as a Theme in Political Thought* (Cambridge, MA: MIT Press).

Wirth, Linda (2001) *Breaking through the Glass Ceiling* (Geneva: International Labour Organization).

Welbourne, Theresa M. (1999) "Wall Street Likes its Women: An Examination of Women in the Top Management Teams of Initial Public Offerings," Center for Advanced Human Resource Studies Working Paper 99-07, Cornell University School of Industrial and Labor Relations.

Westin, Peter (2001) *The Wild East: Negotiating the Russian Financial Frontier* (Upper Saddle River, NJ: Prentice-Hall).

White, Marceline, and Ritu Sharma (1999) "The Asian Financial Crisis: Hearing Women's Voices," an occasional paper from Women's EDGE, at <www.womensedge.org/trade/asiancrisis.htm>, May.

Woods, Ngaire (2000) "The Challenge of Good Governance for the IMF and the World Bank Themselves," *World Development*, 28 (5), May, pp. 823–41.

World Bank (2001) *Engendering Development* (Oxford: Oxford University Press and Washington: World Bank).

World Bank (2002) *Integrating Gender into the World Bank's Work: A Strategy for Action* (Washington, DC: The World Bank).

Young, Brigitte (2002) "Financial Crisis in Asia and the Feminization of Human Security," paper prepared for the International Studies Association Annual Convention, New Orleans, March 23–7.

Zhang, Lan (2002) Unpublished report on China and Global Finance, on file with author.

Zhiqin, Shao (2002) "Women and Social Security: Impact of Financial Crisis," prepared for United Nations University Seminar, "Thinking Outside the Security Box: Non-Traditional Security in Asia," at <www.ony.unu.edu/seminars/securityinasia.htm>.

Index